The
DINAH'S CUPBOARD
COOK·BOOK

The

DINAH'S CUPBOARD
COOK ❦ BOOK

*Recipes and Menus for
elegant home entertaining*

DINAH KOO & JANICE POON

DESIGN AND ILLUSTRATIONS BY JANICE POON

A TOTEM BOOK
Toronto

ON THE COVER

Provimi Veal Stuffed with Spinach and Mushrooms, page 26
Shrimp and Scallops with Chèvre Dressing, page 21

Food photography: Richard and Tina Sharabura, Chatsworth Studio
Authors' photography and imaging: Yolanda and Yanka Van Der Kolk

A NOTE ON METRIC MEASURES

The recipes in this book are given in both imperial and metric measures. Follow the recipes using either imperial or metric, but do not switch from one to the other within one recipe. The metric measurements are not exact conversions of the imperial and the conversions are not always consistent, but the recipes have been devised so that the balance of the ingredients is correct within each system.

First published 1986
by TOTEM BOOKS
a division of Collins Publishers
100 Lesmill Road, Don Mills, Ontario

© 1986 by Dinah Koo and Janice Poon

Canadian Cataloguing in Publication Data

Koo, Dinah.
   The Dinah's Cupboard cookbook

Includes index.
ISBN 0-00-217653-X

1. Cookery. 2. Menus. 3. Entertaining.
I. Dinah's Cupboard (Shop) II. Title.

TX715.K66 1986   641.5   C86-094237-6

Editor: Mary Adachi
Layout: Marg Round
Typesetting: Compeer Typographical Services Ltd.
Printed and bound in Canada by John Deyell Company

To family ties, friendship and working together

ACKNOWLEDGEMENTS

*Our gratitude to all the friends who helped so much;
every one as essential
as each ingredient in a very special recipe.*

Lucy Waverman

IN THE KITCHEN:
Alice, Sonny
Robert
Jackie and Henry
Anne Marie
Dee, Joseph
Chris, Lawrence
Pearl and Paul
Michael Crossman
Creley and Smith

Barry and Nita Koo
Star Poon

RECIPE TESTING –
Karen Boulton

Eve Hansen
Elke McMename
Yanka and Yolanda
Richard and Tina

Robert Mang & Beverly
Tom Bjarnason

Nina
Richard Procunier
Ann Pedum
Richard Teleky
Irene McGuire

Extra special thanks to Mely Jumarang for her untiring, unerring assistance in the kitchen,
and to Mary Adachi for going beyond the call of editorial duty
into the realm of patron saint.

CONTENTS

INTRODUCTION

Good food and creative cooking have always been part of my life. Growing up with Dad's Sunday dinners and Mom's myriad of recipe clippings, our whole family developed a love of food.

For me, this love grew into an idea that, in 1972, became "Dinah's Cupboard," a cubbyhole on fashionable Yorkville Avenue. The first food store of its kind in Toronto, it offered a treasure trove of fine imported teas, coffees, spices and herbs, as well as a wide assortment of condiments from all parts of the world. Janice Poon was our artistic director — creating from her little design shop next door, contributing everything from brochures and labels to her crazy "designer cakes," Easter eggs, Valentine cookies and sugar angels. Business prospered. We brought in new items to meet the needs and burgeoning interest of the city's food lovers. A number of restaurants asked us to blend their coffee, and our name began appearing on some of the smartest menus in town. We did our first catering job.

Before long the little store was bursting at the seams, so we moved to our present location on Cumberland Street. With five times the space, we were able to offer an even greater range of products, including baked goods, cheeses, smoked salmon, caviar, our own pâtés and salads, fresh pasta and pasta toppings. The catering mushroomed into a very important part of our business, and we became known not just for the quality of our food but for our beautiful and unusual presentation.

In this book we share with you some of our favourite recipes and offer you tips on how to make entertaining at home easy and pleasurable. There are guidelines and checklists, and for the party menus, I've produced work-ahead schedules covering as many details as possible, just as I do for my catering staff. Janice's section on garnishing will show you how to make simple but attractive decorations, as well as a spectacular carved-fruit table arranged in the shape of a peacock. The recipes are an eclectic collection drawn from many cuisines and reflect current interest in fresh, healthy ingredients. Follow the recipes, by all means, but don't be afraid to make substitutions. We've always had fun discovering unusual combinations and new taste sensations, and we hope you'll be inspired to do the same.

Dinah Koo

ENTERTAINING

Let's have a party! There are so many reasons to celebrate — personal milestones, auspicious occasions, special holidays, just sharing good times with good friends. Whether large or small, extravagant or modest, formal or casual, zany or sedate, a party should be FUN for both the host/hostess and guests. And there's no reason why it shouldn't be. With our suggestions, schedules, guidelines, menus, recipes and special ideas, you can make each party a resounding success.

GUIDE TO SUCCESSFUL PARTY-GIVING

Who could forget that special evening? The room was filled with candlelight, sparkling laughter and dinner's intoxicating aroma. Moments to remember . . . Unfortunately, memories are not always so sweet. Was it the burnt entrée? Or the shortage of wine? The guests seemed anxious to leave; and the hostess so relieved to have them go.

Successful parties do not simply happen. They are created, and it is thorough and imaginative planning that is the key. If everything has been well thought out and taken care of in advance, then all will go smoothly. You can relax and enjoy the party. Remember that your guests are in your home to see you and that you set the pace and tone of the evening.

Here we offer a checklist to help you organize the details of your party. Pre-planning will leave you unharried and unhurried as your special event unfolds.

PREPARE THE GUEST LIST   The length of your guest list will, in part, determine the type of party best for you. If the number of guests is too large for a sit-down dinner, consider a cocktail party. A buffet of fork food is an excellent solution for the hostess who wishes to serve something substantial but hasn't room in her home for a lot of tables and chairs.

PREPARE AND SEND THE INVITATIONS   For large functions, send out the invitations a month in advance. Make follow-up telephone calls for RSVPs, if necessary. For smaller gatherings, handwritten invitations or telephone calls may suffice. Card stores offer a good variety of blank invitations. If you prefer you can have personalized ones printed at a stationery store, or you can design your own and have them run off at your local photocopy shop.

PLAN THE LAYOUT OF THE PARTY AREA   Walk through the proposed party area and imagine how the activities will best flow through the rooms. In this way you can determine where to place the bar, the buffet, the seating and other focal points.

Decide how many tables and chairs you can accommodate. If it's necessary to borrow or rent additional pieces, make a list. Don't worry about limited seating—at larger parties there is often more mingling and liveliness if the seating is limited.

The capacity of your home can be expanded with careful and inventive use of space, so don't be discouraged if the party area seems small. That large closet can be converted into a bar by opening the doors wide and sliding a table inside. If you have a pool that takes up most of the yard but you want to have your party under the stars, rent a dance floor to cover the pool and suddenly you have a lot of space. The backyard can be made hospitable even in late fall if covered by a tent (rented from a local awning company) and warmed by electric heaters.

PLAN THE DECOR   Create an ambience that sets the mood. Your guests should feel the excitement as soon as they enter the room! Choose decorative touches, lighting and flowers to create a party atmosphere that's special, yet one in which your guests will feel comfortable.

It needn't be elaborate: candles, a few stems of roses and soft music are all you need for a romantic theme. Or pull out all the stops! Rock 'n' Roll Fifties is a theme that will have you filling your home with streamers and balloons, searching through old trunks for poodle skirts, prom dresses and faded high-school pictures. Humming ''Chantilly lace and a pretty face . . .'' you'll arrange Cheez Whiz-filled celery sticks on a Melmac plate. Whatever your theme, your personal touches will create a heightened sense of occasion and put everyone in the mood.

Fresh flowers add immeasurable warmth and beauty. Order them well in advance to be sure you get the varieties you want. If you are planning to put flowers on the dinner table, make sure the arrangement will not obscure the view across the table. Keep candles below eye level as well. Towering flowers and flickering flames are sure to inhibit conversation.

LIST BAR REQUIREMENTS   For many, the trend is now towards wine, especially white wine. Each crowd varies, but here is a guide that you can modify according to the tastes of your friends.

ESTIMATING BAR REQUIREMENTS	
Bar requirements for dinner	
Bottles* per guest	½ bottle of wine
Bar requirements for after dinner	
Bottles* per 12 to 15 guests	1 cognac, 1 Armagnac 1 liqueur or eau-de-vie.
Bar requirements for cocktails	
Bottles* per guest	⅓ bottle of wine
Bottles† per 25 guests	1 vodka, 1 Scotch, 1 gin, 1 rye, 1 rum
Bottles† per 35 guests	2 vodka, 2 Scotch, 1 gin, 1 rye, 1 rum
Bar extras	
Per 25 guests	7(5-lb/2-kilo) bags of ice-cubes 3 lemons, 3 limes
Bottles* per 25 guests	12 mineral water, 3 tonic, 2 ginger ale, 2 diet cola, 2 regular cola
*26 oz/750 mL bottle †40 oz/1.14 L bottle	

For brunch, you might offer Bloody Marys, Screwdrivers, Mimosa (champagne and orange juice) or Kir Royale. Don't forget to add the necessary mixes and garnishes to your list.

In summer, guests may drink more gin — long, cool drinks such as gin and tonic, Tom Collins, and gin and Bitter Lemon. Campari and soda becomes a seasonal favourite, along with sweet and dry vermouth on the rocks. On hot days your guests may drink twice as much, so be sure to buy enough. If you overbuy, check to see if your liquor store has a refund policy. Many will take back unopened bottles if the labels have not been damaged.

You might want to offer mulled wine or cider at Christmas, or a delicate fruit punch at a wedding. Estimate 8 to 10 oz (250 to 300 mL) per guest, along with the full bar.

CHECK SERVICE ITEMS

Sometimes it's necessary to round out your own collection of party supplies with rentals or items borrowed from friends and family. Here's a checklist for your party:

Serving platters—If necessary, modify menu so you have an appropriate platter for each item. Tape a note on each platter to indicate what its use will be. If you're planning a large party, allow 2 platters or bowls per menu item so food can be replenished quickly and efficiently.

China and silverware — Match requirements to the items on your menu. Remember serving spoons, trays and punchbowls.

Glassware—Requirements will be easy to estimate if you follow the chart below. Don't feel you must have a wide assortment of sizes. Large old-fashioned glasses can be used for soda water, highballs and rock drinks. Beer can be served in highball glasses or beer mugs which are often available for rental.

champagne flutes old-fashioned

snifter wine

GLASSWARE REQUIREMENT PER GUEST	
For champagne receptions	3 champagne flutes (Also have on hand a few glasses for mineral water.)
For cocktail reception, 3 to 4 hrs long	3 large old-fashioned glasses
For cocktails with a full bar For *regular drinkers*	1½ wine glasses 1½ large old-fashioned glasses
For *heavy wine drinkers*	2 wine glasses 1 large old-fashioned glass
For cocktails and dinner	2 wine glasses 1 large old-fashioned glass
For *after dinner*	1 snifter
Extras and optional items Bar trays, ashtrays, ice buckets and tongs, champagne buckets, pail for discarding ice and garnishes, towels, napkins, shaker and strainer	

Linens—Order extra dinner napkins for dressing wine bottles, lining bun baskets and carrying hot plates.
For cocktail parties, order at least 3 cocktail napkins per person.

Dressing wine bottles

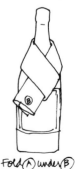

Fold Ⓐ under Ⓑ   Fold Ⓑ under

Rental companies — They are listed in the Yellow Pages of the telephone directory. Most of them will rent in small quantities, so don't hesitate to ask. Here's a rental list from one of our favourite suppliers. Check your requirements against this list to make sure you haven't forgotten anything.

CHECKLIST OF SERVICE ITEMS AND EXTRAS

Old-Fashioned Glasses	Knives	Ice Buckets	Ashtrays
Wine Glasses	Salad Forks	Champagne Buckets	Tablecloths
Champagne Glasses	Forks	Chafing Dishes	Napkins
Dinner Plates	Soup Spoons	Trays	Tables
Sandwich Plates	Teaspoons	Platters	Chairs
Bread and Butter Plates	Cake Forks	Bowls	Coat Racks and Hangers
Soup Plates/Bowls	Dessert Spoons	Punch Bowls	Other
Cups and Saucers	Cheese Knives	Coffee Pots or Urns	
Dessert Nappies	Serving Spoons		
	Serving Forks		
	Cake Servers		
	Cream and Sugar		

DECIDE ON THE MENU WELL IN ADVANCE

Plan a menu that you're comfortable with. Try out any new recipes well in advance. Select dishes that require very little last-minute preparation.

Try to choose recipes using ingredients that are at their seasonal best. Celebrate springtime with asparagus, lamb or softshell crabs. In summer enjoy locally grown fruits and vegetables, full of sun-ripened flavour.

WRITE OUT A SCHEDULE FOR FOOD PREPARATION AND SHOPPING LISTS

With careful organization, you will avoid those moments of crisis that come with the unexpected. Realistic scheduling will ensure that you are not too pressured on the day of the party. Keep in mind the size of your kitchen, your supply of pots and pans, the capacity of the oven, stovetop and refrigerator when you make your plans. Or you'll find yourself chilling the mousse in a snowbank. Determine which items can be made in advance.

List any special grocery requirements and make a note to order them at least seven days in advance.

If the project seems cumbersome, then go back to your menu and simplify. It is far better to make three simple, perfect dishes than several ambitious failures.

ORGANIZE THE MUSIC

Whether you plan to use live musicians or good tapes, check your sound system. Select the music carefully to set the appropriate mood.

GET A HELPING HAND

You may need extra hands to help your party run smoothly. Even at the smallest dinner party it can make a big difference. But don't feel you must hire professionals. Try asking that personable young niece or nephew, or a friendly neighbour. With a little coaching, they can give you just the assistance you need.

Waiters, waitresses and food prep professionals will go about their duties quickly, unobtrusively and efficiently. But however experienced your staff, it is important to go over a list of the details of the party with them before the guests arrive.

☐ If there is a guest of honor, make his or her identity known to the staff so special attention can be paid to his or her needs.

☐ Inform the staff of the layout of the rooms so service can be carried out smoothly and directions (to washrooms, telephones, cloakrooms) can be given without ado.

☐ Advise your staff that dirty ashtrays, abandoned glasses, dirty plates, used cocktail napkins etc. should be removed immediately. However, at a sit-down dinner, dishes for each course should be removed only after everyone at the table is finished. It can be embarrassing for slower eaters to be munching away while dishes are being cleared.

☐ Describe to the waiters and waitresses the menu items and the sequence and timing of service. This way, nothing will be forgotten, and they will be able to provide an enticing description to guests who may be shy about trying a particular dish.

☐ If you are having a sit-down dinner, familiarize your staff with the type of service you wish to use:

Plate service — the first course may be placed on the table before the guests are seated. The remaining courses are served onto plates in the kitchen and each guest is given an individual plate.

Tray service — English — The tray or serving dish is presented to each guest so that he or she may take a portion.

Tray service — French — The waiter or waitress holds the tray or serving dish with one hand, and with the other, serves a portion to each guest.

General rules of service:

Guest of honour is served first; then, women and lastly, the men. The host or hostess usually chooses to be served last.

Wine bottles should be wrapped with a napkin to prevent dripping.

At a sit-down dinner, the traditional way is to serve from the left and remove dishes from the right, except for beverages which are always served from the right.

Between courses, that which is not pertinent to the following courses should be removed from the table; for example, salt and pepper shakers should be whisked away before dessert.

Number of helpers needed for smooth and efficient service:
Cocktail party — 1 waiter/waitress per 15 guests Dinner, sit-down buffet — 1 waiter/waitress per 12 guests Dinner, plate service — 1 waiter/waitress per 10 guests Dinner, French or English service — 1 waiter/waitress per 8 guests

PARTIES
MENUS, RECIPES & SCHEDULES

Whether it's to celebrate a birthday or marriage, or to welcome a new boss or out-of-town visitors, we all have occasion to give a special party now and again. We've designed nine menus, ranging from quiet evenings for eight to sumptuous buffet dinners for twenty or thirty, to meet a variety of needs.

Each party has been planned and outlined, using the same methods we use when we're catering. The menus offer a mix of interesting new dishes and classic favourites. The kitchen-tested recipes include our suggestions for attractive presentations, and the work-ahead schedules provide detailed timetables and helpful hints that leave as little as possible to chance. From the moment the invitations are sent until the last dessert fork is lowered, we'll help make your party a success.

A TASTE OF ELEGANCE
Dinner for Eight in Three Courses

Blueberry Soup

❦

Wild Rice with Pine Nuts
Duck in Mango Sauce

❦

Chocolate Pâté
with White Chocolate Sauce

Here's your chance to use your best dishes and silver to show off this sophisticated dinner. To start, a dark, delicious and cool blueberry soup. Then a beautifully composed plate of duck garnished with a fan of mango slices and served with wild rice. The finishing touch is a chocolate pâté in a pool of rich, white chocolate sauce.

WORK-AHEAD SCHEDULE

2 WEEKS AHEAD
- Telephone invitations.
- Arrange for a kitchen helper, if you wish.

1 WEEK AHEAD
- Make a list of groceries and check supplies. Order ducks, check availability of mangoes.
- Plan wines, flowers, dishes and linens. Arrange for rental or loan of dishes, cutlery, etc., if necessary. See checklist page 13.

3 DAYS AHEAD
- Buy wines and all non-perishable requirements.

1 DAY AHEAD
- Buy all food.
- Make Blueberry Soup.
- Make Chocolate Pâté and Sauce

EARLY IN DAY
- Prepare duck meat and make stock.
- Toast pine nuts.
- Fry duck skin.

3 HOURS AHEAD
- Make mango sauce.
- Set table and arrange flowers.

1 HOUR BEFORE MAIN COURSE
- Make wild rice.
- Peel and slice mangoes for garnish.

TO SERVE
- Cook duck, heat sauce and blanch lettuce leaves.
- Compose each plate individually.

BLUEBERRY SOUP

3 cups	unsweetened pineapple juice	750 mL
2¼ cups	water	550 mL
⅓ cup	sugar	75 mL
1½ cups	frozen grape juice concentrate	375 mL
1 Tbsp	grated lemon rind	15 mL
1	8-inch (20-cm) cinnamon stick, broken into 1-inch (2.5-cm) pieces	1
3 cups	fresh or frozen blueberries	750 mL
3 Tbsp	cornstarch mixed with 4 Tbsp (60 mL) water	45 mL
⅔ cup	medium-dry sherry	150 mL
1 cup	sour cream	250 mL

1. In a large saucepan combine pineapple juice, water, sugar, grape juice, grated lemon rind and cinnamon sticks. Heat together over medium-high heat. Add blueberries and bring to boil.

2. Stir in cornstarch paste and bring to boil again, stirring occasionally until soup loses its milky colour, about 1 or 2 minutes. Adjust sweetness; it should be slightly sweet but still a little tart. Remove from heat and add sherry.

3. Chill for 24 hours. Remove cinnamon sticks.

4. Before serving garnish each bowl with a dollop of sour cream.

This dramatically dark soup has a tart, sassy flavour that's wonderful cold, or deliciously unusual served hot. Make a day ahead so flavours will blend.

WILD RICE WITH PINE NUTS

2 cups	wild rice	500 mL
2½ cups	cold water	625 mL
¼ tsp	salt	1 mL
¼ tsp	pepper	1 mL
2 Tbsp	butter	30 mL
½	medium-sized red onion, chopped	½
20 to 24	iceberg lettuce leaves, blanched	20 to 24
½ cup	chopped fresh parsley	125 mL
6 Tbsp	pine nuts, toasted	90 mL

1. In a large saucepan combine rice, water, salt and pepper and bring to a boil over high heat. Reduce heat and simmer, uncovered, for 45 minutes, or until rice is tender but firm. Add more hot water as necessary.

2. In a medium-sized frying pan melt butter over medium-high heat. Add chopped onions and sauté until tender, about 5 minutes. Stir into cooked rice.

3. For each serving, form a cup from 2 or 3 leaves of lettuce and fill with hot rice mixture. Garnish with parsley and pine nuts.

The nutty, full flavour of wild rice tossed with toasted pine nuts is wonderful, but if you prefer, you may use a mixture of wild and regular rice combined with toasted almonds. If you do use two types of rice, cook them separately as the wild rice takes longer to cook.

In Canada, wild rice is gathered by hand and only by native Indians. The very best grains are long, slender and unbroken. With its delicate nutty flavour, we find it a favourite accompaniment to game.

TO TOAST NUTS

Preheat oven to 350°F (180°C). Spread nuts evenly on baking sheet and brown in the oven for about 5 minutes, or until golden in colour.

DUCK IN MANGO SAUCE

Other fruits such as pears or peaches can be substituted successfully for mangoes.

3	ducks	3
For duck stock:		
1	carrot, chopped	1
1	onion, chopped	1
1	rib celery, chopped	1
to taste	peppercorns	to taste
For marinade:		
1	½-inch (1.25-cm) piece of ginger, sliced	1
3 Tbsp	soy sauce	45 mL
1 clove	garlic, crushed	1 clove
1½ Tbsp	sherry	22 mL
For garnish:		
3 to 4 cups	oil for deep frying	0.75 to 1 L
4	mangoes	4
For sauce:		
1 Tbsp	butter	15 mL
2	mangoes, peeled and chopped	2
2 Tbsp	brandy or sherry	30 mL
2 Tbsp	Cointreau, Triple Sec or apricot brandy	30 mL
to taste	salt and pepper	to taste
For sautéing duck:		
2 Tbsp	oil or butter	30 mL

Although ripe mangoes have the best flavour, underripe mangoes can be used for the sauce. Just cook until very tender.

Serve duck strips sautéd in this way with wild mushrooms such as chanterelles for a quick elegant entrée.

1. Remove skin from ducks and reserve. Remove breast meat in two whole pieces. Disjoint and remove legs. Bone legs and trim off all fat. Remove all tendons and ligaments or meat will be tough.

2. For duck stock, put carcasses and trimmings in a large pot. Add chopped carrots, onions, celery and peppercorns. Cover with cold water and bring to boil over high heat. Reduce heat and simmer for 2 hours. Strain, return stock to pot over medium-high heat and reduce volume to 1½ cups (375 mL). Set aside.

3. Combine all ingredients for marinade in a medium-sized mixing bowl. Cut duck meat diagonally across the grain into slices about ½ inch × 3 inches (1.25 cm × 7.5 cm) and ¼ inch (6 mm) thick. Add to marinade and allow to stand at least 1 hour, refrigerated.

4. For garnish, remove excess fat from reserved skin and cut into strips about ¼ inch × 3 inches (6 mm × 7.5 cm). Heat oil for deep frying to 375°F (190°C) in heavy frying pan over medium-high heat. Add sliced skin and fry until crisp and brown. Set aside. Peel 4 mangoes and cut into thin, long wedges. Set aside.

5. For sauce, melt butter in frying pan over medium-high heat. Add chopped mangoes and sauté for 5 minutes. Add brandy and cook for 1 minute. Pour in reduced duck stock and simmer, uncovered, for 10 to 15 minutes to reduce slightly. Add Cointreau. Remove to blender or food processor fitted with steel blade and

process until smooth. Strain and season to taste with salt and pepper. Set aside.

6. To sauté duck, heat non-stick frying pan over high heat until very hot. Add 1 Tbsp (15 mL) oil. Add half of the duck slices and sauté very quickly for 2 to 3 minutes. Remove from pan. The duck will be pink inside. Repeat with remaining oil and duck.

7. To serve, put about ½ cup (125 mL) of sauce on a warm plate. Arrange several slices of duck on top. Sprinkle with fried duck skin and garnish with a fan of mango slices.

CHOCOLATE PÂTÉ WITH WHITE CHOCOLATE SAUCE

For pâté:

14 oz	semi-sweet chocolate	400 g
1½ cups	whipping cream	375 mL
1 tsp	vanilla	5 mL

For sauce:

6 oz	white chocolate	170 g
1½ cups	whipping cream	375 mL
3 Tbsp	Mandarin Napoleon or Grand Marnier	45 mL

For garnish:

½ cup	toasted slivered almonds	125 mL

White chocolate is not true chocolate but a wickedly rich blend of cocoa butter and milk solids.

1. For the pâté, prepare a 3½-inch × 7-inch (9-cm × 18-cm) loaf pan by coating liberally with vegetable oil.

2. In top of a double boiler melt semi-sweet chocolate over simmering water. Set aside to cool.

3. In a medium-sized mixing bowl whip cream with an electric beater until it holds a firm peak. Beat in vanilla and fold in melted chocolate until well blended. Pour into prepared pan and refrigerate until ready to serve.

4. For sauce, melt white chocolate in top of a double boiler over simmering water. Remove from heat and gradually add cream, stirring constantly. Add Mandarin Napoleon and stir until well blended. Leave in a cool place or refrigerate until ready to serve.

5. To assemble, pour about ¼ cup (60 mL) of sauce per serving onto dessert plates, forming a neat pool on each. Unmould pâté by lowering pan into hot water for about 30 seconds, or until pâté has loosened from pan. Invert onto cutting board and with a knife dipped in hot water cut into ½-inch (1.25-cm) slices. Place one slice of pâté on each pool of sauce. Sprinkle with toasted almond slivers.

FÊTE ACCOMPLIE
Dinner for Eight in Three Courses

**Shrimp and Scallops
with Chèvre Dressing**

❦

**Noisettes of Lamb
White Bean Purée
Onion Marmalade
Radicchio Stir-Fry**

❦

Pear and Ginger Tarte

The wonderful flavours of French country cuisine abound in this dinner, but there's a city slickness in the presentation. The seafood salad is cupped in a ruffle of lettuce and trimmed with a tomato fan. The main course is a composed plate of lamb noisette, onion marmalade, bean purée and radicchio — the portions artistically arranged on each dinner plate. And in the best French tradition, a glossy pear tarte for dessert.

WORK-AHEAD SCHEDULE

2 WEEKS AHEAD
- Telephone invitations.
- Arrange for a kitchen helper, if you wish.

1 WEEK AHEAD
- Make list of groceries and check supplies. Order lamb and check sources for radicchio, shiitake mushrooms and chèvre cheese.
- Plan wines, flowers, dishes, and linens. Arrange for rental or loan of dishes, cutlery, etc., if necessary. See checklist, page 13.

2 DAYS AHEAD
- Buy everything, including wines, except fresh scallops.

1 DAY AHEAD
- Prepare lamb but do not roast.
- Soak beans for White Bean Purée.
- Make Onion Marmalade.
- Prepare pastry for Pear and Ginger Tarte.
- Make crème fraîche for Pear and Ginger Tarte.

EARLY IN DAY
- Buy fresh scallops.
- Poach shrimp for Shrimp and Scallops with Chèvre Dressing.
- Wash all greens.
- Make White Bean Purée.
- Prepare all shredded vegetables for Radicchio Stir-Fry.

3 HOURS AHEAD
- Marinate scallops.
- Set table and arrange flowers.

2 HOURS AHEAD
- Toss together shrimp, scallops and chèvre and prepare lettuce and tomatoes for salad.
- Slice pears and ginger for tarte. Keep pears in solution of vinegar and water to prevent discolouration.

- Complete salad by arranging on individual plates.
- Cook filling for tarte and set aside.

- Cook lamb.
- Slowly heat White Bean Purée and Onion Marmalade.

- Stir fry radicchio mixture, then compose individual plates.

- Put pastry on tarte and bake.

**1 HOUR BEFORE
GUESTS ARRIVE**

**45 MINUTES BEFORE
MAIN COURSE**

**10 MINUTES BEFORE
MAIN COURSE**

**30 MINUTES BEFORE
DESSERT**

SHRIMP AND SCALLOPS WITH CHÈVRE DRESSING

1 ½ lb	shrimp, unshelled	675 g
1 ½ lb	scallops	675 g
⅓ cup	lime juice	75 mL
For dressing:		
4 oz	creamy chèvre cheese	120 g
⅓ tsp	dried mixed Italian herbs	2 mL
⅓ tsp	crushed black peppercorns	2 mL
3 Tbsp	olive oil	45 mL
For greens:		
8 to 12	leaves of leaf lettuce, washed and dried	8 to 12
2	tomatoes, each cut into 16 wedges	2
2 Tbsp	finely chopped green bell peppers	30 mL

You may be able to get marinated Cigalon or marinated Canadian chèvre. It can be crushed lightly into its own herbed oil and used instead of the dressing.

1. In a pot of boiling water poach shrimp for 3 to 5 minutes, or just until they turn pink. Drain, cool and shell. Place in mixing bowl and set aside.

2. Combine scallops and lime juice in another mixing bowl and marinate for at least 1 hour. Drain and add to shrimp.

3. To prepare dressing, crumble chèvre cheese lightly in a small mixing bowl. Stir in Italian herbs, pepper and olive oil, taking care not to mash the cheese. Add to shrimp mixture and toss to coat well.

4. To assemble, for each serving form 1 or 2 leaf lettuce leaves into a cup and fill with shrimp mixture. Place 4 tomato wedges in a fan shape on the lettuce and garnish the shrimp with chopped green pepper. This salad can also be attractively served on radicchio leaves with a fan of snow peas.

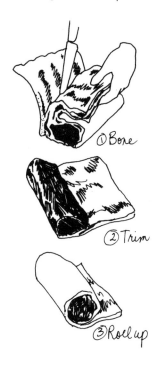

① *Bone*

② *Trim*

③ *Roll up*

To compose the main course plate:

Using a large spoon, shape bean purée

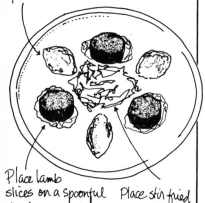

Place lamb slices on a spoonful of onion marmalade.

Place stir-fried vegetables in the centre

ONION MARMALADE

Try this with any meat, poultry or fish. It's a flavourful accompaniment to every savoury from grilled swordfish to meat pie.

NOISETTES OF LAMB

4	racks of lamb	4
6 to 8 cloves	garlic, crushed	6 to 8 cloves
to taste	salt and pepper	to taste
2 to 3 ft	butcher's twine	60 to 90 cm
2 Tbsp	butter	30 mL

1. Preheat oven to 450°F (230°C).

2. Bone racks of lamb. Take one rack, turn lamb meat side up and trim away all excess fat and gristle. Turn over to fat side and trim, leaving a layer of fat ¼ inch (6 mm) thick. Spread 1 tsp (5 mL) crushed garlic over meat and fat and sprinkle with salt and pepper. Roll up tightly so fat completely encircles meat. Tie several times with butcher's twine to make a compact roll. Spread with a little more garlic, and sprinkle with salt and pepper. Repeat with remaining racks.

3. Melt butter in a heavy frying pan over medium-high heat. Add a roll and brown on all sides, about 5 to 8 minutes and remove to roasting pan. Repeat with remaining rolls. Space rolls evenly on pan and roast for 15 minutes for medium rare. Remove from oven and let cool for 5 minutes. Slice into noisettes approximately 1 inch (2.5 cm) thick. Each roll should cut into 6 pieces.

WHITE BEAN PURÉE

2 cups	white navy beans	500 mL
4 cups	water	1 L
¼ tsp	herbes de Provence	1 mL
4 Tbsp	butter	60 mL
to taste	salt and pepper	to taste

1. Place beans in a saucepan and cover with water. Soak overnight and drain. Add 2 cups water and herbes de Provence, place on high heat and bring to boil. Reduce heat to low and simmer until beans are very soft, about 1 hour. Drain off excess water and add butter. Increase heat to medium and continue cooking, stirring constantly, until beans are mashed. Season with salt and pepper.

ONION MARMALADE

1 cup	butter	250 mL
8 lb	Spanish onions, thinly sliced	3.5 kg
1½ cups	red wine	375 mL
1 Tbsp	balsamic vinegar	15 mL
1½ tsp	brown sugar	7 mL
¼ tsp	salt	1 mL

1. In a Dutch oven or heavy casserole melt butter over medium-high heat. Add onions and sauté until lightly browned. Reduce heat to low, cover, and cook for at least 4 hours until onions have almost "melted" and reduced to about 1½ cups (375 mL).

2. Add wine and cook, uncovered, until liquid evaporates, about 20 minutes. Mix in vinegar, sugar and salt, then remove from heat.

RADICCHIO STIR-FRY

4 Tbsp	butter	60 mL
3 cups	fresh shiitake mushrooms, julienned	750 mL
	or 2 cups (500 mL) dried shiitake, soaked in warm water for 20 minutes and julienned, hard stems discarded	
to taste	salt and pepper,	to taste
to taste	soy sauce	to taste
2 cups	bean sprouts	500 mL
3 cups	snow peas, julienned	750 mL
7 cups	shredded radicchio	1.75 L

1. In a large frying pan melt 2 Tbsp (30 mL) of butter over medium-high heat. Add shiitake and sauté until browned. Season with salt and pepper. Remove from pan and set aside.

2. Melt remaining butter over high heat. Add bean sprouts and snow peas and sauté for 2 to 3 minutes. Add shiitake and radicchio and season to taste with soy sauce, salt and pepper. Sauté together for only 1 minute more as radicchio will lose its colour if cooked too long. Serve immediately.

PEAR AND GINGER TARTE

For crème fraîche:

1 cup	sour cream	250 mL
1 cup	whipping cream	250 mL

For tarte:

½ lb	puff pastry	225 g
⅓ cup	butter	75 mL
1 cup	sugar	250 mL
1 tsp	fresh ginger, very finely shredded	5 mL
2 tsp	lemon rind, very finely shredded	10 mL
1 tsp	lemon juice	5 mL
5	Bosc pears, peeled, cored and quartered	5

1. To make crème fraîche, whisk together sour cream and whipping cream in a medium-sized bowl. Cover with plastic wrap and let stand in a warm place overnight or until thickened.

2. For tarte, preheat oven to 425°F (220°C).

3. Roll out puff pastry dough to ⅛-inch (3-mm) thickness. Cut out 12-inch (30-cm) circle. Prick all over with fork and refrigerate.

4. In a heavy 10-inch (25-cm) frying pan with oven-proof handle, melt butter and sugar together over medium heat until sugar starts to turn light brown. Add ginger, lemon rind, lemon juice and pear and cook, turning occasionally, until sugar has caramelized and pears have softened, about 15 minutes. Top with puff pastry. Bake for 15 minutes, or until pastry is golden brown. Invert onto platter and present pear side up. Serve warm, topped with crème fraîche.

RADICCHIO

The darling of cuisine courante. Beautiful white-streaked ruby leaves make a gorgeous addition to a composed plate or a salad. Its slightly bitter taste provides an interesting foil in many combinations. There are many varieties of radicchio; travise is one of our favourites.

SHIITAKE MUSHROOMS

Japanese mushrooms with velvety, pale brown, flat caps. Woodsy and delicate in flavour when fresh. When dried, the flavour intensifies.

SPRING SONATA
Dinner for Eight in Three Courses

Seafood Ravioli

❦

Provimi Veal Stuffed with
Spinach and Mushrooms

Fan Potatoes

❦

Jewel-Box Trifle Cake

There's a touch of Italy in this stylish dinner that's perfect for a cool, spring evening. The repast opens with ravioli filled with shrimp and scallops, and is followed by a roast of veal with a stuffing so simple in its ingredients yet utterly magnificent in flavour. And the finale is a creamy trifle cake brimming with the season's first bounty of fresh strawberries.

WORK-AHEAD SCHEDULE

2 WEEKS AHEAD
- Telephone invitations.
- Arrange for a kitchen helper, if you wish.

1 WEEK AHEAD
- Make list of groceries and check supplies. Order veal and pork fat.
- Plan wines, dishes, flowers and linens. Arrange for rental or loan of dishes, cutlery, etc., if necessary. See checklist page 13.
- Make demi-glace and freeze in small containers.

3 DAYS AHEAD
- Buy wines and all non-perishable supplies.

1 DAY AHEAD
- Buy remaining groceries.
- Prepare Jewel-Box Trifle Cake through to step 13.
- Prepare spinach stuffing for Stuffed Veal. Cover tightly and refrigerate.

EARLY IN DAY
- Make ravioli but do not cook.
- Prepare and stuff veal. Make ready for oven.

2 HOURS BEFORE GUESTS ARRIVE
- Prepare potatoes and cover with water.

1 HOUR BEFORE DINNER
- Bake potatoes.
- Reduce wine and clam juice for Seafood Ravioli.

10 MINUTES BEFORE DINNER
- Cook ravioli and make sauce.

30 MINUTES BEFORE MAIN COURSE
- Roast veal and make Madeira Sauce.

DESSERT TIME
- Add berries to Jewel-Box Trifle Cake.

SEAFOOD RAVIOLI

For ravioli:

½ lb	scallops	225g
1	egg white	1
2 Tbsp	whipping cream	30 mL
1 Tbsp	soft butter	15 mL
¼ tsp	salt	1 mL
⅛ tsp	pepper	0.5 mL
½ lb	shrimp, shelled and cleaned	225 g
1 tsp	chopped fresh dill weed *or* ¼ tsp (1 ml) dried dill weed	5 mL
1 to 2 tsp	corn starch	5 to 10 mL
½ lb	thin wonton wrappers	225 g

For sauce:

½ cup	clam juice (available in bottles)	125 mL
1½ cups	white wine	375 mL
½ cup	cold butter	125 mL

1. In a food processor fitted with a steel blade coarsely chop scallops with egg white, cream, butter, salt and pepper. Remove to mixing bowl.

2. Coarsely chop shrimp and dill weed in processor. Add to mixing bowl and mix thoroughly with scallops.

3. Prepare a baking sheet by dusting lightly with corn starch. Moisten the edges of a wonton wrapper with a little water. Place about one teaspoon (5 mL) of filling in the middle of the wrapper and fold diagonally to form a triangle, sealing well. Place on baking sheet and, with a sieve, sprinkle very lightly with corn starch to prevent sticking. Repeat until all filling is used. Do not stack filled wrappers as they will stick together. If you wish, these may be prepared to this stage and frozen for later use.

4. To prepare sauce, combine clam juice and wine in a large saucepan and bring to boil over medium-high heat. Reduce to one quarter of the original volume. Remove from heat. Cut butter into small pieces and whisk, a little at a time, into reduced clam juice mixture. Sauce will be thin. Keep warm while cooking ravioli.

5. Bring a large pot of water to boil over high heat. Drop in 10 or 15 ravioli and boil for 2 or 3 minutes. When they float to the top, they are cooked. Scoop out with a skimmer or large sieve. Place in a casserole and pour a little sauce over the ravioli. Keep hot in an oven preheated to 200°F (100°C). Repeat until all the ravioli are cooked. Pour rest of sauce into the casserole and serve immediately. Garnish with flat-leaf parsley and diced, seeded, peeled tomatoes, if desired.

Ravioli with an Oriental touch — a cross-cultural combination of paper-thin wonton skins filled with shrimp and scallops in a sinfully rich, buttery sauce. Proving once again that nothing can be too thin or too rich.

Wonton wrappers are thin 3-inch (7-cm) square sheets of uncooked dough made from wheat flour, egg and water. Sold frozen, they are made in two thicknesses. The thick, sometimes called Sui Kow wrappers, has about 100 sheets in a 1-lb (450-g) package. Thin wrappers have about 125 in a 1-lb (450-g) package. Thaw before separating. Keep thawed wrappers covered with a slightly damp cloth as they are quick to dry out.

Don't be surprised by the *unusually large quantities of spinach and mushrooms in this recipe. As they cook, they release moisture, reducing most of their bulk. You may have a little stuffing left over after you fill the veal. Use it the next day to stuff tomatoes for a delicious side dish.*

PROVIMI VEAL

PROtein, **VI**tamins and **MI**nerals *are part of the special baby formula that a calf is fed for its entire brief life. By choosing Provimi veal, you are assured that you are not buying overpriced, anaemic, overaged beef.*

If possible, use Provimi veal, although Choice loin will certainly do. Veal is delicate and lean, so it must not be overcooked. Roast should be slightly tinged with pink, or it will be dry.

Cut slit in loin

Stuff until very plump

PROVIMI VEAL STUFFED WITH SPINACH AND MUSHROOMS

8	10-oz (284-g) bags spinach, well washed and trimmed	8
¾ cup	butter	175 mL
3 lb	mushrooms, sliced ¼ inch (6 mm)	1.35 kg
1½ tsp	crushed garlic	7 mL
1 Tbsp	salt	15 mL
2 tsp	pepper	10 mL
2¼ cups	dry breadcrumbs	550 mL
2	1½- to 2-lb (675- to 900-g) Provimi veal strip loins	2
3 oz	thinly sliced pork fat	80 g
For Madeira sauce:		
2 cups	demi-glace	500 mL
2 to 4 Tbsp	Madeira or port	30 to 60 mL
4 Tbsp	whipping cream	60 mL
to taste	salt and pepper	to taste

1. In a large pot of boiling water blanch spinach for 1 minute and drain. Run under cold water and drain well. Place in a piece of cheesecloth and squeeze dry. Set aside.

2. In a frying pan melt 2 to 3 Tbsp (30 to 45 mL) butter over high heat. Add ¾ to 1 cup (175 mL to 250 mL) of mushrooms and sauté until dry. Season to taste with garlic, salt and pepper. Repeat until all mushrooms and butter have been used. Cook in small amounts so mushrooms cook and dry faster. Set aside to cool.

3. In a food processor fitted with a steel blade process ½ of the spinach for 30 seconds. Add ½ of the mushrooms and ½ of the breadcrumbs. Pulse on/off until mixture is finely chopped. Remove and repeat 3 times with remaining spinach, mushrooms and breadcrumbs.

4. Preheat oven to 425°F (220°C).

5. Trim veal and, in each piece, make a slit in the middle through the length to within ¾ inches (2 cm) of the sides. Using 1 tsp (5 mL) salt and ¾ tsp (3 mL) pepper, season meat inside and out. Into each slit push as much stuffing as possible, making each roast very plump. Any leftover stuffing may be frozen for use at another time. Arrange on baking sheet with as much space as possible between roasts. Cover completely with a layer of pork fat secured with toothpicks. Roast 15 to 20 minutes; meat will be slightly pink. Remove fat and let meat rest for 5 to 10 minutes before slicing. To serve, slice ¼ inch to ½ inch (6 mm to 1.25 cm) thick with a sharp serrated knife, being careful not to push too hard on stuffing. If stuffing falls out, restuff slices after cutting.

6. To make Madeira sauce, combine all ingredients for sauce in a medium-sized saucepan. Bring to boil over medium heat, reduce heat to low and simmer for 3 to 5 minutes. Serve warm with veal slices.

DEMI-GLACE

Yields 2½ cups (625 mL)

8 lb	beef bones	3.5 kg
4 Tbsp	flour	60 mL
1 cup	sliced carrots	250 mL
1 cup	sliced onions	250 mL
½ cup	sliced celery	125 mL
6 quarts	cold water	6 L
½ cup	tomato paste	125 mL
4 cloves	garlic	4 cloves
6	whole cloves	6
3	bay leaves	3
1 Tbsp	rubbed dried thyme	15 mL
10 sprigs	fresh parsley	10 sprigs
1 tsp	pepper	5 mL
2 cups	red wine	500 mL

1. Preheat oven to 450°F (230°C).

2. Dust the beef bones with flour and place in roasting pan. Roast for 2 hours, or until bones are golden brown. Add carrots, onions and celery and continue roasting for another hour, or until vegetables are well browned. Transfer bones and vegetables to large pot and cover with cold water. Add remaining ingredients and bring to boil over high heat. Immediately lower heat and simmer for 8 to 10 hours. Remove from heat and strain out bones. Skim off fat. Strain stock through cheesecloth and return to pot. Simmer over low heat until volume is reduced to about 2½ cups (625 mL). This sauce freezes well.

FAN POTATOES

16	small, round potatoes	16
½ lb	butter	225 g
to taste	salt and pepper	to taste
1 tsp	ground dried rosemary	5 mL

1. Preheat oven to 375°F (190°C).

2. Peel potatoes and trim to oval-shaped uniform sizes. Cover with cold water. Working with one potato at a time, remove from water and make a cut half way through the potato, across the width. Repeat at ⅛-inch (3-mm) intervals along the length of the potato. Remove one slice from the middle to allow the slices to fan out while baking. Return cut potato to water and repeat with the remaining potatoes. When all have been cut, drain, pat dry and place in roasting pan, cut sides up. Brush liberally with butter and season with salt and pepper. Bake for 1 hour, basting with more butter every 10 minutes. Fifteen minutes before baking time is up, sprinkle with rosemary and more salt and pepper. Remove and serve hot, two potatoes per person.

JEWEL-BOX TRIFLE CAKE

For pound cake:

2⅔ cups	sifted cake flour	650 mL
¼ tsp	cream of tartar	1 mL
½ tsp	salt	2 mL
¼ tsp	mace	1 mL
1⅓ cups	butter	325 mL
1⅓ cups	sugar	325 mL
6	eggs, at room temperature	6
1 tsp	vanilla	5 mL

For praline:

3 cups	sugar	750 mL
¾ cup	roasted sliced almonds	175 mL

For pastry cream:

2 cups	milk	500 mL
1 cup	cream (10%)	250 mL
1 tsp	vanilla	5 mL
4 Tbsp	sugar	60 mL
4	egg yolks	4
3	eggs	3
4 Tbsp	flour	60 mL
2 Tbsp	butter	30 mL

To assemble:

3 Tbsp	Amaretto	45 mL
3 Tbsp	Cassis	45 mL
⅓ cup	red currant jelly	75 mL
1 pint	strawberries	500 mL
½ pint	blackberries	250 mL
½ pint	raspberries	250 mL
2	sprigs fresh mint leaves	2

1. For pound cake, preheat oven to 300°F (150°C). Butter and flour a 9-inch × 5-inch × 3-inch (23-cm × 13-cm × 7-cm) pan.

2. Sift together flour, cream of tartar, salt and mace and set aside.

3. In a large mixing bowl cream butter with an electric beater. Beating constantly on medium speed, add sugar a tablespoon (about 15 mL) at a time until light and fluffy. Add eggs, one at a time, beating well after each addition. Stir in vanilla.

4. With beater on low speed, gradually add dry ingredients and beat only until thoroughly blended.

5. Pour into prepared pan and bake for 1 hour. Remove cake from pan and cool on wire rack.

6. Cut top off cake and reserve lid. Hollow out cake to form a box with sides ½ inch (1.25 cm) thick. (Reserve the pieces of cake for another use.) Set aside box.

7. For praline, heat sugar in a heavy frying pan over medium-

low heat. Toss lightly with a fork to ensure that it heats evenly. When it is completely melted and golden brown, remove from heat and stir in almonds.

8. Ladle a thin coating of praline over the entire surface of the top of the cake lid, and the outside sides and top edge of the box. Wear oven mitts or rubber gloves to prevent burns from the hot praline. Work quickly as praline hardens within 5 to 10 minutes. Keep the pan on very low heat while working; do not allow to burn. Set box aside to cool and harden.

9. For pastry cream, scald milk and cream in a heavy saucepan over medium heat. Stir in vanilla. Turn heat down to medium-low.

10. In a medium-sized bowl beat sugar, egg yolks and eggs until mixture falls from whisk in a ribbon. Stir in flour and mix thoroughly. Slowly pour half of the hot liquid into the egg mixture, beating constantly. Return to saucepan and beat. Turn heat up to medium-high and bring to boil. Boil for 1 minute or until thickened. Stir in butter.

11. Transfer to a bowl. Place plastic wrap directly on surface of pastry cream to keep skin from forming. Set aside to cool.

12. To assemble, sprinkle Amaretto and Cassis over the inside of box and lid. Press small spoonfuls of jelly around the inside of the box. Place on platter.

13. Pour cooled pastry cream into box to within ½ inch (1.25 cm) of the top. Reserve remaining pastry cream to pass when serving. At this point, box can be refrigerated for up to 24 hours. The cake is best prepared ahead of time in order to allow the flavour to mature.

14. Just before serving, rinse berries and mound fruit attractively in and around the box. Garnish with mint leaves. Place lid on top and offset slightly to show fruit. Present cake at table before cutting.

Spread praline over top of "lid" and sides of "box"

EVENING IN VENICE
Dinner for Eight in Seven Courses

Eggplant, Red Pepper and Zucchini Salad

❦

Angel Hair with Sun-Dried Tomatoes, Pine Nuts and Asiago

❦

Marinated Tiger Shrimp

❦

Roast Loin of Veal with Tuna Sauce

❦

Tomato Granita with Pesto

❦

Almond Cornucopia of Summer Fruit

❦

Fruit and Cheese

This cold Italian dinner is the ultimate in cool grace and is perfect for a hot summer's night. Each course, a small elegantly designed serving, is arranged on individual plates in advance, so your work is done before the guests arrive.

WORK-AHEAD SCHEDULE

2 WEEKS AHEAD
- Telephone invitations.
- Arrange for a kitchen helper, if you wish.

1 WEEK AHEAD
- Make a list of groceries and check supplies. Order veal roast and tiger shrimp.
- Plan wines, dishes, flowers and linens. Arrange for rental or loan of dishes, cutlery, etc., if necessary. See checklist page 13.
- You will need 7 small plates and corresponding cutlery for each guest as each course is served separately in this dinner. Don't feel that all the plates must match. Get 7 different patterns and serve each course on a different pattern. Or, for a very charming effect, use a different pattern for each guest.

3 DAYS AHEAD
- Shop for all non-perishable groceries, including liquor, wine and other bar requirements.

1 DAY BEFORE
- Shop for remaining groceries.
- Make Almond Cornucopias and store in airtight container.
- Make Tomato Granita, scoop into balls on cookie sheet, wrap in foil and keep in freezer. Make Pesto Sauce and refrigerate.
- Shop for flowers and candles.
- Cut green-onion flowers, immerse in water and refrigerate.

EARLY IN DAY
- Roast veal.
- Prepare Marinated Tiger Shrimp and refrigerate.
- Make Eggplant, Red Pepper and Zucchini Salad and Angel Hair with Sun-dried Tomatoes, Pine Nuts and Asiago.

- Prepare tuna sauce for Roast Loin of Veal.
- Arrange Fruit and Cheese on a platter.
- Buy ice-cubes for drinks.
- Set table and arrange flowers.

- Arrange servings on individual plates, except for Tomato Granita and Almond Cornucopia of Summer Fruit which have to be arranged just prior to serving.

2 HOURS BEFORE GUESTS ARRIVE

½ HOUR BEFORE SERVING

EGGPLANT, RED PEPPER AND ZUCCHINI SALAD

5	red bell peppers	5
1 Tbsp	rosemary-flavoured olive oil or olive oil plus a pinch of powdered rosemary	15 mL
3	medium-sized zucchini, sliced ⅛ inch (3 mm)	3
1 to 2 tsp	olive oil for grilling	5 to 10 mL
2	small eggplants, cut in half lengthwise and sliced ¼ inch (6 mm)	2
1 to 2 Tbsp	salt	15 to 30 mL

For zucchini marinade:

1 Tbsp	malt, cider or red wine vinegar	15 mL
2 cloves	garlic, crushed	2 cloves
1 Tbsp	brown sugar	15 mL
pinch	dried mint	pinch
to taste	salt and pepper	to taste

For eggplant marinade:

⅓ cup	olive oil	75 mL
4 Tbsp	lemon juice	60 mL
2 cloves	garlic, crushed	2 cloves
to taste	salt and pepper	to taste

1. For red bell peppers: Preheat oven to 500°F (260°C) or as high as possible. Place a pan of hot water on the lowest rack of the oven. Put peppers on upper rack and roast for 30 to 45 minutes, rotating once during cooking. Peppers should be sweaty with slightly wrinkled skin. Remove from oven and put in a plastic bag. Close the bag and let peppers steam in their own heat for 15 minutes. Remove from bag and run under cold water. Peel, seed and cut into long ¼-inch (6-mm) strips and place in small bowl. Add rosemary-flavoured olive oil and toss. Set aside.

2. For zucchini: Heat a heavy frying pan—cast iron is best—over medium-high heat. Brush surface lightly with a paper towel moistened with oil. Allow pan to become very hot but not smoking. Add a layer of zucchini and grill 1 to 2 minutes on both sides, until wilted and spotted with brown. Remove to bowl and repeat until all zucchini has been grilled. Set aside.

3. In a small bowl combine all ingredients for zucchini marinade. Add to grilled zucchini and toss well. Set aside.

OLIVE OIL

Wherever we refer to olive oil, it is of the extra-virgin quality — cold pressed oil that comes from the first pressing of the finest olives. In Dinah's Cupboard we occasionally have tastings of olive oil selected from the many varieties we stock. This is an excellent way of acquainting yourself with the rich and complex flavours of fine oils, some costing as much as a fine bottle of wine. Use the very best oils for cold preparations such as salads, pesto, carpaccio, chèvre in herbed oil. And always good olive oil for cooking.

Zona Chianti Classico Hills

Tuscany oil

Product of France

4. For eggplant: Sprinkle eggplant slices with salt and allow to sweat for 30 minutes in a colander. Pat dry with paper towels, then grill, using the same method as for zucchini.

5. In a small bowl combine all ingredients for eggplant marinade. Add to grilled eggplant and toss well.

6. For each serving, arrange peppers, zucchini and eggplant in three separate little groupings on a small plate. Serve at room temperature.

ANGEL-HAIR PASTA WITH SUN-DRIED TOMATOES, PINE NUTS AND ASIAGO

1 lb	capellini (angel hair) or fedelini	450 g
4 Tbsp	olive oil	60 mL
3 Tbsp	oil from sun-dried tomatoes	45 mL
½ cup	julienned sun-dried tomatoes	125 mL
1 cup	toasted pine nuts	250 mL
10 oz	Asiago cheese, crumbled	275 g
¾ tsp	salt	3 mL
½ tsp	pepper	2 mL

1. In a pot of salted boiling water cook pasta *al dente*. Drain and run under cold water. Drain very well and place in large mixing bowl. Add olive oil and oil from tomatoes. Toss to coat well. Add remaining ingredients and toss well.

2. Be sure each serving has a good distribution of nuts. Pine nuts have a tendency to fall to the bottom of the bowl.

SUN-DRIED TOMATOES

Field-ripened plum tomatoes are air dried in the open sun then packed in olive oil. Bursting with concentrated flavour, slices of these tomatoes are fabulous added to any dish that welcomes tomatoes.

ANGEL-HAIR PASTA (CAPELLINI)

Just like spaghetti but ultra thin — as thin as an angel's hair, the name implies. If angel hair is unavailable, substitute spaghettini or fedelini.

MARINATED TIGER SHRIMP

8	tiger shrimp, about 4 to 5 oz (110 to 140 g) each	8
For marinade:		
1 cup	coarsely chopped fresh basil	250 mL
¾ cup	olive oil	175 mL
2 Tbsp	lemon juice	30 mL
to taste	salt and pepper	to taste
garnish	cucumber, lemon and green onions	garnish

1. Steam shrimp over hot water until just cooked, about 5 minutes. Shrimp will turn pink. When cool enough to handle, remove shells, leaving tails on. Set aside.

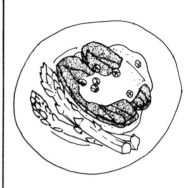

2. In a medium-sized mixing bowl combine all ingredients for marinade. Mix well and add shrimp. Toss to coat well and marinate, refrigerated, for 1 to 2 hours, turning occasionally.

3. For each serving, place one shrimp on a doily of thinly sliced cucumber, spoon a little marinade on top and garnish with a lemon slice or green-onion flower (see page 185).

ROAST LOIN OF VEAL WITH TUNA SAUCE

4 lb	veal strip loin, white Provimi, if possible, or veal tenderloin	2 kg
to taste	salt and pepper	to taste
4 oz	pork fat, thinly sliced	100 g
For sauce:		
2	6.5-oz (184-g) cans white chunk tuna, drained	2
½ cup	olive oil	125 mL
6 Tbsp	lemon juice	90 mL
2 cloves	garlic, crushed	2 cloves
1 tsp	Worcestershire sauce	5 mL
¼ cup	black Greek or Italian olives, pitted	60 mL
6	anchovy fillets	6
1 cup	whipping cream	250 mL
4 tsp	capers	20 mL
4 tsp	chopped fresh flat-leaf parsley	20 mL
24 to 40	steamed asparagus stalks	24 to 40

1. Preheat oven to 400°F (200°C).

2. Cut meat into 2 pieces for more even and quicker roasting. Season each piece liberally with salt and pepper. Place on roasting pan and cover with slices of pork fat. Roast for 15 to 20 minutes, or until medium rare. Set aside to cool. Slice thinly, ⅛ inch to ¼ inch (3 to 6 mm). The meat can be prepared up to this point, earlier in the day.

3. Combine all ingredients for sauce, except whipping cream, in a food processor fitted with a steel blade. Process for about 1 to 2 minutes. The ingredients should be blended, but with olives still in little pieces.

4. In a medium-sized bowl beat whipping cream to soft peak stage. Fold in tuna mixture.

5. For each serving, spoon about ⅓ cup (75 mL) sauce on a small plate. Arrange a few slices of veal on top and garnish with capers and a sprinkling of parsley. Serve with a few stalks of crisp, steamed asparagus.

TOMATO GRANITA WITH PESTO

For granita:

1	28-oz (796-mL) can plum tomatoes, undrained	1
4 tsp	balsamic vinegar	20 mL
1 tsp	salt	5 mL
½ tsp	pepper	2 mL
1 recipe	pesto (page 66)	1 recipe

1. Set freezer at lowest temperature.

2. Into a mixing bowl press tomatoes and their juice through food mill or sieve, removing seeds. Add remaining ingredients. Pour into rectangular baking pan and freeze for at least 5 hours, stirring once an hour to break up ice crystals as they form.

3. Just before serving, spoon 1 to 2 Tbsp (15 to 30 mL) of pesto on each plate. Using a small sherbet scoop or a ⅓-cup (75-mL) measure, pack granita into balls and carefully turn them out onto pesto, one for each serving.

BALSAMIC VINEGAR

Italian vinegar that has been fermented and aged in oak barrels for 7 to 100 years. Highly aromatic and sweetly pungent in flavour.

If the day is very humid, the Almond Cornucopias might not hold their shape. If this is the case, there is no need to shape the cookies. Simply serve each one flat, with a mound of fruit and cream on top.

ALMOND CORNUCOPIA OF SUMMER FRUIT

For cornucopias:

⅓ cup	melted butter	75 mL
3	egg whites	3
1 cup	sugar	250 mL
½ tsp	vanilla	2 mL
3 Tbsp	flour	45 mL
2½ cups	sliced almonds	625 mL

For vanilla cream:

1 lb	soft, deli-style cream cheese	450 g
½ cup	brown sugar	125 mL
2 tsp	vanilla	10 mL
4 Tbsp	whipping cream	60 mL
3 cups	assorted fresh berries	750 mL

1. For cornucopias, preheat oven to 375°F (190°C). Line two cookie sheets with parchment, or butter liberally.

2. In a mixing bowl combine butter, egg whites, sugar and vanilla. Stir for 2 or 3 minutes to dissolve sugar. Stir in flour, then add almonds and mix gently. Drop a 3 Tbsp (45 mL) measure of almond batter onto each prepared baking sheet. Spread out thinly into 5-inch (12-cm) circles. Bake for 10 to 12 minutes, or until edges are golden brown and centres are beginning to brown. Remove and cool for 1 minute. Using a metal spatula, free one cookie from pan, taking care to not tear the still-soft centre, and form by hand into horn shape. Hold for 30 to 45 seconds until it begins to harden. Repeat with second cookie. If it has become too brittle to work with, return to the oven for a minute to soften. Repeat until all batter has been used. Store cornucopias in a dry, airtight container.

3. To make vanilla cream, combine cream cheese, brown sugar and vanilla in a medium-sized mixing bowl, and beat until light and fluffy with an electric beater. Add whipping cream and whip until smooth. Keep refrigerated if not using immediately.

4. To assemble, just before serving, select the 8 best cornucopias and place one on each dessert plate. Using a large star tip, pipe about ⅓ cup (75 mL) vanilla cream into each and fill with an assortment of berries.

FRUIT AND CHEESE

Select one or two Italian dessert cheeses such as Gorgonzola, Torta, Fontina or Mascarpone. Complement them with a Cheddar and a Brie and serve with a colourful assortment of strawberries, apples, pears and grapes. Arrange on a large platter or board.

BRUNCH FOR 12

Bastilla
Brown Rice Salad
Caribbean Shrimp and Cheese
Grapefruit-Avocado-Onion Salad
Apple-Orange Coffee Cake
Melon Basket

Brunch always seems so perfect on Sundays. With none of the weekday's beat-the-clock schedules, it's the ideal time to invite friends for a leisurely meal.

When planning a brunch menu, we look for items that are substantial but not too rich; food that can be kept warm for long periods, or are good at room temperature. That way, guests can come and go at their own pace.

Our brunch offerings cross many borders. From the Caribbean comes a flavoursome mix of shrimp, tomatoes and cheese; from the Middle East, bastilla — sweetly spiced chicken enveloped in light-as-air pastry; and from the health-conscious West Coast, brown rice salad.

Special drinks that go best with brunch: Mimosa (champagne and freshly squeezed orange juice), Kir Royale, Bellini (peach juice and champagne), Screwdriver and Bloody Mary.

As an alternative to our globe-trotting menu, take a simpler route with either of these two easy-going ideas: the omelette party or pasta party.

The Omelette Party

Omelette parties are great fun. Arrange big baskets of eggs and lots of different fillings on a table and cook omelettes to order in front of the guests. Set up an omelette bar in the dining room, with a hot plate, electric frying pan or réchauffé burner, or more informally in the kitchen, where guests seem to congregate naturally. On warm summer mornings, the balcony can be a great place for omelette making. A few loaves of freshly baked bread, sticky buns, hashed brown potatoes and a salad or two will round out the fare.

The Pasta Party

Everybody loves pasta. And a pasta bar is easy on the hostess and a novelty for the guests. We always offer a variety and encourage everyone to try them all. Cook two or three different shapes and colours of pasta and several sauces — Alfredo, tomato, pesto — and keep everything warm in chafing dishes. Load the table with toppings — freshly grated Parmesan, chopped fresh parsley, paprika flakes, salami slices, meatballs, bacon bits. And let your guests create. For accompaniments, serve hot garlic bread, a piquant leafy salad and an assortment of antipasti, such as olives, marinated eggplant and spiced sausage.

WORK-AHEAD SCHEDULE

- Telephone invitations.
- Arrange for a kitchen helper and a bartender/waiter, if you wish.

- Plan usage of serving dishes and arrange for rental or loan of china, cutlery, etc., if necessary. See checklist page 13.

- Make lists for bar requirements and groceries, and shop.

- Prepare but do not bake Caribbean Shrimp and Cheese.
- Assemble but do not bake Bastilla. Coat well with melted butter to keep phyllo from drying out. Refrigerate uncovered.
- Make Brown Rice Salad, cover with a damp cloth then wrap tightly with plastic wrap and refrigerate.
- Make Apple-Orange Coffee Cake.
- Buy flowers and arrange in vases.

- Buy ice-cubes for drinks.
- Make Melon Basket.
- Remove Brown Rice Salad from refrigerator and allow to come to room temperature.
- Bake Bastilla. Can be served at room temperature.

- Bake Caribbean Shrimp and Cheese.
- Assemble Grapefruit-Avocado-Onion Salad.

BASTILLA

Sweetly spiced chicken layered with buttery eggs, enveloped in a dome of light-as-air pastry and dusted with almonds, cinnamon and sugar. This is a sensational-looking dish that will draw raves from the moment of presentation until the last bite has been savoured.

For chicken layer:

1	6- to 7-lb (2.75- to 3.25-kg) capon *or* 2 small chickens	1
1 cup	strong chicken stock	250 mL
¼ tsp	saffron threads	1 mL
1 Tbsp	ground cinnamon	15 mL
1 Tbsp	curry powder	15 mL
1 Tbsp	grated fresh ginger	15 mL
½ tsp	ground cardamom	2 mL
1½ tsp	salt	7 mL
9	eggs	9
4 Tbsp	lemon juice	60 mL
1 Tbsp	butter	15 mL

For almond layer:

½ cup	butter	125 mL
3 cups	sliced almonds	750 mL
½ cup	sugar	125 mL
4 tsp	ground cinnamon	20 mL

For pastry:

1	1-lb (454-g) package phyllo pastry	1
1 cup (approx.)	melted butter	250 mL (approx.)

For topping:

¼ cup	toasted sliced almonds	60 mL
2 tsp	icing sugar	10 mL
1 tsp	ground cinnamon	5 mL

1. Cut the capon or chickens into serving pieces. Place in a single layer in a roasting pan, skin side up. Add chicken stock. Sprinkle with saffron threads, ground cinnamon, curry powder, grated ginger and ground cardamom. Cover tightly with foil and poach in the oven, basting occasionally, until just underdone, about 25 minutes (depending on size of pieces). The meat should still be pink. Cool completely and reserve the pan juices.

2. Remove the bones and skin, reserving skin. Cut or tear meat into strips about ½ inches × 2 inches (1.25 cm × 5 cm). Place in a medium-sized mixing bowl and set aside.

3. In a food processor fitted with a steel blade purée the skin. Most of the spices will have adhered to the skin during poaching. Add to sliced meat with ½ tsp (2 mL) salt, or to taste. Set aside.

4. In a medium-sized mixing bowl beat eggs with lemon juice, all pan juices and fat reserved from poaching and 1 tsp (5 mL) salt. In a frying pan melt 1 tsp (5 mL) butter over medium heat. Add one third of the egg mixture and scramble until quite crumbly and moisture is being released. Remove and place in strainer to drain off excess liquid. Repeat with remaining butter and egg mixture. Set aside to cool.

5. In a frying pan melt ½ cup (125 mL) butter over medium heat.

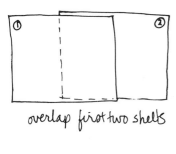

overlap first two shells

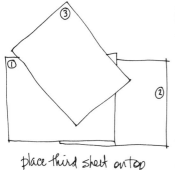

place third sheet on top

Add sliced almonds and sauté until golden brown, stirring constantly. Add sugar and cinnamon, stir to melt sugar and cool.

6. Preheat oven to 400°F (200°C).

7. Unfold phyllo pastry and lay out flat on working surface. Cover with a slightly damp cloth as the thin sheets of pastry dry out very quickly and become difficult to work with. Remove 6 sheets of phyllo and place on a large baking sheet about 11 inches × 16 inches (28 cm × 40 cm), as diagrammed. Brush each one lightly with melted butter. Work quickly to keep phyllo from drying out and cracking. Remove another sheet of phyllo and brush with butter. Fold in four and place in the centre of the baking sheet.

8. Place two thirds of the chicken mixture in the middle of the pastry and form it into a circular mound the width of the pan. Sprinkle half of the almond-butter mixture over the chicken, then heap on the egg mixture to create a little flat-topped mound. Sprinkle on half of the remaining almond-butter mixture and top with the remaining chicken mixture, rounding it off at the top so that the entire mound of filling takes on the shape of an inverted bowl. Sprinkle on remaining almond-butter mixture.

9. Remove another sheet of phyllo and butter it lightly. Fold in four and place over the top of the filling. Bring the sheets of phyllo that form the base up around the top, tucking and smoothing to round the shape nicely. Brush on additional butter if necessary. Remove and lightly butter 4 more sheets of phyllo. Place them over the mound, one at a time and at different angles, smoothing the top and tucking ends snugly under the mound. Brush with melted butter and bake for 30 minutes, or until golden brown.

10. To make topping, combine toasted sliced almonds, icing sugar and cinnamon in a small bowl. Mix well and sprinkle over baked Bastilla. Transfer to large platter or tray and cut in wedges to serve.

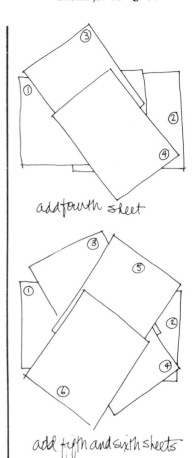

add fourth sheet

add fifth and sixth sheets

BROWN RICE SALAD

4 cups	brown rice	1 L
4 cups	chicken stock	1 L
½ cup	olive oil	125 mL
⅔ cup	freshly squeezed orange juice	150 mL
4 Tbsp	grated orange rind	60 mL
1 cup	roasted pine nuts	250 mL
1 cup	currants	250 mL
1 tsp	salt	5 mL
¼ tsp	pepper	1 mL

1. In a heavy pot with a lid add brown rice and chicken stock. Cover and bring to a boil. Lower heat and simmer for 30 minutes.

2. Transfer rice to a bowl, add oil and orange juice and mix well. Cool to room temperature.

3. Add grated orange rind, pine nuts, currants, salt and pepper and toss together.

CARIBBEAN SHRIMP AND CHEESE

A flavoursome mix of shrimp, tomatoes, olives and gherkins enveloped in a "crust" of Edam cheese.

2 lb	Edam cheese	900 g
2 Tbsp	butter	30 mL
1½ cups	chopped onions	375 mL
2½ cups	diced tomatoes	625 mL
2 lb	medium-sized shrimp, peeled, cleaned, and each cut into three pieces	900 g
½ cup	finely chopped stuffed olives	125 mL
6	sweet pickled gherkins, chopped	6
1½ cups	loosely packed fresh breadcrumbs	375 mL
1	egg, lightly beaten	1
½ cup	raisins	125 mL
½ tsp	cayenne	2 mL
to taste	salt and pepper	to taste

1. Preheat oven to 375°F (190°C).

2. Slice 1½ lb (675 g) of the cheese into ¼-inch (6-mm) slices. Chop the remaining ½ lb (225 g) in a food processor fitted with a steel blade.

3. Line the bottom and sides of a 3-quart (3-L) soufflé dish with the slices of cheese. Reserve enough slices to cover the top.

4. Melt butter in a frying pan over high heat. Add chopped onions and sauté for 2 or 3 minutes. Add chopped tomatoes and cook until liquid evaporates and mixture is quite dry. Set aside to cool.

5. In a large mixing bowl combine the shrimp pieces, chopped stuffed olives, chopped gherkins, breadcrumbs, egg, raisins, cayenne, and a little salt and pepper. Be careful with the amount of salt as Edam cheese tends to be slightly salty. Add the chopped cheese and the cooled tomato mixture and toss well to mix. Spoon into the cheese-lined soufflé dish. Cover with an even layer of reserved cheese slices and bake for 45 minutes, or until browned and bubbly and shrimps are just cooked. Serve hot.

GRAPEFRUIT-AVOCADO-ONION SALAD

2	medium-sized red or Spanish onions	2
4	seedless grapefruit, preferably pink	4
4	small ripe avocados	4
4 to 6 Tbsp	lemon juice	60 to 90 mL
1 cup	Honey-Lemon Dressing (see recipe below)	250 mL

1. Cut onions in ⅛-inch (3-mm) slices. Separate the slices into rings and place in a bowl. Cover with cold water and soak overnight in refrigerator, changing water 2 or 3 times.

2. Using a small, sharp, serrated knife, cut away all pith and rind of grapefruit. Try to avoid cutting into the flesh as much as possible. Remove segments by carefully cutting between membrane and flesh, keeping segments whole. Set aside.

3. Just before serving, peel avocados and cut each into 10 to 12 long wedges. Sprinkle liberally with lemon juice to prevent discolouration. Arrange on serving platter. Drain onions and scatter over avocados. Arrange grapefruit segments on top. Drizzle Honey-Lemon Dressing over salad and serve.

To prepare grapefruit trim away rind and pith with a paring knife.

HONEY-LEMON DRESSING

Yields 1 cup (250 mL)

⅔ cup	lemon juice	150 mL
⅓ cup	olive oil	75 mL
3 Tbsp	honey	45 mL
1	egg yolk	1
½ tsp	finely minced garlic	2 mL
½ tsp	salt	2 mL
¼ tsp	pepper	1 mL

1. Combine all ingredients in bowl and whisk together, or put all ingredients in a blender and process until thoroughly mixed. Toss with salad greens.

This dressing goes wonderfully with so many different flavours. Toss a salad of as many varieties of greens as possible and, if you like, fresh fruit. Try combinations of leaf, bibb or romaine lettuce with greens like spinach, watercress, mâche (lamb's quarters), arugula or dandelion greens. The honey-lemon flavour is especially complementary to bittersweet chicories, so add radicchio, Belgian endive or curly endive.

APPLE-ORANGE COFFEE CAKE

Moist chunks of apple are nestled in a tender cake drizzled with a creamy caramel glaze. Who can resist?

APPEALING ZEST

When grating the rind of oranges and lemons, use a light hand to take only the zippy fragrant peel and avoid the bitter white pith. Or, use a zester. This little tool, with tiny holes across the top of a small stainless steel head, produces delicate strands of peel.

For cake:

4	apples, cored and peeled	4
5 Tbsp	sugar	75 mL
5 tsp	ground cinnamon	25 mL
1 cup	vegetable oil	250 mL
4	eggs	4
¼ cup	freshly squeezed orange juice	60 mL
1 tsp	grated orange rind	5 mL
1 Tbsp	vanilla	15 mL
3 cups	flour	750 mL
1 Tbsp	baking powder	15 mL
1 tsp	salt	5 mL
2 cups	sugar	500 mL

For caramel glaze:

½ cup	butter	125 mL
½ cup	brown sugar	125 mL
¼ cup	whipping cream	60 mL

1. Preheat oven to 375°F (190°C). Line a 9-inch × 12-inch (23-cm × 30-cm) cake pan with parchment, or butter and dust with flour.

2. Cut each apple into 12 wedges and combine with sugar and cinnamon in a small bowl.

3. In a large mixing bowl beat together the oil, eggs, orange juice, orange rind and vanilla.

4. Sift together flour, baking powder, salt and sugar. Add all at once to the oil and egg mixture and stir lightly just until well blended. Batter will be very thick.

5. Spread half of the batter in the prepared cake pan. Arrange half of the apple wedges on the batter. Cover with the remaining batter and arrange the rest of the apples on top. Sprinkle excess cinnamon and sugar from apples over the top. Bake for 1 hour or until a toothpick inserted into the middle of the cake comes out clean.

6. Combine butter, brown sugar and whipping cream in a small saucepan to make glaze. Bring to boil over medium heat and stir until melted and smooth. While cake is still hot, make small holes all over the top with a toothpick and pour on the warm glaze.

MELON BASKET

1	large watermelon	1
1	gold watermelon, *or* 2 cantaloupe and 1 honeydew melon	1
½ cup	liqueur (optional)	125 mL
3 to 5 bunches	green and purple grapes	3 to 5 bunches
assort-ment	seasonal fruit	assort-ment

1. Cut large watermelon into a basket, as described on page 189. Using a small ice-cream scoop approximately 1½ inches (3 cm) in diameter, make large melon balls out of the flesh of the watermelon. If gold watermelon is available, make large yellow melon balls to mix with the pink for striking colour contrast. If not, use cantaloupe and honeydew melon cut into large chunks. Sprinkle liqueur on melon, if desired, then pile into basket. Around the base of the basket, arrange several bunches of green and purple grapes, and strawberries, or a few peaches, plums and apricots.

HORS D'OEUVRE DINNER FOR 20

Olive, Artichoke and Mozzarella Salad
Little Filled Tortillas
Braised Country-Style Chicken Wings
Potato Skins
Antipasto Salad
Hot Cajun Shrimp
Lemon-Garlic Meatballs
Mini Scotch Eggs
Deep-Fried Mushrooms and Zucchini

S panish taverns are famous for their tapas. Little dishes of fork and finger foods are served all night to hungry patrons—bites of everything from garlic shrimp and grilled spicy sausage to frittata and stuffed squid.

Chinese, the world over, engage in the venerable custom of dim sum. Tea taken with many small and varied savouries such as shrimp dumplings, stuffed crab claws, sticky rice in banana leaves, and other exotica.

In North America, we too are showing a fondness for a style of eating that is best described as grazing. Leisurely sampling a variety of tantalizing little servings; eating to your own rhythm. Making a meal of three or four hors d'oeuvres that leave you satisfied, yet not stuffed.

If this serendipitous way of eating appeals to you, you'll love our hors d'oeuvre dinner. The menu includes lots of different flavours and textures. Some dishes can be kept warm in chafing dishes, others can be passed around. Set up a buffet and replenish from the kitchen as necessary.

Relax; this is an evening that flows by itself. Guests eat at their own pace and serve themselves. Just make sure you have lots of small dishes and napkins available, and encourage your guests to nibble through the evening as they sip, chat and mingle.

WORK-AHEAD SCHEDULE

4 WEEKS AHEAD

- Send out invitations.
- Plan layout of room(s).
- Organize music.

2 WEEKS AHEAD

- Plan usage of serving dishes and chafing dishes.
- Arrange rental or loan of any dishes, cutlery, etc., if necessary. See checklist page 13.
- Arrange for a kitchen helper and a bartender/waiter.

1 WEEK AHEAD

- Make grocery list and shop for non-perishable items. Don't forget to get lots of cocktail napkins and fuel for the chafing dishes.
- Make list and shop for bar requirements.

- Make Little Filled Tortillas.
- Make Olive, Artichoke and Mozzarella Salad.
- Make Antipasto Salad.
- Prepare but do not fry meatballs for Lemon-Garlic Meatballs.
- Shop for flowers and arrange them in vases.
- Buy remaining groceries.

- Peel and clean shrimp for Hot Cajun Shrimp. Make sauce and marinate shrimp.
- Bake potatoes for Potato Skins, cut and fry.
- Prepare Mini Scotch Eggs but do not fry.
- Cut up zucchini and clean mushrooms for Deep-Fried Mushrooms and Zucchini.

- Buy ice-cubes for the drinks.
- Make Country-Style Chicken Wings.
- Fry meatballs.
- Fry Scotch eggs
- Make Lemon-Garlic Sauce.
- Fry tortillas.

- Heat chicken wings.
- Broil shrimp.
- Heat tortillas in oven or serve at room temperature.
- Broil potato skins.
- Prepare batter and deep fry zucchini and mushrooms.
- Heat meatballs in sauce.

OLIVE, ARTICHOKE AND MOZZARELLA SALAD

1 lb	green olives (in olive oil and coated with chilies, if desired)	450 g
1 lb	black or Greek olives	450 g
2 lb	fresh Mozzarella cheese, sliced ¼ inch (6 mm), *or* feta cheese or regular Mozzarella, cubed ½ inch (1.25 cm)	900 g
½	lemon, quartered and thinly sliced	½
4 to 6	6-oz (170-mL) jars marinated artichoke hearts, slightly drained	4 to 6
⅓ cup	olive oil	75 mL
4 cloves	garlic, finely minced	4 cloves
¾ cup	coarsely chopped Italian parsley	175 mL

Use Greek or Italian olives and Bocconcini-style Mozzarella cheese. Search out the best quality ingredients and you will be rewarded with their wonderful flavour and texture.

1. In a large mixing bowl combine all ingredients. Mix well and allow flavours to blend for at least 2 hours. Serve at room temperature.

LITTLE FILLED TORTILLAS

Masa harina, a very fine cornmeal ground from white or yellow corn, is used to make Mexican tortillas and tamales. Texture resembles chickpea flour.

For filling:

2 lb	ground pork	900 g
1 cup	water	250 mL
4 Tbsp	red wine vinegar	60 mL
8 cloves	garlic, crushed	8 cloves
4 Tbsp	tomato paste	60 mL
2 to 5 tsp	chili powder	10 to 25 mL
½ tsp	ground cinnamon	2 mL
2 tsp	salt	10 mL
½ tsp	pepper	2 mL
to taste	Tabasco sauce	to taste
to taste	cayenne	to taste

For shells:

½ cup	lard, softened	125 mL
3 cups	corn flour (masa harina)	750 mL
3 to 3½ cups	water	750 to 875 mL
1	egg, lightly beaten	1
3 to 4 cups	vegetable oil for deep frying	0.75 to 1 L

1. In a frying pan, over medium-high heat, fry pork until golden brown. Add water and vinegar to deglaze pan, scraping up bits from the bottom of the pan. Add remaining filling ingredients to season. Continue cooking until fat is released. Tilt pan and spoon off excess fat. Remove from heat and cool. Set aside.

2. To make shells, beat lard until creamed. Stir in flour and add enough water to make a soft dough. Roll out dough on floured surface to ¹⁄₁₆-inch (2-mm) thickness. Cut into 2-inch (5-cm) rounds with cookie cutter.

3. To assemble, place ½ Tbsp (7 mL) filling in the middle of one round of pastry. Brush the edges with egg wash and top with another round of pastry. Crimp edges closed, using the tip of a fork and taking care not to crack the top. Set aside and repeat with remaining filling and pastry.

4. In a heavy frying pan or deep fryer heat oil to 350°F (180°C). Deep fry tortillas a few at a time, until golden brown. Drain on paper towels.

5. Serve with hot sauce, if desired.

place filling on round

top with another round and crimp closed with fork tines.

BRAISED COUNTRY-STYLE CHICKEN WINGS

5 lb	chicken wings (about 28 pieces)	2.25 kg
4 Tbsp	butter	60 mL
2 cups	sliced onions	500 mL
1 cup	slivered green bell peppers	250 mL
1 cup	sliced celery	250 mL
¾ cup	red wine	175 mL
2 Tbsp	Dijon mustard	30 mL
2 tsp	crushed garlic	10 mL
2 tsp	salt	10 mL
1 tsp	pepper	5 mL

1. Split chicken wings in two and discard tips.

2. In a Dutch oven or heavy casserole that has a lid melt 2 Tbsp (30 mL) butter over medium-high heat. Add onions, bell peppers and celery. Sauté for 5 minutes, then remove from pot. Melt remaining butter, add chicken wings, and sauté until golden brown. Return sautéed onion mixture to the pot. Add remaining ingredients and mix together. Cover, reduce heat to low and simmer for 45 minutes, stirring occasionally. Adjust seasonings and serve in a chafing dish.

To split chicken wing

Discard

cut in two at joint

POTATO SKINS

15	medium-sized baking potatoes	15
3 to 4 cups	oil for deep frying	0.75 to 1 L
2 lb	Cheddar cheese, thinly sliced	900 g
1½ cups	sour cream for garnishing	375 mL

1. Preheat oven to 375°F (190°C).

2. Scrub potatoes clean and pierce skins with fork. Bake for 50 to 60 minutes, or until a knife can be inserted easily but with a little resistance. Potatoes should still be a little crispy. Cut into quarters lengthwise and scoop out some of the pulp, leaving about ¼ inch (6 mm) of pulp on the skin. Reserve the pulp for another use.

3. In a heavy frying pan or saucepan heat oil over medium-high heat to 375°F (190°C). Add several pieces of potato skin and fry until golden brown. Remove to baking sheet. Repeat until all potatoes are fried, allowing oil to return to original temperature between batches. Place a slice of cheese on each potato skin and broil until cheese melts. Serve warm with sour cream.

ANTIPASTO SALAD

Mixed Italian Herbs or Italian Bouquet is a fragrant mixture of dried herbs usually based on oregano and basil.

For marinade:

1 cup	tomato paste	250 mL
1½ cups	chopped tomatoes	375 mL
1 tsp	dried mixed Italian herbs	5 mL
3 Tbsp	balsamic vinegar	45 mL
1 tsp	crushed garlic	5 mL
2 tsp	sugar	10 mL
2 tsp	salt	10 mL
½ tsp	pepper	2 mL
3 cups	cauliflower florets (1 medium-sized head)	750 mL
2 cups	sliced zucchini, ¼-inch (6-mm) slices (2 medium-sized zucchini)	500 mL
2 cups	diagonally sliced green or yellow beans, 1½-inch (4-cm) slices (about 12 oz/350 g)	500 mL
1 cup	pickled onions	250 mL
2	large red, green, yellow or purple bell peppers, cut into 1-inch × 1-inch (2.5-cm × 2.5-cm) pieces	2

1. In a large bowl combine all ingredients for marinade and set aside.

2. Bring a large pot of water to a boil. Blanch cauliflower for 3 minutes, until slightly soft but crispy. Remove and drain well. Add immediately to marinade. Blanch zucchini for 30 seconds. Remove and drain well and add to marinade. Blanch beans for 4 to 5 minutes. Drain and add to marinade. Add onions and peppers to marinade and mix vegetables to coat well. Refrigerate overnight before serving.

CAJUN DIP

2 cups/500 mL
    tomato sauce

1 Tbsp/15 mL
    Tabasco sauce

4 cloves
    garlic, crushed

2 Tbsp/30 mL
    red wine

2 Tbsp/30 mL
    olive oil

1. Combine ingredients in a small saucepan and stir over medium heat for 5 minutes.

HOT CAJUN SHRIMP

1 cup	olive oil	250 mL
1 cup	finely chopped onions	250 mL
2 cups	tomato paste	500 mL
1 cup	red wine	250 mL
2 Tbsp	crushed garlic	30 mL
½ tsp	cayenne	2 mL
1½ tsp	salt	7 mL
2 Tbsp	pepper	30 mL
1 cup	finely chopped fresh parsley or fresh basil	250 mL
4 lb	medium-sized shrimps, shelled	2 kg

1. In a frying pan heat olive oil over medium-high heat. Add

onions and sauté until translucent, about 5 minutes. Add tomato paste and red wine and bring to boil. Stir in garlic, cayenne, salt and pepper and continue cooking for 5 minutes. Remove from heat and mix in parsley. Transfer to large mixing bowl and cool completely.

2. Add shrimp to bowl and toss to coat well. Marinate in the refrigerator for several hours. Mix occasionally to ensure even marination.

3. Line a baking sheet with foil and spread with a layer of shrimp and marinade. Broil for 1 to 2 minutes, turn over and broil for an additional minute. Transfer to a chafing dish. Repeat until all shrimp have been cooked. Serve hot from chafing dish.

LEMON-GARLIC MEATBALLS

For meatballs:

1 Tbsp	butter	15 mL
1 cup	minced onion	250 mL
2 Tbsp	crushed garlic	30 mL
3 lb	lean ground pork or lamb	1.35 kg
½ cup	chopped fresh parsley	125 mL
1½ cups	fresh breadcrumbs	375 mL
2	eggs	2
4 Tbsp	table cream (18%)	60 mL
1 Tbsp	salt	15 mL
½ tsp	pepper	2 mL

For sauce:

1 cup	hot melted butter	250 mL
1 Tbsp	crushed garlic	15 mL
3 Tbsp	lemon juice	45 mL
1 tsp	salt	5 mL
½ cup	olive oil for frying	125 mL

1. In frying pan melt butter and sauté minced onion and garlic for 2 to 3 minutes. Let cool and combine with all ingredients for meatballs in a large mixing bowl. Mix very well and with wet hands roll into 1¼-inch (3-cm) balls.

2. In frying pan heat butter, add garlic and cook for 2 to 3 minutes. Add lemon juice and salt and remove from heat. Place mixture in blender and process until smooth. Set aside and keep warm.

3. In frying pan heat about 2 Tbsp (30 mL) oil over medium-high heat. Add 10 to 15 meatballs (do not crowd in pan) and fry until cooked, shaking pan to brown meatballs on all sides. Remove and keep warm in oven. Repeat until all meatballs are cooked.

4. To serve, place meatballs in chafing dish and pour lemon-garlic sauce over them.

MINI SCOTCH EGGS

24	quail eggs	24
1 lb	lean ground pork	450 g
2 cups	fresh breadcrumbs	500 mL
2	eggs	2
2 Tbsp	chopped fresh parsley	30 mL
2 tsp	ground poultry spice	10 mL
2 cloves	garlic, crushed	2 cloves
1 tsp	salt	5 mL
1 tsp	pepper	5 mL
1 cup	dry breadcrumbs for coating	250 mL
3 to 4 cups	oil for deep frying	0.75 to 1 L

If you can't get quail eggs, use peewee or pullet eggs which are available at poultry stores. You will have to double the quantity of meat since peewees are larger than quail eggs.

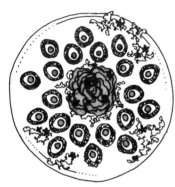

Garnish a plate of Mini Scotch Eggs with a radicchio rose surrounded by curly endive & small flowers. To make rose, just spread open the leaves of a small head of radicchio.

1. Place eggs in a large saucepan. Cover with cold water and bring to boil over medium-high heat. Immediately reduce heat to low and simmer for 7 minutes. Remove eggs and plunge into cold water until well chilled. Peel immediately.

2. In a food processor fitted with a steel blade combine pork, fresh breadcrumbs, eggs, parsley, poultry spice, garlic, salt and pepper. Process until finely ground and well blended.

3. Divide pork mixture into 24 equal parts, about 1½ Tbsp (25 mL), and wrap each egg with a portion of pork. Roll in dry breadcrumbs.

4. Heat oil in heavy deep frying pan, or deep fryer, to 375°F (190°C). Drop in 5 to 7 eggs and fry for 2 to 3 minutes, or until golden brown. Remove and drain on paper towels. Cool for 10 minutes, then slice in half to reveal egg and serve.

DEEP-FRIED MUSHROOMS AND ZUCCHINI

2 cups	flour	500 mL
2 cups	beer	500 mL
1 tsp	salt	5 mL
6	zucchini, sliced into ⅛-inch (3-mm) rounds	6
2 lb	medium-sized mushrooms, cleaned and trimmed	900 g
4 to 6 cups	oil for deep frying	1 to 1.5 L

1. In a large bowl combine flour, beer and salt. Stir ingredients together just until blended.

2. Heat oil to 375°F (190°C).

3. Dip a few vegetables at a time into the batter and drop into heated oil. Do not overcrowd. Deep fry until golden brown. Drain on paper towels. Repeat with remaining vegetables.

HAWAIIAN LUAU FOR 20

Crab Wonton Crisps
Stuffed Plantain Slices
Tofu Pockets
Sesame Shrimp

Korean Barbecued Short Ribs
Mely's Coconut Chicken
Stir-Fried Vermicelli Salad
Fried Rice
Duck Salad
Glazed Yams and Bananas

Pineapple-Coconut Rice Pudding
Macadamia Nut Pie
Peacock Fruit Tablescape

Rum Punch
Strawberry Colada

What could relieve winter doldrums better than an evening with friends in Hawaii. Can't jet everyone south for the night? Then make your own Hawaii here. Get out the grass skirts . . . we're having a luau!

So many of our clients request this theme that it's become a specialty of ours. We're old hands at transforming winter-bound homes into lush tropical gardens, and we can help you create the same magic. First, set the scene with tropical plants rented from a local greenhouse or borrowed from friends. Or for a more whimsical touch, make your own palm trees. Cover your bar with straw thatching, fish net and shells, and presto — it's a little grass shack! Try renting live parrots — their chatter can really liven up the party. And scatter flowers everywhere. Real, paper, silk or plastic — they are the essence of Hawaii.

The theme is great for summer, too. The casual spirit of a backyard barbecue is made even more lively with colourful Hawaiian touches. Bamboo torches to light the night. Fish nets, seashells and bamboo blinds to drape the buffet table. And pots of cheerful flowers that can later be planted into the garden to commemorate the evening.

Leis are an essential part of a luau. String together carnations, daisies, gladiola blossoms of vivid hues to make fresh leis, or buy plastic or paper leis.

Have your waiters and waitresses dress for the occasion. Hawaiian shirts and flowered sarongs will add a lot of fun and colour to the night.

And, of course, there should be Hawaiian music. If the budget allows, hire Hawaiian musicians and dancers from a local talent agency. Or dig out those old Don Ho tapes.

The menu given here is eclectic Polynesian, and always popular.

MAKE YOUR OWN PALM TREES
For each tree:
4-in (10-cm) styrofoam ball
Spanish moss (available at florist)
1 bunch Mexican palm leaves (available at florist)
4- to 6-feet (1.5 to 2-m) length of bamboo cane
10-inch (25-cm) clay flower pot packed with wet sand

Wrap styrofoam ball with moss and imbed stems of palm leaves all over the ball. Impale the ball on one end of the bamboo pole and push the other end into the flower pot.

Trays of hors d'oeuvres are decorated with big bright flowers. Tiny paper parasols top icy glasses of rum punch and strawberry coladas. On the buffet, grilled short ribs, unusually cut in thin strips, are piled high on platters lined with palm leaves. Coconut Chicken is displayed enticingly in big wooden bowls decorated with tiny orchids. Vermicelli Salad and Duck Salad, Fried Rice, and Glazed Yams and Bananas are served from giant scallop shells.

For a larger group, you can order a roast suckling pig from a merchant in Chinatown that specializes in barbecued meats. Surrounded with blossoms, this can be a dazzling centrepiece dish.

WORK-AHEAD SCHEDULE

4 WEEKS AHEAD

- Send out invitations.
- Plan layout of room(s) and decor.
- Arrange rental or construction of any special decorative items.
- Organize music and entertainment.

2 WEEKS AHEAD

- Order flowers and palm leaves, including leis.
- Arrange rental or loan of any dishes, cutlery, etc., if necessary. See checklist page 13.
- Arrange for kitchen helpers and one or two bartender/waiters.

1 WEEK AHEAD

- Make grocery list and shop for non-perishable items.
- Order, if necessary, any of the exotic fruits in the Peacock Tablescape.
- Order short ribs.
- Plan serving dishes and garnishes.

3 DAYS AHEAD

- Marinate short ribs for Korean Barbecued Short Ribs.
- Shop for bar requirements and remaining groceries, except barbecued duck.

1 DAY AHEAD

- Prepare garnishes and immerse in water or wrap tightly in plastic wrap. Refrigerate.
- Decorate room and tables.
- Make Mely's Coconut Chicken and refrigerate.
- Julienne all vegetables for Stir-Fried Vermicelli Salad. Wrap individually in plastic wrap or store in covered bowl and refrigerate.
- Chop carrots and celery for Fried Rice, cover and refrigerate.
- Julienne duck, celery and snow peas for Duck Salad. Cover and refrigerate.
- Make pie shells for Macadamia Nut Pie. Roast nuts.
- Carve fruit for Peacock Fruit Tablescape, wrap each fruit separately in plastic wrap and refrigerate.

EARLY IN DAY

- Buy barbecued duck.
- Arrange flowers.
- Cook rice for Fried Rice. Do not refrigerate.
- Complete Macadamia Nut Pie.
- Prepare crab filling for Crab Wonton Crisps. Do not fill until ready to fry.
- Prepare filling for Stuffed Plantain Slices.
- Make Tofu Pockets.

- Cook shrimp for Sesame Shrimp and marinate.
- Cook and peel yams for Glazed Yams and Bananas.

- Prepare Pineapple-Coconut Rice Pudding.
- Prepare rest of ingredients for Duck Salad. Do not assemble.
- Prepare Stir-Fried Vermicelli Salad. Can be reheated just before serving.
- Peel shrimp for Sesame Shrimp, leaving tails on. Return to marinade.
- Prepare Fried Rice. Can be reheated just before serving.

- Assemble Peacock Fruit Tablescape.

- Assemble ingredients for drinks and set up bar.

- Garnish serving platters and plan their positioning on buffet table.
- Assemble Glazed Yams and Bananas. Bake 45 minutes before serving.
- Assemble Stuffed Plantain Slices. Fry just before guests arrive.
- Assemble Crab Wonton Crisps. Fry just before serving.
- Warm up Fried Rice in oven or on stove top.
- Reheat Mely's Coconut Chicken.
- Drain shrimp for Sesame Shrimp and roll in sesame seeds just prior to serving.

- If barbecuing, light the coals.

- Cook Korean Barbecued Short Ribs.
- Assemble Duck Salad.

The Peacock Fruit Table-scape is spectacular and well worth the 4 to 5 hours it takes to carve and assemble. But if you prefer a simpler presentation, select an assortment of tropical fruits and display them whole and in pieces on large platters or in baskets. Call your green-grocer a week in advance to ascertain which fruits will be available.

CRAB WONTON CRISPS

1 lb	frozen crab meat, thawed and lightly squeezed	450 g
½ lb	processed cream cheese	225 g
1½ tsp	Worcestershire sauce	7 mL
½ tsp	finely minced garlic	2 mL
to taste	salt and pepper	to taste
1	16-oz (450-g) package thick wonton wrappers	1
3 to 4 cups	oil for deep frying	0.75 to 1 L

1. In a mixing bowl combine crab, cream cheese, Worcestershire sauce and garlic. Mix well and season to taste with salt and pepper.

2. Using one wonton wrapper at a time, put 1½ tsp (7 mL) crab mixture in the centre. Moisten edges with water and fold wrapper, handkerchief style, as diagrammed. Pinch to seal well. Place on a baking sheet lined with waxed paper. Repeat until all crab mixture has been used. The wontons can be prepared to this stage several hours in advance.

3. Fill a deep heavy frying pan or deep fryer half full of oil. Heat oil to 350°F (180°C) over medium heat. Carefully add 4 to 6 wontons and fry until golden brown. Remove to drain on paper towels. Repeat until all wontons have been fried. Serve immediately, or keep warm in oven for short time until ready to serve.

A simpler method of folding is to place crab mixture on wrapper, moisten edges with water, fold on the diagonal to form a triangle, and pinch to seal well. The wonton won't be as crispy, but it still makes a tasty mouthful.

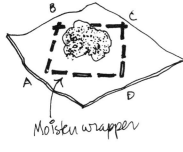

Moisten wrapper

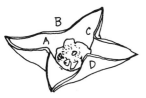

STUFFED PLANTAIN SLICES

¾ lb	chicken meat, cubed	350 g
½ lb	raw shrimp, shelled and cut in half	225 g
4 Tbsp	finely chopped green onions	60 mL
to taste	salt and pepper	to taste
4	large ripe plantains *or* 6 to 8 very firm bananas	4
2	eggs, well beaten	2
4 to 6 cups	oil for deep frying	1 to 1.5 L

1. In a food processor fitted with a steel blade purée chicken. Add shrimp and process until coarsely chopped. Mix in green onions and season with salt and pepper to taste. Set aside.

2. Peel plantains and slice into ¼-inch (6-mm) rounds. Place a heaping teaspoonful (approx. 7 mL), or enough to make a ¼-inch (6-mm) layer, of chicken and shrimp mixture on a slice of plantain and top with a second slice of plantain. Press together lightly. Repeat until all slices have been filled.

3. In a heavy frying pan add oil to a depth of 1 inch (2.5 cm). Heat over medium-high heat to 375°F (190°C). Dip filled plantain slices into beaten egg and deep fry until golden brown on each side, turning once. Remove to drain on paper towels. Serve immediately.

Plantains are sold in stores specializing in Caribbean food. If unavailable, substitute large, firm bananas.

TOFU POCKETS

For sushi rice:

2 cups	Japanese rice	500 mL
2¾ cups	water	675 mL
⅔ cup	rice vinegar	150 mL
4 Tbsp	mirin	60 mL
7 Tbsp	sugar	105 mL
1 tsp	salt	5 mL

For pockets:

1	3-oz (85-g) package Japanese dried gourd strips (*kanpyo*), cut into 10-inch (25-cm) lengths	1
15 cakes	deep-fried tofu (*age*), approx. 4 inches × 2 inches × ½ inch (10 cm × 5 cm × 1.25 cm)	15 cakes
12 cups	water	3 L
1 cup	dried bonito flakes	250 mL
1½ cups	sugar	375 mL
1 cup	soy sauce	250 mL
3 Tbsp	shredded pink pickled ginger	45 mL

1. In a heavy saucepan with a lid combine rice and water, and bring to boil over high heat. Cover, reduce heat and simmer for 20 to 30 minutes, or until rice is soft.

2. In a small bowl combine vinegar, mirin, sugar and salt. Mix into hot cooked rice. Set aside.

3. Place gourd strips in a bowl, cover with water and allow to soak for 20 minutes.

4. Cut each cake of deep-fried tofu in half across width and gently pull open to form a pocket. Bring a pot of water to boil and add deep-fried tofu. Cook for 5 minutes to remove excess oil. Drain and set aside.

5. In a large pot combine 12 cups water and bonito flakes. Boil over high heat for 5 minutes. Remove from heat, cover and allow to steep for 5 minutes. Strain, discard bonito flakes and return liquid to pot. Add sugar and soy sauce and stir over high heat to dissolve sugar. Add deep-fried tofu and boil rapidly for 15 minutes. Remove deep-fried tofu and set aside to drain. Add gourd to liquid and boil for 5 minutes. Remove and drain.

6. Carefully fill a deep-fried tofu pocket with about 1½ Tbsp (20 mL) sushi rice. Loosely gather top closed and tie with a gourd strip. Place a garnish of pink pickled ginger on top. Repeat with remaining deep-fried tofu pockets.

DEEP-FRIED TOFU
Cake of soybean curd that has been deep fried, giving it a browned crust and a drier texture inside. Available in packages of four from stores specializing in Japanese or Chinese foods. If unavailable, slice fresh tofu into appropriate size, pat dry and deep fry until golden brown.

JAPANESE RICE
Short-grain rice. Sweeter, richer flavour than long-grain rice and slightly sticky in texture when cooked.

MIRIN
Sweet rice wine for cooking. Substitute equal parts of pale dry sherry (or sake) and sugar.

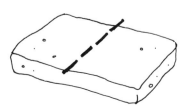

SESAME SHRIMP

These shrimp look marvellous piled up in generous mounds on large platters. Large scallop shells can be provided as receptacles for discarded shrimp tails.

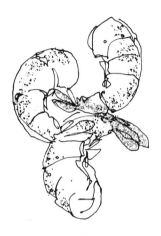

For marinade:

¼ cup	rice vinegar	60 mL
¼ cup	light soy sauce	60 mL
2 Tbsp	sesame oil	30 mL
3 cloves	garlic, crushed	3 cloves
10	very thin slices fresh ginger	10
¼ cup	brown sugar, well packed	60 mL
1 Tbsp	sherry	15 mL
2½ lb	unshelled jumbo shrimp	1.15 kg
1½ cups	roasted sesame seeds	375 mL

1. Combine all ingredients for marinade in a large mixing bowl.

2. Bring a large pot of salted water to boil over high heat. Add shrimp and cook for 2 minutes. Remove from heat. Drain well and add to marinade. Allow to stand, refrigerated, for 2 hours or more. Toss occasionally to ensure even marination.

3. Drain off marinade and reserve. Shell shrimp, leaving tails on and replace in marinade.

4. Just before serving, roll shrimp in sesame seeds.

"Miami Ribs"
Great for the BBQ

KOREAN BARBECUED SHORT RIBS

MIAMI RIBS
Beef short ribs cut across the bones into ¹/₂-inch (1.25-cm) strips are called Miami ribs or flanken ribs. Buy them from a specialty meat store or ask your butcher to cut them for you. These flavourful strips are improved even more with long marination.

For marinade:

1 cup	grated fresh ginger	250 mL
2 Tbsp	crushed garlic	30 mL
2 cups	well-packed brown sugar	500 mL
2 cups	medium-dry sherry	500 mL
2 cups	soy sauce	500 mL
10 lb	short ribs, Miami or flanken cut	4.5 kg

1. In a large mixing bowl combine all ingredients for marinade. Add ribs, tossing to coat well. Marinate, refrigerated, for three days, turning occasionally. Barbecue or broil for 3 to 5 minutes on each side.

MELY'S COCONUT CHICKEN

4 lb	Spanish onions, thinly sliced	1.8 kg
36 cloves	garlic, finely minced (large cloves)	36 cloves
3 cups	white vinegar	750 mL
¾ cup	soy sauce	175 mL
⅓ cup	oyster sauce (optional)	75 mL
1½ tsp	Tabasco sauce	7 mL
3 Tbsp	salt	45 mL
3 Tbsp	coarsely ground pepper	45 mL
6	3-lb (1.4-kg) chickens, cut into serving pieces	6
6	coconuts	6
2½ cups	boiling water	625 mL

1. In a very large bowl or foil roasting pan combine Spanish onions, garlic, vinegar, soy sauce, oyster sauce, Tabasco sauce, salt and pepper. Mix well and add chicken pieces. Marinate overnight, refrigerated.

2. With a screwdriver and hammer poke hole through two of the eyes of each coconut. Shake out liquid and discard or save for use at another time. Using a hammer, crack open coconuts. Pry the white meat off the shells and discard shells. In a food processor fitted with a steel blade chop coconut very finely. Remove to large mixing bowl. Add ½ cup (125 mL) of boiling water to coconut, allow to cool for 3 minutes, then strain and squeeze dry, reserving this liquid which is coconut milk. Do not discard coconut meat.

3. Remove chicken pieces from marinade. In a large non-stick frying pan, over medium-high heat, brown chicken pieces, skin side first, to render the fat. Cook 10 to 15 minutes. Set aside browned chicken pieces. Add marinade to frying pan and reduce by half over high heat. While marinade is reducing, pour the remaining boiling water over the coconut in a mixing bowl. Cool for 2 or 3 minutes, strain and squeeze dry. Add this coconut milk to the reduced marinade. Discard coconut meat.

4. In a very large Dutch oven or casserole combine the marinade-coconut milk mixture and the chicken pieces. Simmer over medium-low heat for 10 or 15 minutes, or until chicken is just cooked. Stir in the reserved ½ cup (125 mL) of coconut milk and simmer for 1 to 2 minutes. Transfer chicken and juices to a large bowl and serve hot.

If you have had a long day and don't feel like cracking coconuts, use this shortcut for making coconut milk: Melt a 7-oz/198-g bar of coconut cream in a saucepan over medium heat. Remove from heat and, beating constantly, slowly add 2 cups/500 mL water in a steady stream. This liquid can be substituted for the coconut milk described in steps 2 and 3.

Poke out "eyes" and shake out liquid.

Tap coconut all over until you locate the "fault line" which will crack easily

OYSTER SAUCE

A soy-based sauce flavoured with oysters. Buy the best quality available, such as Lee Kum Kee Old Brand.

KETJAP BENTENG

A spicy-sweet sauce used in Indonesian cooking. If unavailable, substitute this mixture:

1 *cup*/250 mL
    dark soy sauce
1/2 *cup*/125 mL
    sugar
1/2 *cup*/125 mL
    molasses
1/2 *tsp*/2 mL
    Chinese five-spice

1. Mix together all ingredients in a small bowl. Keep in a jar, refrigerated.

STIR-FRIED VERMICELLI SALAD

1 lb	vermicelli cellophane noodles	450 g
8 Tbsp	peanut oil	120 mL
1	1-inch (2.5-cm) piece fresh ginger, thinly sliced	1
2 cups	sliced onions	500 mL
6 cups	diagonally sliced green beans	1.5 L
½ head	cabbage, shredded	½ head
9 cups	grated carrots, about 10 to 15 carrots	2.25 L
1 cup	cloud ears (dried black fungus), soaked in warm water for 20 minutes, well washed and drained	1 cup
4 cups	julienned bamboo shoots	1 L
2 cups	julienned water chestnuts	500 mL
5 cups	strong chicken stock	1.25 L
1 cup	oyster sauce	250 mL
½ cup	ketjap benteng	125 mL
4 Tbsp	soy sauce	60 mL
2 tsp	crushed garlic	10 mL
2 tsp	salt	10 mL
2 tsp	pepper	10 mL
2 Tbsp	sesame oil	30 mL
1 bunch	fresh coriander, stems removed	1 bunch

1. In a large bowl cover noodles with warm water and allow to soak for 5 minutes. Drain and cut into 3-inch (7-cm) lengths with scissors. Set aside.

2. In a large frying pan heat 2 Tbsp (30 mL) peanut oil over high heat. Add 3 slices of ginger, brown and discard. Add onions and sauté until translucent. Add 1½ cups (375 mL) green beans and cook for 2 minutes. Add ¼ of all the remaining vegetables — cabbage, carrots, cloud ears, bamboo shoots, water chestnuts — and continue cooking for 6 to 8 minutes. Add ¼ of the noodles, mixing it very well with the vegetables. Cook for 5 minutes. Add 1¼ cup (300 mL) chicken stock and continue cooking until all the liquid has been absorbed by the noodles. Add ¼ of each of the seasonings — ¼ cup (60 mL) oyster sauce, 2 Tbsp (30 mL) ketjap benteng, 1 Tbsp (15 mL) soy sauce, ½ tsp (2 mL) garlic, ½ tsp (2 mL) salt, ½ tsp (2 mL) pepper, ½ Tbsp (7 mL) sesame oil. Transfer cooked noodles and vegetables into a foil roasting pan and keep warm, if serving hot.

3. Repeat the procedure three times, until all the vegetables and noodles are used up.

4. Garnish with fresh coriander. May be served hot or cold.

FRIED RICE

5 cups	parboiled rice	1.25 L
7½ cups	cold water	1.875 L
8 Tbsp	peanut oil	120 mL
4 Tbsp	butter	60 mL
2 cups	diced celery, ⅛-inch (3-mm) cubes	500 mL
2 cups	diced carrots, ⅛-inch (3-mm) cubes	500 mL
2 cups	sliced green onions	500 mL
12 cups	sliced mushrooms	3 L
6 Tbsp	soy sauce	90 mL
2 Tbsp	oyster sauce	30 mL
8 Tbsp	ketjap benteng	120 mL
1 tsp	pepper	5 mL
3 cups	frozen peas	750 mL

Parboiled rice, such as Uncle Ben's Converted, is ideal for this dish. The grains stay perfectly shaped and separate and will absorb a lot of liquid without becoming mushy.

1. In a large saucepan with a lid combine rice with water and place over high heat. Cover and bring to boil, lower heat and simmer for 20 to 30 minutes. Fluff with fork and set aside.

2. In a very large frying pan combine 2 Tbsp (30 mL) oil and 1 Tbsp (15 mL) butter over medium-high heat. Add celery and carrots and sauté until softened, about 2 to 3 minutes. Add green onions and sauté for an additional minute. Remove to large pot or foil roasting pan. Heat 2 Tbsp (30 mL) oil and 1 Tbsp (15 mL) butter in frying pan and add mushrooms. Sauté until juices begin to run, about 3 to 4 minutes. Add to celery mixture. Heat 2 Tbsp (30 mL) oil and 1 Tbsp (15 mL) butter in frying pan and add half the cooked rice. Add half the soy sauce, oyster sauce, ketjap benteng and pepper and sauté over medium heat until well mixed and hot. Add to vegetable mixture. Repeat with remaining rice and seasonings.

3. Place peas in a large sieve and pour boiling water over them. Drain well and add to rice mixture, tossing well to mix all ingredients. Adjust seasonings if necessary. The rice may be held in a warm oven (200°F/100°C) for up to one hour if tightly covered.

Fried rice can be served from a hollowed pineapple half.

DUCK SALAD

Barbecued duck can be purchased from Chinese stores specializing in barbecued meats. Smoked duck or chicken, or duck roasted with a honey glaze can be used if Chinese barbecued duck is not available.

4	Chinese barbecued ducks, meat and skin julienned	4
1 head	iceberg lettuce, julienned	1 head
4 cups	julienned snow peas	1 L
2	14-oz (398-mL) cans pineapple, drained, cut into ¼-inch (6-mm) wedges, juice reserved	2
2	10-oz (284-mL) cans mandarin orange segments, drained	2
2	19-oz (540-mL) cans lichee nuts, drained, quartered	2
4 cups	thinly diagonally sliced celery	1 L
1	19-oz (540-mL) can water chestnuts, drained, sliced into thin rounds	1

For dressing:

4 Tbsp	juice reserved from pineapple	60 mL
4 Tbsp	sesame oil	60 mL
2 Tbsp	light soy sauce	30 mL
2 Tbsp	rice vinegar	30 mL
1 tsp	salt	5 mL
½ tsp	pepper	2 mL

1. In a large mixing bowl combine the duck, lettuce and snow peas with the pineapple, mandarin oranges, lichee nuts, celery and water chestnuts. Mix together.

2. In a small mixing bowl combine fruit juices, sesame oil, soy sauce, rice vinegar, salt and pepper. Stir together and pour over duck mixture. Toss well and serve.

GLAZED YAMS AND BANANAS

12	large yams or sweet potatoes	12
8	bananas, sliced ⅓ inch (1 cm)	8
1 cup	brown sugar	250 mL
2 cups	whipping cream	500 mL
½ cup	dark rum	125 mL
½ cup	butter	125 mL

Yams baked with bananas under a boozy blanket of heavy cream and rum.

1. In a large pot cover yams with water and bring to boil over high heat. Cover and boil until yams are just barely cooked. Drain, cool, peel and slice ⅓ inch (1 cm) thick.

2. Preheat oven to 400°F (200°C).

3. Layer the slices of yams and bananas in two 9-inch × 12-inch (23-cm × 30-cm) baking dishes. Sprinkle half the brown sugar over each. Pour half of the cream and rum over each and dot each with half the butter. Bake for 30 minutes, mixing occasionally. Serve warm.

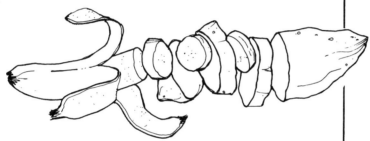

PINEAPPLE-COCONUT RICE PUDDING

2 cups	short-grain rice	500 mL
3 cups	cold water	750 mL
4 cups	whipping cream	1 L
2	12-oz (355-mL) cans cream of coconut syrup	2
1	19-oz (540-mL) can crushed pineapple, undrained	1

1. In a heavy saucepan with a lid combine rice and water over high heat. Cover and bring to boil. Reduce heat to simmer and cook for 20 to 30 minutes, or until soft.

2. Preheat oven to 350°F (180°C).

3. In a medium-sized bowl combine whipping cream, cream of coconut syrup, crushed pineapple and hot cooked rice. Stir together and pour into two 9-inch × 12-inch (23-cm × 30-cm) rectangular glass baking dishes. Bake for 1½ hours until set. The top will still be syrupy and runny but will set as pudding cools. Serve at room temperature.

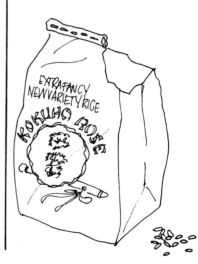

MACADAMIA NUT PIE

Visitors to Hawaii often return home laden with macadamia nuts. One taste tells you why: these big round gems are crunchy, buttery and very, very rich.

All nuts have their own very distinct taste, but cashews will substitute quite nicely in our pie if macadamia nuts are un-available.

For pastry:

3 cups	flour	750 mL
1 tsp	salt	5 mL
1 cup	cold butter	250 mL
1 Tbsp	white vinegar	15 mL
5 Tbsp	cold milk	75 mL
1	egg	1

For filling:

1 lb	butter	450 g
3 cups	sugar	750 mL
12	eggs, lightly beaten	12
3 cups	dark corn syrup	750 mL
½ tsp	salt	2 mL
4 tsp	vanilla	20 mL
4 cups	unsalted roasted macadamia nuts, coarsely chopped	1 L

1. To make pastry, combine flour and salt in a mixing bowl. Add butter and work with pastry cutter until texture resembles coarse meal. In a small bowl beat together vinegar, milk and egg. Sprinkle over flour mixture and mix lightly with a fork until liquid is incorporated into flour in a lumpy dough. Turn out onto lightly floured board and press into a ball. Wrap in plastic wrap and refrigerate at least 20 minutes.

2. Preheat oven to 425°F (220°C).

3. Divide dough into two equal portions. Roll each portion into a circle about 15 inches (38 cm) in diameter and slide each into a deep 10-inch (25-cm) pie pan. Crimp overhanging dough of pie shell into decorative edge. Place a square of waxed paper on each pie shell and fill with rice or pastry beans. Bake for 10 minutes. Cool slightly and remove rice and waxed paper.

4. Lower oven temperature to 350°F (180°C).

5. To make filling, cream butter and gradually add sugar. When light and lemon-coloured, add beaten eggs. Blend in corn syrup, salt, vanilla and nuts. Mix well and pour half into each baked pie shell. Bake for 45 to 55 minutes, or until set.

macadamia nuts and cashews

RUM PUNCH

Yields 30 drinks

3	12-oz (355-mL) cans grapefruit juice concentrate	3
3	12-oz (355-mL) cans orange juice concentrate	3
4½ cups	water	1.125 L
2 cups	grenadine	500 mL
¾ cup	lemon juice	175 mL
1½ cups	passion fruit syrup *or* ¾ cup (175 mL) almond-flavoured syrup	375 mL
3 to 4 cups	dark rum	0.75 to 1 L
30	slices of orange	30
30	maraschino cherries	30
30	paper parasols	30

1. Combine ingredients in a large punch bowl and mix well. To serve, fill a glass with ice and pour in punch. Garnish with a slice of orange, maraschino cherry and paper parasol.

Serve in double old-fashioned or sling glasses.

STRAWBERRY COLADA

Yields 30 drinks

3	48-oz (1.36-L) cans unsweetened pineapple juice	3
1½	12-oz (355 mL) cans cream of coconut syrup	1½
1	2.2-lb (1-kg) bag frozen strawberries *or* 6 cups (1.5 L) fresh strawberries	1
1½	12-oz (355-mL) cans orange juice concentrate	1½
3 to 4 cups	light rum or vodka	0.75 to 1 L
2	fresh pineapples, cut into 30 spears	2

1. In a blender purée ingredients together in small quantities and combine in large punch bowl. To serve, fill glass with ice, pour in colada and garnish with a fresh pineapple spear. Or, fill a blender ¾ full of crushed ice, add colada mixture and blend until ice is finely chopped. Fill glass and serve with a straw.

Serve in large glasses. Brandy snifters or sling or wine glasses are ideal.

COCKTAIL PARTY FOR 25

Pesto Shrimp
Smoked Capon Canapés
Stuffed Vegetables
Mandarin Duck Rolls
Cocktail Spanakopita
Prunes in Bacon
Savoury Tarts
Chicken Satay

Give a grand cocktail party. Make it an event, not just a hasty preludial drink before an evening at the theatre, or a pre-restaurant pit stop for Scotch and thaw-and-serve rumakis. Make it a knock-down, talked-about, smart and smashing party that lasts all night and long into memory.

For this cocktail party menu we've chosen a wide variety of appetizers selected to please even the most eclectic crowd — some seafood, some fowl, others vegetable. Half are served at room temperature and half served hot, not only for variety but for ease in preparation. So you won't find yourself juggling the deep fryer with the broiling pan all evening.

It's a menu that allows you to make most of the items in advance, leaving you free to mingle with your guests and personally accept all the compliments! It's a good idea to hire one or two waiters or waitresses to pass around the food and drinks.

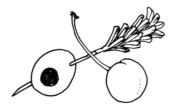

WORK-AHEAD SCHEDULE

4 WEEKS AHEAD
- Send out invitations.
- Organize music.
- Decide on location of bar.

2 WEEKS AHEAD
- Arrange for rental or loan of serving trays, glassware, ice buckets, ashtrays, coatracks, etc., if necessary. See checklist page 13.
- Arrange for a kitchen helper and 1 or 2 waiters.

1 WEEK AHEAD
- Make list of bar requirements and groceries. Check supplies and shop for required non-perishables and groceries required to make Cocktail Spanakopita.
- Make but do not bake Cocktail Spanakopita. Brush well with melted butter, wrap well and freeze.
- Plan garnishes for serving trays and list requirements.

- Shop for bar requirements and remaining groceries, except barbecued duck.

2 DAYS AHEAD

- Prepare toast bases, hazelnut butter and sliced kumquats for Smoked Capon Canapés.
- Prepare but do not broil Prunes in Bacon.
- Bake tart shells for Mediterranean and Leek and Stilton Tarts and fry onion and leeks.
- Marinate and skewer Chicken Satay.
- Cut vegetables for Mandarin Duck Rolls.
- Buy flowers and arrange.
- Prepare cut vegetable garnishes for trays.

1 DAY AHEAD

- Buy barbecued duck.
- Cook, peel and marinate shrimp for Pesto Shrimp.
- Prepare vegetables and stuffing for Stuffed Vegetables but do not assemble.
- Make pancakes and shred duck for Mandarin Duck Rolls.
- Slice smoked capon.
- Fill tart shells.
- Remove Cocktail Spanakopita from freezer and allow to thaw wrapped.

EARLY IN DAY

- Roll Mandarin Duck Rolls.
- Assemble Smoked Capon Canapés.
- Prepare trays and platters for presentation of hors d'oeuvres.

3 HOURS AHEAD

- Roll shrimp in Parmesan and arrange 2 or 3 dozen on platter or tray.
- Fill Stuffed Vegetables and arrange 2 or 3 dozen pieces on platter.
- Bake Cocktail Spanakopita and arrange on platter.
- Broil Prunes in Bacon and arrange on platter.
- Bake Savoury Tarts and arrange on platter.
- Broil Chicken Satay and arrange on platter.

TO SERVE

BASIL

PESTO SHRIMP

For pesto:

½ cup	fresh basil leaves	125 mL
4 Tbsp	roasted pine nuts	60 mL
½ cup	olive oil	125 mL
1 tsp	finely minced garlic	5 mL
½ tsp	salt	2 mL
1½ lb	shrimp	700 g
1 cup	freshly grated Parmesan cheese	250 mL

1. To make pesto, in a food processor fitted with a steel blade chop together basil, pine nuts, olive oil, garlic and salt. Process, scraping down the bowl often, until puréed. Set aside.

2. Rinse shrimp well, then add to a pot of boiling water and cook for 3 to 5 minutes, or just until they turn red. Cool completely. Remove shells, leaving tails on, and place in a mixing bowl. Add pesto and mix to coat well. Marinate, refrigerated, for 2 hours.

3. Place Parmesan cheese on a plate and lightly dip each shrimp into the cheese. Arrange shrimp on platter and serve immediately.

Decorate a platter of canapés with an onion chrysanthemum, carrot lilies and green leaves.

SMOKED CAPON CANAPÉS

1 cup	whole hazelnuts	250 mL
9 slices	thinly sliced whole-wheat bread (sandwich loaf)	9 slices
8 Tbsp	butter, softened	120 mL
1	smoked capon or pheasant, *or* 2 lb (900 g) smoked turkey meat	1
1	10-oz (284-g) jar kumquats	1

1. Preheat oven to 350°F (160°C). Roast hazelnuts until very lightly brown, remove to cool and reduce heat to 250°F (120°C).

2. Remove crusts from bread slices and spread a thin even layer of butter on each side, using about 3 Tbsp (45 mL) butter all together. Quarter each slice into 1¼-inch (3-cm) squares. Place on baking sheet and bake until crisp, about 15 minutes. Set aside.

3. Remove skin from smoked capon, then bone, keeping meat in large pieces. Slice meat into ⅛-inch (3-mm) slices, then cut into 1¼-inch (3-cm) squares. Set aside.

4. Drain kumquats and cut into thin strips, approximately 14 slices per kumquat. Remove and discard seeds.

5. Rub roasted hazelnuts in a tea towel to remove hulls. Shake nuts and blow away hulls. Put hazelnuts into a food processor fitted with a steel blade and process, pulsing on/off until chopped. Add 5 Tbsp (75 mL) butter and process just enough to combine. Do not purée. Mixture should be coarse.

6. To assemble, spread ¾ tsp (4 mL) hazelnut butter on each piece of toasted bread. Top with 2 slices of smoked capon and garnish with 2 slices of kumquat.

STUFFED VEGETABLES

For filling:

1 lb	processed cream cheese	450 g
1½ Tbsp	Dinah's Chive Salad Mix or dried chives	20 mL
2½ Tbsp	chopped fresh dill weed or other chopped fresh herb	37 mL
2½ Tbsp	chopped fresh parsley	37 mL
2 Tbsp	finely chopped green onions	30 mL
to taste	salt	to taste

For vegetables:

¼ lb	snow peas	100 g
2	red bell peppers	2
1 pint	cherry tomatoes	0.5 L
2	Belgian endives	2
1 lb	Brussels sprouts	450 g
1	English cucumber	1
2	zucchini	2
¼ lb	uniformly sized mushrooms	100 g

1. In a food processor fitted with a steel blade process cheese until soft. Add Chive Salad Mix and process for another 30 seconds, or until well blended. Transfer to mixing bowl and add dill weed, parsley, green onions and salt. Stir to mix well and put into a piping bag fitted with a large star tip. Set aside.

2. Wash and dry all vegetables except mushrooms. Remove tips and strings of snow peas. With the tip of a round toothpick, slit open one edge of each snow pea. Cut red peppers into ¾-inch (2-cm) strips. Cut off top quarter of each cherry tomato (rounded end, not stem end). Scoop out seeds with a demitasse spoon and drain upside down on paper towels. Separate the leaves of endives, trim bottom edge of each leaf and dip in lemon juice to prevent browning. Trim bottom of each Brussels sprout so it will stand. Cut a deep X through the top. Pull apart slightly and remove a little of the inside leaves to form a cavity. Blanch in boiling salted water for 1 to 2 minutes. Slice cucumber and zucchini into ½-inch (1.25-cm) rounds. Using melon baller, scoop out a depression in each slice. Clean mushrooms by gently brushing with paper towels or mushroom brush. Remove stems.

3. To assemble, pipe a dab of filling into each cavity. Arrange stuffed vegetables on platter lined with leaves of lettuce or cabbage, and serve.

MANDARIN DUCK ROLLS

For pancakes:

2 cups	flour	500 mL
¾ cup	boiling water	180 mL
3 to 4 tsp	sesame oil	15 to 20 mL

For filling:

1½	Chinese barbecued duck or duck roasted with a honey glaze	1½
6	medium-sized carrots, cut in 4-inch (10-cm) long julienne	6
2 bunches	green onions, cut in 4-inch (10-cm) long julienne	2 bunches
5 Tbsp	hoisin sauce	75 mL
2 bunches	Chinese chives (garlic chives), at least 8 inches (20 cm) long, or green onion tops halved lengthwise.	2 bunches

1. Put flour into mixing bowl and add boiling water, stirring constantly. Turn out dough onto lightly floured surface and knead for 10 minutes. Dough will be soft and elastic but not sticky. Wrap with plastic wrap and let rest for 5 to 10 minutes.

2. To form pancakes, pinch off a small piece of dough and form a ball ¾ inches (2 cm) in diameter. Pat out and roll into a 2-inch (5-cm) circle. Brush the surface with a few drops of sesame oil. Make another circle in the same way and place on top of the first. Roll into a 4-inch (10-cm) circle. Repeat with remaining dough.

3. Heat a heavy frying pan over medium-high heat. Oil surface very lightly. Place several pancakes in pan (do not overcrowd) and cook about 1 minute on each side, or until layers begins to bubble and steam apart. Remove from heat and peel apart. Stack under a damp towel, or wrap immediately in plastic wrap. Repeat until all pancakes are cooked. Set aside.

4. Remove skin from duck and cut into strips about 4 inches × ⅛ inch (10 cm × 3 mm). Set aside. Remove meat, keeping pieces as large as possible, and cut into strips about 4 inches × ⅛ inch (10 cm × 3 mm).

5. In a pot of boiling water blanch chives just until limp, about 15 seconds. Immediately run under cold water to stop cooking. Set aside.

6. To assemble pancakes, spread ⅛ tsp (0.5 mL) hoisin sauce on each pancake. If brown spots have formed on the pancake during cooking, spread hoisin sauce on that side. Place an equal amount of duck meat on each pancake. Repeat with duck skin, carrots and green onions. Roll each pancake into a ¾-inch (2-cm) cylinder and tie with a blanched chive knotted with a bow. Serve at room temperature.

COCKTAIL SPANAKOPITA

1	10-oz (284-g) bag spinach, well washed	1
½ lb	feta cheese	225 g
¾ tsp	ground or freshly grated nutmeg	3 mL
5 sheets	phyllo pastry, each sheet cut into 8 strips 4 inches × 6 inches (10 cm × 15 cm)	5 sheets
½ cup	melted butter	125 mL

1. Preheat oven to 450°F (230°C).

2. Blanch spinach in boiling water for 2 minutes, or just until limp. Drain well. Place in cheesecloth and squeeze very dry. Chop into small pieces and put into small mixing bowl.

3. Crumble feta cheese with fork and add to spinach. Add nutmeg and toss to mix well.

4. Working with only 3 or 4 strips of phyllo at a time, brush each with melted butter. Cover the rest of the phyllo with a slightly damp cloth as it dries out rapidly and becomes very brittle.

5. Place about ¾ tsp (3 mL) spinach mixture in the centre of one end of a strip of buttered phyllo. Leave a 1-inch (2.5-cm) margin of pastry on either side of the filling. Roll up the pastry, but not too tightly. Put a drop of butter in each end of the roll and pinch ends closed. Brush top and bottom of roll with butter and place on a baking sheet. Repeat with the remaining phyllo strips.

6. Bake for 5 to 6 minutes or until golden brown. These can be made ahead of time and frozen, unbaked. A half hour before serving, remove from freezer, place on baking sheet, and cover with plastic wrap. When thawed, remove wrap and bake as above.

PRUNES IN BACON

2 lb	sliced bacon (about 40 slices)	900 g
½ lb	raw milk Cheddar cheese, or other firm white cheese, cut into pieces ⅜ inch × ⅜ inch × ¾ inch (1 cm × 1 cm × 2 cm)	225 g
40	flat toothpicks	40
10 oz	large dried prunes, pitted (about 40)	300 g

1. In a large frying pan fry bacon slices over medium-high heat or place under broiler for a few minutes to render some of the fat. Remove and drain on paper towels.

2. Insert one piece of cheese into the pit cavity of each prune. Repeat until all prunes are filled. Wrap each prune with a strip of bacon, covering the opening. Secure bacon with toothpick and cut off excess bacon. (Excess bacon can be chopped and frozen for later use.)

3. Just before serving, broil prunes for 2 to 3 minutes on each side and serve hot.

Crispy little rolls of phyllo pastry are a cocktail favourite and can be made with a variety of fillings. These are filled with spinach and cheese in the Greek tradition.
For variations on filling, try these combinations:
- *Cooked, chopped chicken and spinach*
- *Chopped walnuts and jam*
- *Curried shrimp and raisins*

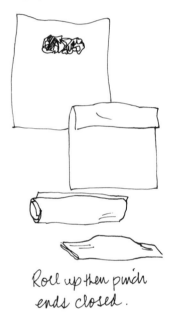

Roll up then pinch ends closed.

SAVOURY TARTS

LEEK AND STILTON TARTS AND MEDITERRANEAN TARTS

For tart shells:

1 recipe	Wine Pastry, see page 133	1 recipe

For Leek and Stilton filling:

4 Tbsp	butter	60 mL
1	large leek, well washed and thinly sliced	1
to taste	salt	to taste
1	egg	1
1 cup	whipping cream	250 mL
1 tsp	ground or freshly grated nutmeg	5 mL
to taste	cayenne	to taste
1¼ lb	Stilton cheese, cubed ⅜ inch (1 cm)	550 g

For Mediterranean filling:

4 Tbsp	butter	60 mL
2	medium-sized Spanish onions, diced ⅜ inch (1 cm)	2
2 cloves	garlic, crushed	2 cloves
to taste	salt and pepper	to taste
5	anchovy fillets, coarsely chopped	5
4 Tbsp	chopped olives	60 mL
10	cherry tomatoes, sliced in four	10
4 Tbsp	freshly grated Parmesan cheese	60 mL

1. Using Wine Pastry recipe, bake 3 dozen tart shells, 1¾ inches (4.5 cm) across and ¾ inch (2 cm) deep.

2. For Leek and Stilton: In a frying pan that has a lid melt butter over medium heat. Add leeks and sauté for 4 to 6 minutes. Cover, reduce heat to low, and cook until soft, about 5 minutes. Remove cover, raise heat to medium and boil off all liquid, stirring occasionally. Season to taste with salt. Set aside to cool.

3. Preheat oven to 350°F (180°C). Place 18 shells on a baking sheet lined with parchment.

4. In a small mixing bowl beat together egg, whipping cream, nutmeg and cayenne. Set aside.

5. Spoon ½ tsp (2 mL) cooled leek mixture into each of the 18 tart shells. Place a cube of Stilton cheese in each. Pour 1½ tsp (7 mL) egg mixture into each and bake for 12 to 15 minutes, or until tip of a knife inserted in the centre of a tart comes out clean.

6. For Mediterranean: In a frying pan that has a lid melt butter over medium-high heat. Add onions and sauté until lightly browned, about 5 minutes. Cover, reduce heat to low, and cook until soft, about 8 minutes. Remove cover, raise heat to medium and boil off liquid, stirring occasionally. Add garlic and season to taste with salt and pepper. Set aside to cool.

PARCHMENT PAPER

We recommend the use of parchment paper to line baking pans in many of our recipes. You can buy this coated paper in shops specializing in cookware, and once you use it, you will appreciate its virtues. Heavier than waxed paper, it withstands all the soggy egg wash, burnt pie filling and sticky meringues your oven can dish out, and it won't stick or tear like aluminum foil. It makes washing up a breeze.

7. Preheat oven to 350°F (180°C). Place the remaining 18 tart shells on baking sheet lined with parchment.

8. Put an equal amount of chopped anchovies in each shell. Add to each: ⅛ tsp (0.5 mL) chopped olives, ½ tsp (2 mL) sautéd onions, 1 slice tomato and a sprinkle of Parmesan cheese. Bake for 8 to 10 minutes, or until cheese begins to brown. Serve warm or at room temperature.

VARIATIONS

Here are three other fillings that you might like to try.

SMOKED SALMON TARTS

36	baked tart shells, as above	36
¾ lb	smoked salmon, diced ⅜ inch (1 cm)	300 g
1½ Tbsp	chopped fresh dill weed	22 mL
1	egg	1
1 cup	whipping cream	250 mL
to taste	pepper	to taste

1. Preheat oven to 350°F (180°C). Place tart shells on two baking sheets lined with parchment.

2. Place an equal amount of smoked salmon in each shell. Top with a bit of dill weed.

3. In a mixing bowl beat together egg, whipping cream and pepper to taste. Spoon 1½ tsp (7 mL) into each shell. Bake for 8 to 10 minutes, or until tip of knife inserted into centre of tart comes out clean.

SEAFOOD TARTS

Substitute 1 lb (450 g) crab meat and ½ cup (125 mL) grated Swiss cheese for smoked salmon and dill in preceding recipe.

SPINACH TARTS

Trim and clean 1½ bags or 3 bunches of spinach. Blanch, squeeze dry and chop. Use this spinach and ½ cup (125 mL) freshly grated Parmesan cheese instead of smoked salmon and dill in Smoked Salmon Tart recipe.

Garnish 'Savoury Tarts' with a leek chrysanthemum and a few green onion flowers

CHICKEN SATAY

SATAY SAUCE

If satay sauce is unavailable, substitute with a mixture of 3 Tbsp (45 mL) soy sauce, 2 Tbsp (30 mL) peanut butter, a dash of sesame seed oil and a dash of hot pepper sauce.

For marinade:

1	4-oz (125-g) bar unsweetened coconut cream	1
2 Tbsp	water	30 mL
6 Tbsp	natural peanut butter	90 mL
2 Tbsp	soy sauce	30 mL
2 Tbsp	spicy soy sauce	30 mL
3 Tbsp	bottled satay sauce	45 mL
1 Tbsp	brandy	15 mL
2 cloves	garlic, crushed	2 cloves
5	whole chicken breasts, about 5 lb (2.25 kg)	5
36	6-inch (15-cm) bamboo skewers, soaked in water for 2 hours	36

1. In a large bowl combine all ingredients for marinade. Remove 4 Tbsp (60 mL) and reserve.

2. Skin and bone chicken breasts. Slice into pieces about 1 inch × 1 inch × ¼ inch (2.5 cm × 2.5 cm × 6 mm). Add to marinade and toss well to coat all pieces evenly. Marinate overnight, refrigerated.

3. Thread 3 or 4 pieces of chicken on each skewer. Just before serving, place on rack and broil 2 to 3 minutes on each side. Brush with reserved marinade and serve hot.

ORIENTAL BUFFET FOR 30

Spring Rolls
Snow Peas Stuffed with Crab
Mandarin Duck Rolls

🍒

Sticky Rice Chicken
Home-style Egg Rolls
Gold Coin Beef
Buddha's Delight
Green Mango Salad

🍒

Almond Float
Fortune Cookies

O ur families came to Canada three generations ago and adapted to a Canadian lifestyle, leaving the Orient behind. But a love and affinity for Chinese cooking is part of the heritage that lingers in us still. And it shows up in the oddest places! Italian pasta with Chinese black-bean sauce. French bistro filet mignon with radicchio stir-fried in butter. East-west crossover cuisine that combines the best of everything.

This menu features authentic Chinese dishes, just slightly altered to suit our Canadian tastes and entertaining style; a little gutsier, a little bigger, a little richer.

The Mandarin Duck Rolls are our special creation, inspired by the traditional Peking Duck. These and the buttery little crab-stuffed snow peas have become a trademark. Chicken with sticky rice is a true banquet dish. Gilded with hoisin sauce and studded with bits of Chinese sausage, it gleams with a sense of occasion. Buddha's Delight is a traditional vegetarian dish made by Chinese monks. It is usually made from dried vegetables, which gives it a dense, musky flavour, but we've chopped fresh vegetables into ours to lighten the flavour and add colour.

The fortune cookies are the most fun of all. Our recipe is French, but the shape is strictly Chinatown. It may take a little practice to get the knack of folding, but the fun of making up the fortunes and sharing them after the meal makes the effort worthwhile.

CHINESE TEA

Formosa Oolong — a semi-fermented tea, much gentler in flavour and lower in caffeine than black (fully fermented) tea. There is a wide variety of fine Oolongs now being exported from Taiwan, each with characteristics so complex as to be compared to a fine wine. Tipsy Poet Tea, a favourite of ours, is first-flush Oolong scented with ginseng wine.

Semi-fermented tea is always taken without milk or sugar as the delicate fruity flavour is best enjoyed unadulterated.

Poonih — a semi-fermented tea popular with Chinese restaurants as it can steep for long periods without becoming overly bitter. As with all Chinese and Japanese teas, it is drunk without the addition of milk or sugar.

Jasmine — tea scented with the sweetly fragrant blossoms of the jasmine tree. Sometimes, in the finer qualities, the blossoms are removed before packaging. More often, they are not, and will float to the surface of the amber liquid as it brews.

Lapsang Soochong — an unusual tea with an earthy, smoky flavour.

Young Hyson — a green tea, it has less caffeine than semi-fermented tea. It is light and herby, or "green" in flavour.

For centrepieces, place small pots of red and yellow flowers in Chinese food take-out containers lined with black tissue paper.

WORK-AHEAD SCHEDULE

4 WEEKS AHEAD	• Send out invitations. • Plan layout of rooms and determine seating arrangements. • Organize music.
2 WEEKS AHEAD	• Arrange rental or loan of any dishes, cutlery, etc., if necessary. See checklist page 13. • Order flowers. • Arrange for two kitchen helpers and a bartender/waiter.
1 WEEK AHEAD	• Make list of bar requirements and groceries. Check supplies and shop for non-perishables. • Plan serving dishes and garnishes. • Prepare Spring Rolls and freeze.
2 DAYS AHEAD	• Buy all groceries, except barbecued duck.
1 DAY AHEAD	• Bone and marinate chicken. • Make Egg-Roll wrappers. • Prepare all vegetables for Buddha's Delight, except fresh greens. Cook, cool and refrigerate. • Make almond cream for Almond Float. • Prepare Fortune Cookies. • Prepare Egg-Roll filling, cool and refrigerate.
EARLY IN DAY	• Buy barbecued duck. • Prepare vegetables for all dishes other than Buddha's Delight. • Make rice stuffing for Sticky Rice Chicken. • Make crab filling for Snow Peas Stuffed with Crab; open snow peas. • Make pancakes for Mandarin Duck Rolls; wrap in plastic wrap and keep in cool place. Julienne duck. • Prepare Egg-Roll batter. Roll filling in wrappers. • Prepare fruit for Almond Float.
MIDDAY	• Remove Spring Rolls from freezer and deep fry. • Assemble Mandarin Duck Rolls. Cover with damp paper towels. • Assemble Sticky Rice Chicken and place on baking sheets. • Slice and marinate beef for Gold Coin Beef. • Prepare greens for Buddha's Delight.
1 HOUR AHEAD	• Combine fruit for Almond Float. • Stuff Snow Peas. • Make Green Mango Salad.
½ HOUR AHEAD	• Arrange Snow Peas Stuffed with Crab and Mandarin Duck Rolls on platters. • Prepare a platter for Spring Rolls. • Cook greens for Buddha's Delight. • Preheat oven and bake Spring Rolls. • Serve hors d'oeuvres.
45 MINUTES BEFORE DINNER	• Bake chicken for Sticky Rice Chicken. • Heat oil for deep frying. Dip Egg Rolls in batter and deep fry. • Heat Buddha's Delight and add greens.
15 MINUTES BEFORE DINNER	• Fry beef for Gold Coin Beef.

SPRING ROLLS

1 Tbsp	peanut oil	15 mL
1 Tbsp	butter	15 mL
2 Tbsp	chopped onion	30 mL
½ cup	finely shredded cabbage	125 mL
½ cup	julienned green beans	125 mL
¾ cup	shredded carrots	175 mL
4 Tbsp	julienned cloud ears (dried black fungus), first soaked in warm water for 20 minutes and well washed	60 mL
½ cup	julienned bamboo shoots	125 mL
½ cup	julienned water chestnuts	125 mL
1 tsp	soy sauce	5 mL
2 Tbsp	oyster sauce	30 mL
3 cloves	garlic, crushed	3 cloves
½ tsp	pepper	2 mL
1 Tbsp	cornstarch	15 mL
1 Tbsp	water	15 mL
1 cup	bean sprouts	250 mL
2	14-oz (400-g) packages spring-roll wrappers 6 inches × 6 inches (15 cm × 15 cm)	2
1	egg, lightly beaten	1
2 to 3 cups	oil for deep frying	500 to 750 mL
½ cup	plum sauce	125 mL

Spring-roll wrappers are very thin, cooked sheets made from wheat flour, water and oil. They are sold frozen, in packages of about 20 sheets. They can be round or square, but they usually measure 6 inches (15 cm) or 9 inches (23 cm). Thaw completely before separating as they are very thin and may tear.

If spring-roll wrappers are unavailable, mini egg rolls can be made by using wonton wrappers. They will not be as crispy but will be delicious all the same.

1. In a large frying pan combine oil and butter over medium-high heat. Add onion and sauté until translucent, about 2 minutes. Add cabbage, beans and carrots and sauté for 4 minutes. Add cloud ears, bamboo shoots and water chestnuts and continue cooking for 5 minutes. Season with soy sauce, oyster sauce, garlic and pepper. Dissolve cornstarch in water and add to vegetable mixture. Cook for another 3 to 4 minutes until cornstarch becomes transparent and liquid thickens. Mixture should be quite dry. Remove from heat and mix in bean sprouts. Set aside to cool.

2. Separate spring-roll wrappers, place in a single layer, and cover with a slightly damp tea towel. This will keep wrappers moist and easy to roll. Spray towel occasionally with a fine mist of water, if necessary, to keep towel moist. Remove one wrapper from under towel and place about 1 Tbsp (15 mL) filling on corner, as diagrammed. Fold in side corners and roll up. Moisten end well with egg to seal. Set aside and repeat with remaining wrappers until all filling is used.

3. Heat oil for deep frying to 375°F (190°C) in a heavy frying pan over medium heat. Add 4 to 6 rolls and deep fry until golden brown, approximately 5 minutes. Remove to drain on rack over paper towels. Allow temperature of oil to return to 375°F (190°C). Repeat until all rolls are cooked. Serve immediately. These can also be made ahead of time and reheated in an oven preheated to 375°F (190°C). Serve with plum sauce.

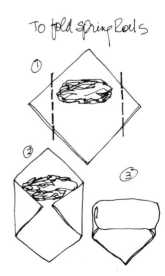

To fold spring Rolls

① ② ③

SNOW PEAS STUFFED WITH CRAB

PEAS PLEASE

Our clients request this hors d'oeuvre so frequently that it has become a signature dish for us. No one ever seems to tire of these crunchy crab-filled snow peas.

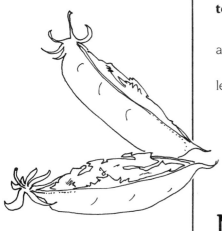

50	snow peas	50
1 lb	crab meat (if using frozen, thaw and squeeze dry)	500 g
2 Tbsp	mayonnaise	30 mL
1 tsp	lemon juice	5 mL
dash	Worcestershire sauce	dash
½ tsp	crumbled dried tarragon	2 mL
to taste	salt and pepper	to taste

1. Wash snow peas and pat dry. With a toothpick slit open along string side and set aside.

2. In a medium-sized bowl combine crab meat, mayonnaise, lemon juice, Worcestershire sauce, tarragon, salt and pepper.

3. Just before serving, stuff snow peas with crab mixture.

MANDARIN DUCK ROLLS

For recipe, see page 68.

STICKY RICE CHICKEN

3	3- to 4-lb (1.5- to 2-kg) chickens	3
For marinade:		
1½ cups	hoisin sauce	375 mL
3 Tbsp	sherry	45 mL
3 Tbsp	soy sauce	45 mL
For stuffing:		
9 cups	glutinous rice	2.25 L
9 cups	water	2.25 L
2 cups	oyster sauce	500 mL
2½ cups	dried black Chinese mushrooms, soaked in warm water for 2 hours	625 mL
12	Chinese sausages	12
2 cups	water chestnuts, diced ¼ inch (6 mm)	500 mL
1 bunch	green onions, thinly sliced	1 bunch
to taste	soy sauce (optional)	to taste

1. Bone each chicken by cutting along backbone and with the point of a boning knife or sharp paring knife freeing the meat from the bone with small cuts, working away from the backbone. Keep the flat of the knife blade as close to the bone as possible. At the thighs and wings, cut through the joints and continue working around to the breastbone. As you release the breast meat, take care not to pierce the skin where it attaches to the breastbone. When the meat has been completely released from the carcass, remove the upper wing, thigh and drumstick bones. The double bones of the lower wing may be left in. Set aside boned chickens.

2. For marinade, combine hoisin sauce, sherry and soy sauce in a small mixing bowl. Brush this mixture liberally over the boned chickens, inside and out. Place chickens in a large bowl or pan and allow to marinate overnight, refrigerated.

3. Prepare rice for stuffing by soaking in water for 2 hours in a large heavy pot with a tight-fitting lid. Add oyster sauce, cover and bring to boil over medium-high heat. Lower heat and simmer until cooked, about 30 minutes. Add more water if necessary. Grains of rice should be quite dry and separate. Fluff up with fork and set aside.

4. Preheat oven to 425°F (220°C). Prepare 3 baking sheets by lining with parchment or spraying with vegetable oil coating, or use non-stick baking sheets. Baking sheets must have a rim of at least ½ inch (1.25 cm) as fat and juices are released during roasting.

5. Cut soaked mushrooms into ¼-inch (6-mm) dice, discarding any stems that may not have softened. Add to rice. Steam sausages for 15 minutes, cool and cut in ¼-inch (6-mm) dice. Add to rice mixture along with diced water chestnuts and sliced green onions and stir to combine ingredients. Add a little soy sauce, if desired. Place one third of the rice mixture on each prepared baking sheet. Spread rice out to the approximate shape and size of the boned chickens. Lay the chickens out flat, skin side up, over the rice. (Chickens can be prepared in advance to this stage and kept in the refrigerator.) Roast for 25 to 30 minutes, or until chicken is just done. Transfer to serving platters and cut into 2-inch (5-cm) squares to serve.

CHINESE SAUSAGE

Sweet dried sausages made from pork. Sold in vacuum-sealed packages of ½ or 1 lb (450 or 900 g).

If you have a friendly butcher, you might ask him to bone the chickens for you. Otherwise, follow this diagram.

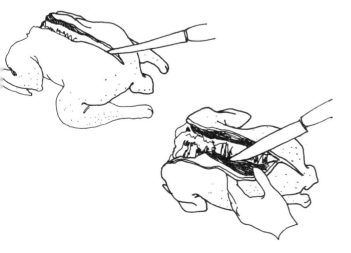

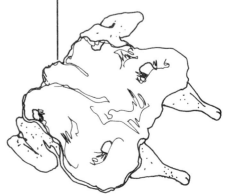

HOME-STYLE EGG ROLLS

Serve egg rolls with hot mustard and plum sauce.

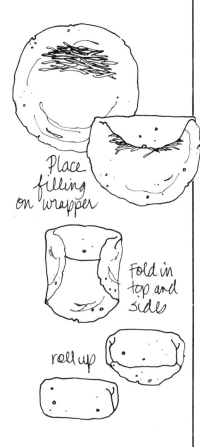

Place filling on wrapper

Fold in top and side

roll up

For filling:

2 cups	wood ears (dried large black fungus)	500 mL
4 Tbsp	butter	60 mL
1 cup	thinly sliced onions	250 mL
2 cups	thinly diagonally sliced celery	500 mL
3 cups	julienned snow peas	750 mL
4 cups	julienned bamboo shoots	1 L
4 cups	julienned deep-fried tofu	1 L
1 lb	julienned Chinese barbecued pork	450 g
1 cup	julienned Szechwan preserved radish	250 mL
4 cups	julienned water chestnuts	1 L
½ cup	oyster sauce	125 mL
1 tsp	crushed garlic	5 mL
½ tsp	pepper	2 mL
3 cups	bean sprouts	750 mL

For wrappers:

18	eggs	18
2 cups	flour	500 mL
3 cups	water	750 mL
2 Tbsp	peanut oil or butter, for frying	30 mL
1	egg, lightly beaten	1

For deep frying:

3 to 4 cups	oil	0.75 to 1 L

For batter:

2	eggs	2
2 cups	flour	500 mL
2 cups	milk	500 mL
2 cups	water	500 mL
2 Tbsp	corn starch	30 mL
3 Tbsp	baking powder	45 mL
2 Tbsp	sugar	30 mL
1 Tbsp	salt	15 mL

1. For filling, soak wood ears in water for 1 hour. Drain. Remove hard stems and wash well to remove sand. Julienne and set aside.

2. In a large frying pan melt butter over medium heat. Add onions and celery and sauté for 2 to 3 minutes. Add snow peas and sauté for 1 minute. Add wood ears, bamboo shoots, tofu, pork, radish and water chestnuts and sauté for 5 minutes, until completely heated through. Stir in oyster sauce, garlic and pepper. Add bean sprouts and sauté for 2 minutes. Remove from heat, drain off any liquid and set aside to cool while making the wrappers.

3. For wrappers, combine eggs, flour and water in a mixing bowl or blender and whisk together until well blended.

If desired, substitute regular mushrooms for wood ears, chicken or shrimp for barbecued pork, and cabbage or carrots for Szechwan preserved radish.

4. Heat an omelette or non-stick pan over medium heat. Brush with a little peanut oil or butter. Pour about 4 Tbsp (60 mL) egg mixture into pan and swirl to form a crêpe-like pancake. Fry on one side only for 1 to 2 minutes, or until cooked. Remove to large plate and repeat until all egg mixture is used, stacking cooked pancakes on a plate.

5. To assemble, place ½ cup (125 mL) filling on one end of a wrapper. Fold sides in and roll up, as diagrammed. Seal with egg wash. Repeat until all filling has been used.

6. Into a heavy frying pan add deep-frying oil to a depth of 2 inches (5 cm). Heat to 375°F (190°C) over medium heat.

7. Combine all ingredients for batter in a mixing bowl or blender and whisk until smooth. Batter will be thin. Dip prepared rolls into batter, let excess drip off, and lower gently into hot oil. Fry 2 or 3 rolls at a time, on both sides, until golden brown. Remove and drain on paper towels. Allow oil to return to original temperature and repeat until all rolls have been fried. Serve immediately.

GOLD COIN BEEF

For marinade:

1 cup	tomato catsup	250 mL
½ cup	hoisin sauce	125 mL
4 Tbsp	bourbon or rum	60 mL
10 cloves	garlic, crushed	10 cloves
3 Tbsp	Worcestershire sauce	45 mL
3 Tbsp	soy sauce	45 mL
5 lb	beef tenderloin, sliced ¼ inch (6 mm)	2.25 kg
4 to 6 Tbsp	peanut oil	60 to 90 mL
6	Spanish onions, sliced	6
to taste	salt and pepper	to taste

1. In a large mixing bowl combine all ingredients for marinade. Add sliced beef and mix to coat well. Marinate, refrigerated, for 1 to 2 hours.

2. In a large frying pan heat 4 Tbsp (60 mL) oil over high heat. Add onions and sauté until lightly browned but still crispy, about 5 to 10 minutes. Season to taste with salt and pepper. Set aside and keep warm.

3. In a non-stick frying pan heat 1 tsp (5 mL) oil over high heat until very hot. Add 8 to 12 pieces of beef (do not crowd in pan) and fry 1 to 2 minutes on each side, until browned and medium rare. Remove from pan to warming oven. Repeat until all beef has been fried. Add marinade to pan and cook for 2 to 3 minutes.

4. To serve, make a bed of fried onions on serving platter and arrange meat slices on top. Pour heated marinade over meat. Serve immediately.

HOISIN SAUCE

A spicy, sweet, thick sauce made from beans and spices. Often used to brush on roasted and barbecued meat, the most famous being Peking Duck.

BUDDHA'S DELIGHT

Our version of a traditional dish originated by Chinese Buddhist monks. An interesting and savoury dish, full of wondrous flavours. Try it, it could be a religious experience!

A trip to your nearest Chinatown will probably be in order as your corner store may not have many of the special dried and canned ingredients. But make an adventure of it; you may make some interesting discoveries as you forage for wood ears through the noisy Chinese market.

BLACK FUNGUS

Cloud Ears (Wun Yee): thin black chips when in their dried state. After a 30-minute soak in warm water, they become floppy ruffles. The hard stem must be pinched off and sand washed out of the little wrinkles. They add subtle flavour and crunchy texture to stir-fried dishes.

Wood Ears (Mook Yee): Very similar to Cloud Ears but larger and lighter in colour. Soak for an hour and clean in the same way as Cloud Ears. Both types of fungus are sold by weight in their dried state and can be used interchangeably.

½ cup	peanut oil	125 mL
12 slices	fresh ginger root	12 slices
1 cup	wood ears (dried large black fungus), soaked in warm water for 1 hr, well washed and cut into ¼-inch (6-mm) strips	250 mL
1 cup	sliced bamboo shoots, drained, liquid reserved	250 mL
1 cup	sliced fresh lotus root, ⅛-inch (3-mm) slices	250 mL
1	14-oz (398-mL) can straw mushrooms, drained, liquid reserved	1
1 cup	sliced water chestnuts	250 mL
1	12-oz (334-mL) can baby corn, drained, liquid reserved	1
½ cup	dried lily buds, soaked in warm water for ½ hour	125 mL
3 cakes	deep-fried tofu, sliced ½ inch (1.25 cm)	3 cakes
1	9-oz (250-g) can white ginko nuts	1
2 oz	cellophane vermicelli noodles, soaked in warm water for ½ hr, then cut into 2-inch (5-cm) lengths	60 g
15 pieces	dried bean-curd skin, soaked for ½ hr, then sliced 1 inch (2.5 cm)	15 pieces
½ cup	soy sauce	125 mL
¾ tsp	Chinese five-spice	3 mL
3 cloves	garlic, crushed	3 cloves
4 Tbsp	sherry	60 mL
2 Tbsp	corn starch	30 mL
1 cup	liquid from canned vegetables	250 mL
1 cup	snow peas, tips and strings removed	250 mL
3 cups	broccoli florets	750 mL
to taste	soy sauce	to taste
to taste	salt and pepper	to taste
6 Tbsp	sesame oil	90 mL
1 bunch	green onions, chopped	1 bunch

1. In a wok or large frying pan heat ⅓ of the peanut oil over high heat. Add 4 slices of ginger, fry for 2 or 3 minutes to brown, then discard ginger. Add wood ears, bamboo shoots, lotus root, straw mushrooms, water chestnuts, baby corn and lily buds. Cook for 5 minutes, tossing constantly.

2. Reduce heat to medium-low. Add deep-fried tofu, ginko nuts, vermicelli, bean-curd skin, ½ cup (125 mL) soy sauce, five-spice, garlic and sherry. Toss gently to mix. Cover and let simmer for 10 minutes.

3. Mix corn starch with liquid reserved from canned vegetables.

Add enough to the wok to coat the vegetables. Cook gently for 5 minutes.

4. In another wok or frying pan heat ⅓ of the peanut oil over high heat. Add 4 slices of ginger. Fry for 2 or 3 minutes until brown, then discard ginger. Add snow peas and stir fry for 1 minute. Remove to a bowl.

5. Add more peanut oil and 4 more slices of ginger to the wok. Brown and remove the ginger. Add broccoli and stir fry for 3 minutes.

6. Add broccoli and snow peas to the other vegetables. Toss to mix. Simmer for 5 more minutes. Adjust seasoning, adding soy sauce and salt and pepper to taste.

7. Sprinkle on sesame oil. Toss to mix. Remove to serving platter and sprinkle with chopped green onions.

GREEN MANGO SALAD

10 cups	shredded green mangoes (approximately 15 unripe mangoes)	2.5 L
4½ tsp	salt	22 mL
12 to 14 Tbsp	sugar, depending on tartness of mangoes	175 to 200 mL
½ tsp	crushed chilies	2 mL
3	large tomatoes, diced	3

1. In a large mixing bowl combine all ingredients except tomatoes. Toss together and marinate for 15 minutes. Add tomatoes, toss and serve immediately.

ALMOND FLOAT

For almond cream:

3 pkg	gelatin	3 pkg
¾ cup	water	175 mL
5¼ cups	whipping cream	1.3 L
¾ cup	sugar	175 mL
1 Tbsp	almond extract	15 mL

For fruit:

12 cups	any combination of canned lichee nuts and juice, canned mandarin oranges and juice, fresh strawberries, grapes, fresh pineapple, sliced bananas, sliced mangoes, sliced peaches	3 L

1. In a small saucepan sprinkle gelatin over cold water and allow to dissolve. Place over low heat, just to melt. Do not boil. Remove from heat and set aside.

2. In a large saucepan scald 3 cups (750 mL) cream. Remove

LILY BUDS

Also called Lotus Blossoms or Golden Needles, these are the dried unopened buds of the tiger lily. Soak in warm water for 30 minutes to soften before cooking. For best flavour and texture, tie a single knot in the middle of each bud after softening.

For the best flavour and texture use mangoes in which the flesh is still very green.

from heat, add sugar and stir until dissolved. Stir in gelatin mixture, almond extract and remaining cream. Add more almond extract if you like. Pour into large round-bottomed bowl and refrigerate until set.

3. In a large bowl combine fruit and their juices and allow flavours to blend for 1 hour.

4. When almond cream has set, invert into a large decorative bowl so it unmoulds with the rounded side up. Top with fruit and juice. For each serving, scoop out a portion of almond cream and an assortment of fruit.

FORTUNE COOKIES

The fun of these is in making up the fortunes to suit your guests. And the cookies taste so good because they're home made.

1½ cups	sugar	375 mL
¾ cup	egg whites	175 mL
1 cup	melted butter	250 mL
⅛ tsp	salt	0.5 mL
½ tsp	vanilla	2 mL
1 cup	flour	250 mL

1. Type or print 24 messages on paper and cut apart into strips for folding into cookies.

2. Preheat oven to 375°F (190°C).

3. In a small mixing bowl combine sugar and egg whites. Stir to dissolve sugar. Add butter, salt and vanilla. Beat lightly to mix. Stir in flour.

4. With a metal spatula, thinly spread 1 Tbsp (15 mL) of batter in a 4-inch (10-cm) circle on baking sheet. Repeat, making a second circle of batter. Bake for 6 minutes, or until lightly browned around the edges. Remove from oven and allow to cool for 1 minute, when it will be cool enough to handle but still supple. You may wish to wear rubber gloves so you can handle the cookies while they are hot. Form each cookie around a fortune, as diagrammed. If cookie cools too much and becomes too crisp to shape, return to the oven for a minute, or until softened. Repeat until all batter has been used.

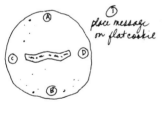

① place message on flat cookie

② lift sides A and B up to form a cylinder

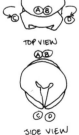

TOP VIEW

③ Holding A B together pull C and D down to meet directly behind A B.

SIDE VIEW

SERENDIPARTIES

T hrowing a party needn't always be a serious matter; the best times are often on the offbeat side. Consider a Weekday Breakfast Party, Supper at Midnight, Dinner on Mars or Mid-winter Beach Blanket Bingo Party. Or why not have a black and white party where everything—the food, the decor, the flowers, the dress code and even the Scotch — are black and white.

We are well known for our unusual theme parties, and we've described two of them here: A Chocoholic Dinner and a Mad Hatter's Tea Dance. Use them as inspiration for your own party creations. And have fun!

CHOCOHOLIC DINNER PARTY

A client came to us one day with a request for something special: she wanted to celebrate her husband's birthday in a way that was really fun and unusual. "He loves chocolate," was all she said.

And we came up with the idea of a chocoholic dinner—chocolate in EVERYTHING, from soup to dessert. The main dish was easy. It had to be Chicken Mole, that magical Mexican preparation, memorable for the remarkable richness that unsweetened chocolate gives the chili and nut sauce.

In developing the recipes we found that chocolate combines surprisingly well with many different foods. Its scented, bitter richness is an unexpected counterpoint in many combinations. When we began to think of chocolate as a flavouring agent, the rest followed naturally.

For your own party, experiment with some of these combinations: shrimp and apple fritters in chocolate batter, chocolate tomato soup, banana and chocolate rolled in buttered phyllo pastry, crudités with a dip of chocolate cream cheese, brie cheese studded with chocolate chips and almonds, pasta with orange sauce drizzled with chocolate sauce, braised beef with mole sauce, chocolate chips tossed into cole slaw, chocolate fondue, chocolate bread or biscuits, chocolate cocktails and coffee served with chocolate swizzle sticks. Then finish with a selection of chocolate desserts or ice-cream with a variety of chocolate toppings — chocolate shot, Smarties, hot fudge sauce, to name a few.

For our chocolate party everything was served buffet style so the rich meal could be sampled at leisure. Of course, the table decorations were made of chocolate. Baskets piped from pure chocolate were filled with fresh strawberries. "Paper" bags were made from chocolate to hold whipped cream. Little chocolate butterflies were everywhere, and giant roses formed from chocolate paste graced the platters.

You might consider doing a chocolate party at Halloween and combining the theme with witches and pumpkins. A word of warning: remember that chocolate is said to be a stimulant and an aphrodisiac!

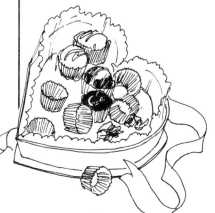

CHICKEN MOLE

Yields 8 servings

2	3- to 4-lb (1.5- to 1.75-kg) chickens, cut into serving-size pieces	2
4 Tbsp	flour	60 mL
½ cup	vegetable oil	125 mL
2	19-oz (540-mL) cans tomatoes, undrained	2
1 cup	ground almonds	250 mL
4 cloves	garlic, crushed	4 cloves
2 to 4 Tbsp	chili powder	30 to 60 mL
4 Tbsp	dry breadcrumbs	60 mL
1 tsp	ground coriander	5 mL
1 tsp	ground cinnamon	5 mL
1 tsp	ground dried oregano	5 mL
2 tsp	salt	10 mL
2 cups	strong chicken stock	500 mL
1½ oz	unsweetened chocolate, chopped	40 g

1. This dish can be cooked in the oven or on top of the stove. Preheat oven to 350°F (180°C), if desired.

2. Sprinkle chicken pieces with flour and toss to coat well.

3. In a large frying pan heat oil over medium-high heat. Sauté chicken pieces, a few at a time, until browned. Remove from pan and keep warm.

4. Add tomatoes, almonds, garlic, chili, breadcrumbs, coriander, cinnamon, oregano and salt and simmer for 5 minutes, stirring occasionally.

5. Lower heat and add chicken stock and chocolate. Cook, stirring occasionally, until chocolate has melted. Add chicken and simmer on low heat for 30 minutes or bake in oven for 30 minutes.

Mole sauce:
Tomatoes, onions, peanuts, peppers and ... CHOCOLATE!

BLACK-AND-WHITE TRUFFLES

Yields approximately 30 candies

6 oz	white chocolate, grated	170 g
½ cup	whipping cream	125 mL
3 Tbsp	Grand Marnier liqueur	45 mL
6 oz	semi-sweet chocolate, grated	170 g

1. In top of double boiler combine white chocolate, ¼ cup (60 mL) whipping cream and 1½ Tbsp (22 mL) Grand Marnier. Melt over barely simmering water, stirring occasionally. Transfer to a bowl and place over hot water to maintain temperature.

2. In top of double boiler combine semi-sweet chocolate, remaining whipping cream and Grand Marnier. Melt over barely simmering water, stirring occasionally. Transfer to a bowl.

3. Place both bowls in refrigerator to cool, stirring occasionally. When mixtures begin to harden (about 10 minutes), combine into one bowl and swirl together with a few strokes just enough to marbleize. Cool for 5 to 10 more minutes, until hard enough to hold its shape.

4. Scoop up chocolate with a teaspoon, incorporating a bit of white and a bit of dark chocolate in each spoonful, and drop in 1-inch (2.5-cm) balls onto cookie sheet lined with waxed paper. Refrigerate until ready to serve. Dust with cocoa or icing sugar, if desired.

MAD HATTER'S TEA DANCE

A mad hatter's tea dance is the kind of felicitous afternoon party that is great fun for adults and children alike. Our party began with pop-up Alice in Wonderland invitations that urged guests to wear mad hats or costumes. They didn't let us down. Kings and queens arrived, rabbits, Cheshire cats, cards galore, a smoking caterpillar and a remarkable array of hats.

Our make-up artist painted the waiters' faces white and decorated them with hearts, diamonds, clubs and spades. For the waitresses we made special aprons with appliqués of playing-card motifs. Giant cut-outs of Alice and her Wonderland company were placed around the room. Pots of spring flowers and brightly coloured balloons added gaiety. And rock-and-roll music prompted a lively tea dance. Our menu of silly sandwiches, storybook sweets and heart-shaped scones evolved into a delightful assortment of tea dainties. All of this created a mood of tongue-in-cheek madness that continued throughout the afternoon.

Here are some menu ideas for your own Mad Hatter's Tea Dance. Use them as fuel for thought. With this theme, you can be as creative as you like. Make your own Wonderland, and invite the children to participate. With their imagination and inquisitiveness, they add fresh charm to an afternoon like this.

COLOURED SANDWICH BREAD

Order pastel coloured sandwich bread from your local bakery. Pink and green are the colours most often available. Ask them to slice it thinly lengthwise, if possible, so you will have large pieces of bread to work with. Bread will be easier to cut and roll if it is a day old or partially frozen.

HEART-SHAPED SCONES

Use your favourite scone or baking-powder biscuit recipe, toss a handful of currants into the dough and cut into heart shapes with a cookie cutter before baking. Serve with lots of sweet butter, Devon cream or crème fraîche, fruit preserves and fresh strawberries.

CUPCAKE FLOWERS

Make small cupcakes and decorate the tops with flowers piped from pastel coloured buttercream icing. Don't be discouraged if your cake decorating skills are less than professional. The pastel colours will work for you. Or ice the cupcakes with pastel coloured buttercream icing and place a single chocolate chip, candied violet, silver dragee or candy heart in the centre of each.

Dainty Pastel Sandwiches

From pink sandwich bread cut hearts and diamonds using cookie cutters. Make diamond sandwiches filled with chocolate-nut spread and heart sandwiches with cream cheese mixed with chopped maraschino cherries. In keeping with the light-hearted spirit of this party, use fun, light spreads.

With green bread use any "Fifties" party sandwich filling, such as devilled ham, or cheese spread mixed with bacon bits and Worcestershire sauce. Or make asparagus pinwheel sandwiches and cut-out rounds topped with butter, cucumber and watercress for a very pretty green on green.

An Assortment of Tea

Offer a brisk black tea, such as English Breakfast (we favour a blend of Darjeeling and Assam), a scented tea like Earl Grey, and a fruity tea, such as Apricot or Blackcurrant. And have lots of milk, lemon and sugar on hand.

In the summer, you may wish to offer a fruit punch as well as the tea. In winter, espresso and hot chocolate hit the spot. Whatever the time of year, you and your friends are sure to enjoy the frivolity of an afternoon spent mad as a hatter.

RECIPES

12 cups all-purpose flour, 8 eggs, 4 lbs. butter, 6 cups brown sugar, 4 cups chopped nuts 2 Tbsp. vanilla. Put in a bowl and beat til

What's for dinner? Desperately bored with beef bourgignon, you flip through last month's *Dinerama* magazine but come up empty handed. You call up Dial-a-Menu, but everyone's out to lunch.

That's where this chapter comes in — like a gourmet friend with a ready supply of interesting, reliable recipes and menu ideas that you can't wait to try.

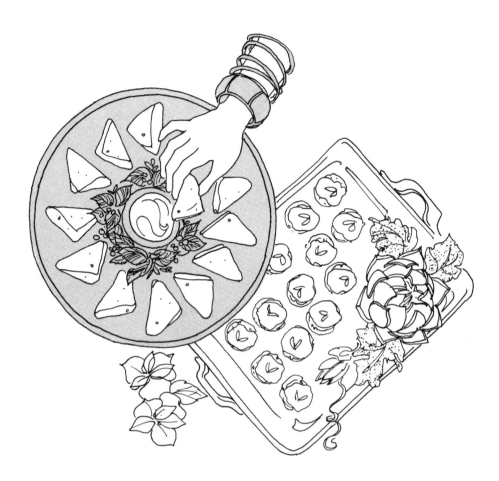

STARTERS

MINIATURE PIZZA

Yields 45 2-inch (5-cm) pizzas

These tiny cocktail pizzas are absolutely delightful. This crust can be topped with our California pizza fillings or your own favourite combinations.

3 cups	flour	750 mL
1 pkg	active dry yeast	1 pkg
1 Tbsp	honey	15 mL
1 cup	warm water	250 mL
1 tsp	salt	5 mL
6 Tbsp	olive oil	100 mL
2 tsp	Dinah's Chive Salad Mix or dried chives	10 mL

1. In a food processor fitted with a steel blade briefly mix the flour and yeast.

2. In a small bowl mix together honey, water, salt and 3 Tbsp (45 mL) of the olive oil. Slowly pour honey mixture through feed tube of processor with motor running and continue processing until dough forms a ball in the middle. Turn out dough onto floured surface and knead in the Chive Salad Mix. Dust with flour if dough is too sticky. Continue kneading for about 10 minutes until dough is smooth and elastic. Form into a ball and oil surface lightly. Place in bowl, cover with clean towel and allow to rise in a warm place until it doubles in volume, about 30 minutes.

3. After dough has doubled, punch down and pinch into 1-inch (2.5-cm) balls. Cover and allow to rest for 10 to 15 minutes.

4. Preheat oven to 425°F (220°F).

5. On a lightly floured surface roll out each ball into a circle about 2 to 2½ inches (5 to 6 cm) in diameter. Place on baking sheet and bake for 8 to 10 minutes. Brush with olive oil as soon as they come out of the oven. These can be made earlier in the day and refrigerated, covered with plastic wrap. Just before serving, top with any filling and heat in the oven for 3 to 5 minutes.

TOP THESE CALIFORNIA FILLINGS!

- Fried mushrooms, green onions and chèvre cheese
- Sun-dried tomatoes and Mozzarella cheese
- Tomato relish, garlic and escargot
- Smoked oysters and fried bacon bits
- Smoked salmon, crème fraîche and capers
- Black olives, fried peppers and anchovies
- Roasted garlic cloves and Gruyère cheese

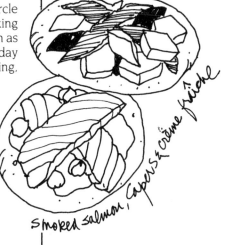

black olives, fried peppers & anchovies

Smoked salmon, Capers & crème fraîche

California mini Pizzas

mushrooms, Green Onions and Chèvre

Sun-dried Tomatoes & Mozzarella

APPLE AND CHEESE IN PHYLLO

Yields 36 pieces

Golden triangles of crisp pastry filled with apple and melted Cheddar cheese. A sweet twist to traditional Greek spanakopita.

PHYLLO PASTRY

These miraculously thin sheets of dough are sold in packages of about 20 sheets. Each sheet should be well buttered before folding or layering for best flavour and texture. Greek desserts are well known for their use of phyllo. Keep a box of phyllo on hand, and you will be able to whip up fabulous little hors d'oeuvres or sweets at a moment's notice.

1½ cups	coarsely grated mild Cheddar cheese	375 mL
2 cups	coarsely grated apples	500 mL
2 tsp	ground cinnamon	10 mL
6 sheets	phyllo pastry, cut into 1½-inch × 17-inch (4-cm × 43-cm) strips	6 sheets
½ cup	butter, melted	125 mL

1. Preheat oven to 400°F (200°C). Line a baking sheet with parchment paper.

2. In a medium-sized bowl combine cheese, apples and cinnamon.

3. Cover the phyllo pastry with a slightly damp cloth to keep it from drying out.

4. Remove 3 strips of pastry and brush with melted butter. Place a heaping teaspoon (7 mL) of filling on bottom corner of one strip and fold on the diagonal to form a triangle as diagrammed. Brush triangle with butter. Repeat with remaining 2 strips. Remove 3 more strips and repeat until pastry and filling are used up.

5. Place on baking sheet and bake for 8 to 10 minutes, or until golden brown.

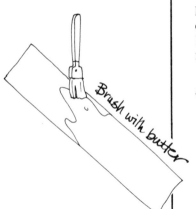

Brush with butter

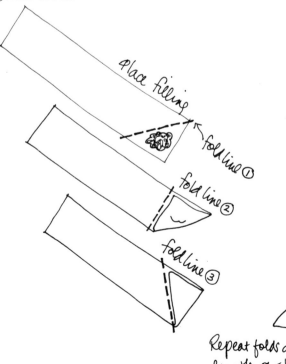

Place filling
fold line ①
fold line ②
fold line ③

Repeat folds along entire length of strip.

CHEDDAR BISCUITS

Yields 25 biscuits

These flaky Cheddar biscuits filled with spiced Cheddar cheese are terrific cocktail fare. Serve them with everything from port to Cajun Martinis.

For biscuits:

1 cup	flour	250 mL
⅛ tsp	salt	0.5 mL
⅛ tsp	cayenne	0.5 mL
½ cup	butter	125 mL
1 cup	shredded Cheddar cheese (about 4 oz/100 g)	250 mL
⅛ tsp	Worcestershire sauce	0.5 mL
½ tsp	Dijon mustard	2 mL
1	egg, lightly beaten	1
2 to 4 Tbsp	toasted black sesame seeds	30 to 60 mL

For filling:

1¼ cups	shredded Cheddar cheese (about 5 oz/130 g)	310 mL
¼ cup	butter, cubed	60 mL
¼ tsp	salt	1 mL
½ tsp	paprika	2 mL
2 tsp	finely chopped green onions	10 mL
2 tsp	finely chopped fresh parsley	10 mL
2 tsp	finely chopped fresh dill weed	10 mL

1. To prepare biscuits, add flour, salt and cayenne to food processor. Process a few seconds. Add butter and process with on/off pulses until mixture resembles corn meal. Do not over-process. Add cheese, Worcestershire sauce and mustard and process for 30 seconds or until blended. Dough will be very dry.

2. Transfer dough to a bowl and knead lightly only until dough gathers together.

3. Preheat oven to 375°F (190°C). Line a baking sheet with parchment paper.

4. On a lightly floured surface roll dough to ⅜-inch (1-cm) thickness. Using a 1-inch (2.5-cm) cookie cutter cut out 50 biscuits. Place on a baking sheet ½ inch (1.25 cm) apart.

5. Brush the tops of 25 of the biscuits with beaten egg. Sprinkle each biscuit with a few sesame seeds.

6. Bake for 18 to 20 minutes, or until browned on the bottom. Remove to wire rack and cool completely.

7. To prepare filling, add cheese, butter, salt and paprika to food processor. Process until mixture is completely blended.

8. Transfer mixture to a bowl. Add green onions, parsley and dill weed and mix well.

9. Spread ½ Tbsp (7 mL) filling on top of a plain biscuit. Place a biscuit decorated with sesame seeds on top of filling.

CAJUN MARTINIS

Cut 1 to 4 jalapeño peppers in half and drop them into a bottle of gin. Allow flavours to blend for at least a week, then stir with ice and a few drops of dry vermouth. Strain into glasses and serve with a twist of lemon.

MINIATURE CHÈVRE TARTS

Yields 16 tarts

These tiny hors d'oeuvres with a delicate toast shell can be made up in minutes. The filling is equally delicious baked in shells of rich pastry.

CHÈVRE CHEESE

Chèvre, an earthy-flavoured cheese made from goat's milk, has been a favoured cheese in France for hundreds of years. It's now very popular in North America, and an excellent, although milder, chèvre is being made in Canada. Chèvre comes in all shapes and sizes, covered in everything from ashes to grapeleaves. A favourite of ours is packed in herbed olive oil.

For tart shells:

16 slices	thinly sliced white bread	16 slices
3 to 4 Tbsp	melted butter	45 to 60 mL

For filling:

1 bunch	watercress, large stems removed	1 bunch
¼ lb	chèvre cheese, crumbled	110 g

1. Preheat oven to 325°F (160°C).

2. Using a 3-inch (8-cm) round cookie cutter, cut the bread into 16 rounds. Using tart tins approximately 1½ inches (4 cm) in diameter and ¾ inch (2 cm) deep, lightly press a round of bread into the bottom and up the sides of each tin. Brush the bread with a little melted butter. Bake for 10 to 15 minutes, until crisp. These tart shells can be prepared up to a day in advance and stored in an airtight container.

3. Wash watercress and dry very well. Coarsely chop leaves and tender top stems. Spoon a generous ½ teaspoon (2 mL) of chopped watercress into the bottom of each tart shell. Top with 1 teaspoon (5 mL) of chèvre and an additional sprinkle of watercress. The tarts can be prepared up to this point and left, unrefrigerated, for up to 2 hours.

4. Preheat oven to 375°F (190°C).

5. Bake tarts just until the cheese melts, about 3 to 5 minutes. Serve immediately.

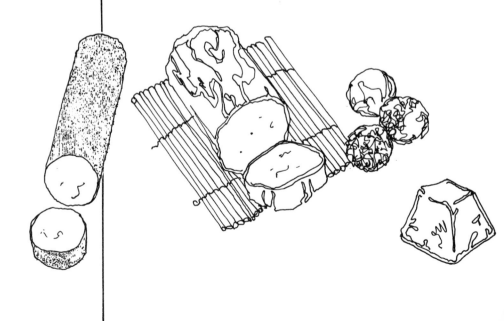

CHEESE AND CRAB BOUCHÉES

Yields approximately 60 rounds

Warm little bites of crab toast, laced with brandy. Just right with a glass of white wine. Lobster meat is a delicious alternative to crab.

1 loaf	white bread, sliced	1 loaf
1½ lb	frozen crab meat, thawed and drained	680 g
2 cups	shredded Gruyère cheese or any mix of Swiss cheese (about ½ lb/225 g)	500 mL
3	eggs, lightly beaten	3
3 Tbsp	whipping cream	45 mL
4 Tbsp	brandy	60 mL
¾ tsp	ground or freshly grated nutmeg	3 mL
2 Tbsp	flour	30 mL
1 to 2 Tbsp	black sesame seeds (optional)	15 to 30 mL

1. Preheat oven to 350°F (180°C).

2. Using a 1½-inch (4-cm) round cookie cutter, cut three rounds out of each slice of bread. Place on a baking sheet. Bake for 12 minutes, or until lightly browned. Rounds can be made a day or two in advance and stored in an airtight container.

3. Increase oven temperature to 425°F (220°C).

4. In a mixing bowl combine crab meat, cheese, eggs, whipping cream, brandy, nutmeg and flour. Mix until well blended.

5. Spoon a generous spoonful of filling on each toasted round. If you like, sprinkle a garnish of black sesame seeds on top. Place on a baking sheet and bake for 5 to 10 minutes, or until hot. Serve warm.

To present bouchées:
Line platter with leaves of
radicchio and leaf lettuce
accented with a full-blown
red rose.

CAJUN CRAB BALLS

Yields 30 pieces

Serve these gently spiced nuggets of crab with Cajun Sauce or a dip of mustard-flavoured mayonnaise.

1 lb	frozen crab meat, thawed and drained well	450 g
4 Tbsp	matzo meal	60 mL
4 Tbsp	mayonnaise	60 mL
1	egg, lightly beaten	1
1 Tbsp	minced onion	15 mL
¼ tsp	Worcestershire sauce	1 mL
½ tsp	dry mustard	2 mL
¼ tsp	salt	1 mL
1 cup	dry breadcrumbs	250 mL
3 to 4 cups	oil for deep frying	0.75 to 1 L

1. In a large mixing bowl combine all ingredients except bread crumbs and oil. Mix well and form into ¾-inch (2-cm) balls. Roll in breadcrumbs to coat and set aside.

2. In a heavy pot or deep fryer heat oil to 375°F (190°C). Deep fry 6 to 10 crab balls at a time, until golden brown, about 3 minutes. Drain on paper towels. These may be served warm or at room temperature.

SHRIMP ROLLS

Yields 5 dozen rolls

Once you've tried these crispy morsels of shrimp and potato gently flavoured with cheese, they're sure to become a favourite.

Shrimp Rolls look great fanned out on a dramatically large platter and garnished with an arrangement of flowers carved from onions. Cut a chrysanthemum from a large red onion (page 184) and make 5 or 6 green-onion flowers (page 185). Arrange leaves from a globe artichoke around onion, and green-onion flowers in sprays around the red-onion mum.

4	medium-sized potatoes, scrubbed	4
2 Tbsp	butter	30 mL
¼ cup	chopped green onions	60 mL
¼ cup	chopped fresh parsley	60 mL
2½ lb	raw shrimp, shelled and cleaned	1.1 kg
5 oz	raw milk or Swiss cheese	150 g
1 tsp	salt	5 mL
1 tsp	pepper	5 mL
2 cups	flour	500 mL
5 to 6	eggs, well beaten	5 to 6
2 cups	dry breadcrumbs	500 mL
3 to 4 cups	oil for deep frying	0.75 to 1 L

1. Boil or steam potatoes until tender. Peel, put into medium-sized bowl and mash them while still hot. Add butter and mix in. Add green onions and parsley.

2. In a food processor fitted with a steel blade chop shrimp coarsely. Add to potato mixture.

3. Chop cheese in food processor to the size of peppercorns. Add to potato mixture, season with salt and pepper and mix well. The mixture will be sticky.

4. With wet fingers make rolls approximately 2 inches × ¾ inch (5 cm × 2 cm). Dust with flour and dip into beaten eggs. Coat with breadcrumbs and shape rolls to resemble whole shrimp. Refrigerate for at least 2 hours.

5. In deep fryer or heavy frying pan heat oil to 375°F (190°C) and deep fry the rolls, a few at a time, until golden brown. Keep the oil hot and fry quickly, otherwise the cheese will melt before the crust has formed and the rolls will crumble.

6. Rolls can be fried in advance, then, just before serving, warmed in an oven preheated to 400°F (200°C). Serve with mustard-mayonnaise dip.

MUSTARD-MAYONNAISE DIP

½ cup/125 mL
mayonnaise

½ cup/125 mL
Russian-style sweet mustard

¼ cup/60 mL
water

1. Combine ingredients well.

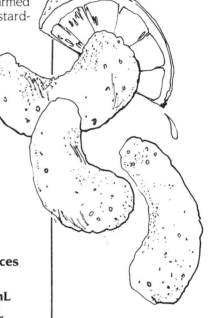

SHRIMP-BACON WRAPS

Yields 50 to 60 pieces

Rumaki at sea — our version of that ever-popular hors d'oeuvre.

30 slices	bacon	30 slices
15	water chestnuts	15
½ cup	hoisin sauce	125 mL
2 Tbsp	soy sauce	30 mL
2 Tbsp	sherry	30 mL
2 lb	medium-sized shrimp, shelled and deveined (approx. 55)	1 kg
60	flat toothpicks	60

1. In a large frying pan sauté bacon over medium heat only until most of the fat is rendered. Do not crisp bacon. Drain on paper towels. Slice in half and set aside.

2. Cut each water chestnut into 4 pieces and set aside.

3. In a small bowl mix together hoisin sauce, soy sauce and sherry. Set aside.

4. Wrap one shrimp and one piece of water chestnut together with a slice of bacon, securing bacon ends with a toothpick. Repeat until all shrimp are wrapped. Place in a large bowl. Add marinade and toss gently to coat completely. Marinate for 1 hour at room temperature or overnight, refrigerated.

5. Preheat broiler.

6. Broil 2 minutes per side. Serve warm.

SCALLOPS TUCKED IN SHRIMP

Yields 24 *pieces*

Scallops wrapped in snow peas are tucked into pink shrimp. The taste and the look are absolutely smashing!

NO GUESSWORK

Here's a general rule of thumb for estimating quantities of hors d'oeuvres: before dinner, 4 to 5 pieces per person; 3-hour cocktail party, 12 to 15 pieces per person; business cocktail reception, 6 to 8 pieces per person.

1½ Tbsp	olive oil	23 mL
pinch	dried mixed Italian herbs	pinch
24	medium-sized shrimp, shelled and deveined	24
pinch	dried thyme	pinch
1 Tbsp	lime juice	15 mL
24	bay scallops *or* 7 to 10 sea scallops cut into ½-inch (1.25-cm) cubes	24
12	large snow peas	12
24	flat toothpicks	24
3 to 4 tsp	soy sauce	15 to 20 mL

1. In a mixing bowl stir together 1 Tbsp (15 mL) olive oil and mixed Italian herbs. Add shrimp and toss to coat well. Marinate 1 hour.

2. In a mixing bowl stir together ½ Tbsp (8 mL) olive oil, thyme and lime juice. Add scallops, toss well to coat and marinate 1 hour.

3. In a pot of boiling water blanch snow peas for 30 seconds. Drain and run under cold water to stop cooking. Split apart each pod and separate into halves, removing string and any overly large peas inside.

4. To assemble, as diagrammed, wrap a scallop with a snow pea and curl a shrimp over it. Skewer with toothpick to keep everything in place and arrange on a baking sheet lined with foil. Repeat with remaining scallops and brush all with a little soy sauce. Broil for 2 minutes on one side, turn over and broil 1 minute on second side. Sprinkle with lemon juice, if desired, and serve immediately.

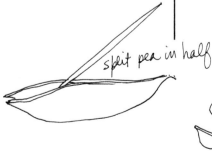

split pea in half

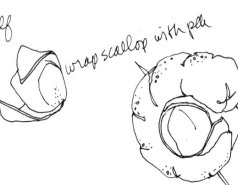

wrap scallop with pea

use toothpick to secure shrimp

DEEP-FRIED WONTONS

Yields 60 pieces

Every country has its own version of pastry-wrapped snacks. These wrappers are Oriental but the fillings are international.

CHICKEN WONTONS WITH SWEET GINGER DIP

For wontons:

2½ lb	chicken breast	1.4 kg
2½ tsp	sesame oil	12 mL
1½ tsp	soy sauce	7 mL
to taste	salt and pepper	to taste
½ cup	finely chopped water chestnuts	125 mL
2 Tbsp	finely chopped green onions	30 mL
1	8-oz (225-g) package thick wonton wrappers	1
3 to 4 cups	vegetable oil for deep frying	0.75 to 1 L

For dip:

⅔ cup	light soy sauce	150 mL
⅓ cup	rice vinegar	75 mL
3 Tbsp	brown sugar	45 mL
1 Tbsp	grated fresh ginger	15 mL
3 cloves	garlic, crushed	3 cloves
4 to 6 dashes	Tabasco sauce	4 to 6 dashes
1 Tbsp	sesame oil	15 mL

1. Remove skin and bones of chicken. Cut meat into cubes and chop for 30 seconds in food processor fitted with steel blade. Add sesame oil, soy sauce, salt and pepper and continue processing, for 1 to 2 minutes, until smooth. Remove to bowl. Add water chestnuts and green onions and mix in well.

2. Working with one wonton wrapper at a time, put 1 heaping teaspoon (7 mL) of filling in the centre of wrapper. Bring up the sides, handkerchief-style, and pinch to seal. The filling is sticky enough to hold the wrapper together. Place on a baking sheet lined with waxed paper. Repeat until all filling has been used. Do not stack uncooked wontons as they may stick.

3. In a heavy saucepan or deep fryer heat vegetable oil to 350°F (180°C) over medium-high heat. Add 4 to 6 wontons and deep fry until golden brown, 1 to 2 minutes. Remove to drain on paper towels. Repeat until all wontons have been fried. These can be made ahead of time and reheated in a very hot oven just before serving. Serve with Sweet Ginger Dip.

4. To make dip, combine all ingredients in a bowl and whisk together or place in a jar and shake well.

LIGHT AND DARK SOY SAUCE

Soy sauce, the ubiquitous dark salty sauce of fermented soy beans is available in light and dark. Light soy sauce is lighter in colour, cleaner in taste and saltier than dark soy. The dark is thicker and very dark brown in colour. It is less salty and has a stronger, more complex flavour than light soy. If you are confused by the strange markings on the Oriental labels, you can distinguish light from dark by turning the bottle upside down, then upright. The dark soy will leave a thin brown film that lingers on the neck of the bottle for a few seconds. The light soy will leave no trace on the glass at all.

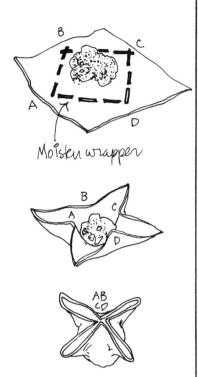

Moisten wrapper

FISH WONTONS

Use exactly the same procedure as for Chicken Wontons, but use 1½ lb (675 g) haddock fillets or any firm-fleshed boneless white fish instead of chicken. The Sweet Ginger Dip is also great with fish-filled wontons.

LAMB WONTONS WITH YOGHURT DIP

For wontons:

1 lb	untrimmed boneless lamb	450 g
¾ tsp	ground cumin	3 mL
¾ tsp	minced garlic	3 mL
1 tsp	olive oil	5 mL
½ tsp	salt	2 mL
¼ tsp	pepper	1 mL
1	8-oz (225-g) package thick wonton wrappers	1
3 to 4 cups	vegetable oil for deep frying	0.75 to 1 L

For dip:

1 cup	natural yoghurt	250 mL
2 tsp	ground cumin or garam masala	10 mL
1 tsp	salt	5 mL

1. Trim excess fat from lamb. Cut meat into cubes and chop for 30 seconds in a food processor fitted with a steel blade. Add cumin, garlic, oil, salt and pepper and process until smooth.

2. Working with one wrapper at a time, place 1 heaping teaspoon (7 mL) of filling in the centre of wrapper. Bring up the sides, handkerchief-style, moisten edges and pinch to seal. Place on a baking sheet lined with waxed paper. Repeat until all filling has been used. Do not stack uncooked wontons as they may stick.

3. In a heavy saucepan or deep fryer heat vegetable oil to 350°F (180°C) over medium-high heat. Add 4 to 6 wontons and deep fry until golden brown, 1 to 2 minutes. Remove to drain on paper towels. Repeat until all wontons have been fried. These can be made ahead of time and reheated in a very hot oven just before serving. Serve with Yoghurt Dip.

4. Combine all ingredients for Yoghurt Dip in a bowl and mix well.

CHICKEN GUMBO SOUP

Yields 15 to 18 servings

Rich, warm flavours from a Cajun kitchen bubble together in a wonderful, thick soup. This is a traditional preparation, but you can give it your own signature by adding chunks of smoked sausage or shrimp, corn, asparagus, or basil and garlic.

⅔ cup	flour	150 mL
⅔ cup	oil	150 mL
6 strips	bacon, julienned, some fat removed	6 strips
1	medium-sized onion, chopped	1
3 ribs	celery, diced ½ inch (1.25 cm)	3 ribs
6	carrots, diced ½ inch (1.25 cm)	6
4 cups	strong chicken stock	1 L
2 lb	okra, sliced ½ inch (1.25 cm)	900 g
2	bay leaves	2
½	hot pepper, slivered	½
2 tsp	dried thyme	10 mL
¼ tsp	coarsely ground black pepper	1 mL
6	tomatoes, diced ½ inch (1.25 cm)	6
4 to 6 cups	diced cooked chicken, ½-inch (1.25-cm) cubes	1 to 1.15 L
2	red, green and/or yellow bell peppers, diced very finely	2
2 tsp	filé powder	10 mL

1. Make a dark roux by slowly browning the flour and oil together in a heavy frying pan. (Cast iron is ideal.) Stir constantly over medium-low heat for at least an hour, or until the mixture is a deep rich brown. Take care not to let the roux burn in the final stages of browning.

2. In a large heavy pot sauté the bacon, onion, celery and carrots over medium-high heat until soft. Add chicken stock, okra, bay leaves, hot pepper, thyme and black pepper. Simmer until okra is cooked, about 5 to 8 minutes. Add tomatoes.

3. Add prepared roux to soup one spoonful at a time, stirring constantly. Simmer gently to thicken slightly.

4. Just before serving, add the cooked chicken, red and green bell peppers and filé powder. Do not allow soup to boil after the addition of the filé powder. (If the soup is reheated, be sure to remove it from the heat as soon as it is hot but not boiling.) Traditionally, a small scoop of cooked rice is placed in the bottom of the bowl before ladling in the gumbo.

FILÉ POWDER

This special Cajun herb made from the dried leaves of the sassafras tree acts as a thickener, while adding a flavour similar to thyme. You can still make our Chicken Gumbo Soup even if you don't have this ingredient; the roux and okra provide thickening and the thyme and bay leaf contribute their herby flavour.

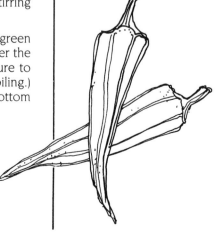

CLAMMING IT UP

Clam juice has always been great and gutsy in cocktails, but cooked into sauces, soups and stews, it adds a deliciously rich undertone. If you keep a few bottles on hand, you just might find yourself sloshing it into almost every seafood dish you make.

COLD SPINACH AND SMOKED SALMON SOUP

Yields 10 to 12 servings

A cool, elegant soup. With a few effortless moments in the kitchen you can create this memorable soup of subtle flavours. The secret ingredient: clam juice!

4 cups	clam juice (available in bottles)	1 L
1½	10-oz (284-g) bags spinach, well washed and trimmed	1½
2 cups	natural yoghurt	500 mL
4 cups	table cream (18%)	1 L
1 lb	smoked salmon, chopped	500 g
to taste	salt	to taste

1. In a medium-sized saucepan bring clam juice to simmer over medium heat. Add spinach and cook until leaves are wilted, about three minutes.

2. In a food processor fitted with a steel blade, purée spinach mixture. Remove to a large bowl and cool.

3. Mix together yoghurt, cream, salmon and salt. Add to spinach mixture and stir. Chill.

4. If you wish, reserve a little of the smoked salmon to garnish each bowl just before serving.

SPRING VEGETABLE SOUP

Yields 4 to 5 servings

Welcome spring with a refreshing soup of asparagus, leeks and cream.

1½ lb	asparagus	700 g
1 Tbsp	butter	15 mL
¾ cup	well-washed, chopped leeks	175 mL
2 cups	strong chicken stock	500 mL
½ cup	whipping cream	125 mL
pinch	ground or freshly grated nutmeg	pinch
to taste	salt and pepper	to taste
For garnish:		
1 cup	finely julienned carrots, leeks, asparagus and/or snow peas	250 mL
1 to 2 Tbsp	chopped roasted pistachios	15 to 30 mL

1. Wash asparagus well to remove all fine sand. Cut off woody ends and discard. Slice into 1-inch (2.5-cm) lengths. You should have approximately 4 cups (1 L).

2. In a large heavy saucepan melt butter over medium-high heat. Add leeks and sauté until translucent but not browned. Stir

in asparagus and chicken stock. Bring to boil, then reduce heat and simmer for 5 minutes, or until tender. Cool slightly.

3. In a food processor fitted with a steel blade purée cooled mixture. Strain and return to saucepan. Stir in cream and season to taste with nutmeg, salt and pepper. Warm over medium heat.

4. Prepare garnish by blanching julienned vegetables in boiling water for 1 minute. Drain and divide among soup bowls, then pour in soup. Top with chopped pistachio nuts.

HEARTY FISH SOUP

Yields 6 to 8 servings

A steaming bowl of soup full of tender fish and fragrant with herbs to warm and satisfy on those brisk autumn days.

For strong fish stock:

3 to 4 lb	fish bones	1.5 to 2 kg
5 cups	water	1.25 L
½ cup	white wine	125 mL
1 tsp	Herbes de Provence	5 mL
½ cup	well-washed, chopped leeks	125 mL

For soup:

2 Tbsp	olive oil	30 mL
1	small leek, well washed and sliced ½ inch (1.25 cm)	1
1	small onion, diced	1
to taste	salt and pepper	to taste
5	medium-sized tomatoes, peeled and diced	5
¼ tsp	saffron threads	1 mL
2 cups	diced monkfish or other firm-fleshed fish, ¾-inch (2-cm) cubes	500 mL
2 cloves	garlic, crushed	2 cloves
⅓ to ½ cup	chopped fresh herbs, such as dill weed, flat-leaf parsley, coriander	75 to 125 mL

1. To make fish stock, combine the fish bones, water, white wine, Herbes de Provence and chopped leeks in a large stock pot. Simmer for 45 minutes only; stock will become bitter if left to simmer longer. Strain and set aside.

2. In a medium-sized frying pan heat olive oil over medium-high heat. Add sliced leeks, diced onion, salt and pepper to taste, and sauté until soft. Add diced tomatoes and toss for one minute.

3. In a large soup pot place fish stock over medium heat. Add the tomato mixture and saffron, then bring to a light boil. Add diced fish and garlic cloves. Simmer for 3 to 5 minutes, until fish is barely cooked. Add salt and pepper to taste. Serve steaming hot, sprinkled liberally with chopped herbs.

Great with lots of crusty garlic bread. Served with a salad, this soup makes a satisfying meal.

Herbes de Provence is a mixture of French herbs including rosemary, bay leaf, savory, coriander, thyme, basil and sometimes lavender.

SAFFRON

Saffron, the tiny hand-picked stigmas of the crocus, is legendary for its high cost and prized for its flavour. The fragile threads should be purchased whole and, at the time of use, infused in warm water or wine to release their powerful flavour.

PÂTÉS

SMOKED SALMON CHEESECAKE

Yields one 10-inch (25-cm) round

Smooth, rich, flecked with pink salmon and dressed in gossamer-thin slices of cucumber. Here's a black-tie version of cream cheese and lox.

2½ lb	soft, deli-style cream cheese	1.1 kg
1½ lb	ricotta cheese or cottage cheese	680 g
7	eggs, lightly beaten	7
1 cup	grated Gruyère cheese	250 mL
⅔ cup	whipping cream	150 mL
2 Tbsp	flour	30 mL
1 tsp	salt	5 mL
1 lb	smoked salmon, coarsely chopped*	450 g
¼ cup	finely chopped fresh chives	60 mL
2 Tbsp	finely chopped fresh dill *or* 2 tsp (10 mL) dried dill weed	30 mL
2 cups	sour cream	500 mL
1	English cucumber, thinly sliced	1

1. Preheat oven to 325°F (160°C). Prepare a 10-inch (25-cm) springform pan by lining bottom with a circle of parchment.

2. In a large mixing bowl beat the cream cheese until smooth. Stir in ricotta or cottage cheese, eggs, Gruyère cheese, whipping cream, flour, salt, smoked salmon, chives and dill. Beat together until thoroughly blended.

3. Pour into prepared pan. Bake for 1½ hours in a water bath.

4. Remove from oven. Reduce heat to 300°F (150°C). Spread sour cream evenly over surface of cheesecake. Return to oven for 5 minutes.

5. Remove from oven and cool. Remove outer ring of pan and cover the top of the cooled cheesecake with thinly sliced cucumber. Cover with a square of parchment paper. Invert carefully onto a large plate. Peel off the circle of parchment. Place serving platter, upside down, on the cheesecake. Turn right side up and remove square of parchment. Rearrange any cucumber slices that may have slipped out of place.

6. For a more elegant presentation, when the circle of parchment is peeled off, cover the bottom of the cheesecake with a layer of thinly sliced cucumbers. Extend the outer row of slices slightly beyond the outer edge of the cheesecake, like the brim of a hat. Then place the platter on top and turn right side up. As wedges of the cheesecake are removed for serving, the "doily" of cucumber is revealed.

BAGEL CRISPS

Perfect with this cheesecake: Slice day-old bagels into thin rounds, about ⅛-inch (3-mm) thick. Preheat oven to 300°F (150°C) and place slices about 1 inch (2.5 cm) apart on the racks. Bake until brown and crisp, about 20 minutes. Store in an airtight container.

*Salmon can be chopped in a food processor fitted with a steel blade by pulsing off/on a few times.

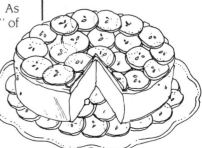

LOBSTER-SALMON TERRINE

Yields one 9-inch × 5-inch (23-cm × 12-cm) terrine

Perfect for a summer buffet, this sparklingly chic seafood terrine is flecked with the cool green of dill and cucumber. Balsamic vinegar and Worcestershire sauce contribute to the intriguing spicy flavour.

For aspic:

4 cups	cold water	1 L
5 pkg	unflavoured gelatin	5 pkg
5 Tbsp	balsamic vinegar	75 mL
2 to 3 Tbsp	grated lemon rind (about 3 lemons)	30 to 45 mL
½ tsp	salt	2 mL
¼ tsp	pepper	1 mL
5 drops	Worcestershire sauce	5 drops
1 drop	Tabasco sauce	1 drop

For garnish:

2 to 4 stems	fresh parsley, dill weed or chives	2 to 3 stems
2 to 4 slices	pimento, carrot or olive	2 to 4 slices

For terrine:

½ lb	fresh salmon, lightly poached and diced ½ inch (1.25 cm)	220 g
1 to 1½ lb	lobster, cooked and meat cut into ¼-inch × ½-inch (6-mm × 1.25-cm) pieces	450 to 670 g
1 cup	sliced English cucumber, quartered and cut into ¼-inch (6-mm) slices	250 mL
3	medium-sized tomatoes, peeled, seeded and cut into ¼-inch (6-mm) strips	3
¼ cup	fresh dill weed sprigs (about ¼ bunch)	60 mL
⅓ cup	capers	75 mL
4 oz	smoked salmon, sliced very thinly or diced ¼ inch (6 mm)	110 g

SMOKED SALMON

There are many varieties available: Canadian smoked salmon from the Pacific, softer in texture, sweeter and gentler in flavour than Atlantic Canadian smoked salmon. Scottish salmon, considered by many to be the best for its lightly sweet-salty, oak-smoked undertones. And Norwegian, favourite of many connoisseurs who admire its meltingly tender, yet firm, pink-gold flesh.

When buying smoked salmon, avoid varieties that are very bright red or orange in colour as these are usually over-processed or oversalted. To economize, buy trimmings and ends cut from a whole side if salmon is to be used in bits or puréed. Try to avoid vacuum-packed, canned or frozen slices, most of which are inferior.

1. Prepare a 9-inch × 5-inch (23-cm × 12-cm) loaf pan by brushing very lightly with oil.

2. To make aspic, in a small saucepan sprinkle gelatin over cold water and allow to soften. Place over low heat until melted. Do not allow to boil. Add the balsamic vinegar, grated lemon rind, salt, pepper, Worcestershire sauce and Tabasco sauce. Stir to combine.

3. Pour just enough aspic into prepared loaf pan to cover a depth of ⅛ inch (3 mm), about ½ cup (125 mL). Refrigerate until completely gelled. Remove from refrigerator and decorate with sprigs of parsley, dill weed or chives, and pieces of pimento,

carrot or olive. Pour a thin layer of aspic over the decorations to keep them in place and return to the refrigerator until gelled.

4. In a large mixing bowl combine poached salmon, lobster, cucumber, tomatoes, dill weed and capers. Add 1 cup (250 mL) aspic and stir gently to mix. Set aside.

5. If you wish, you may cover the terrine with a thin layer of smoked salmon. Dip slices of smoked salmon in aspic and line the bottom and sides of pan. Or, add pieces of diced smoked salmon to the salmon-lobster mixture.

6. Pour salmon-lobster mixture into pan and refrigerate until set. Unmould onto serving platter and slice. If you have difficulty releasing the terrine from the pan, dip the pan very briefly in hot water before unmoulding onto platter.

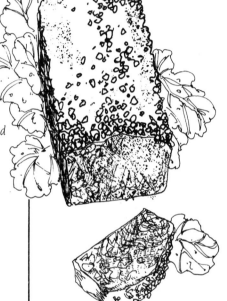

PÂTÉ MAISON

Yields one 2-quart (8-L) terrine

Our country-style pâté, a specialty of the house, is roughly textured, moist and redolent with herbs and spices.

⅓ cup	red wine	75 mL
4 tsp	rubbed dried thyme	20 mL
1 Tbsp	ground or freshly grated nutmeg	15 mL
½ tsp	ground allspice	2 mL
1¼ tsp	pepper	6 mL
1 tsp	salt	5 mL
1	small onion, minced	1
3 cloves	garlic, crushed	3 cloves
1¼ lb	pork, coarsely ground	570 g
½ lb	pork fat, coarsely ground	225 g
1¼ lb	chicken livers, trimmed and coarsely ground	570 g
½ lb	salted pork or bacon, coarsely ground	225 g
1	egg	1
2 Tbsp	flour	30 mL
1	bay leaf	1

1. Preheat oven to 425°F (220°C). Oil a heavy terrine with a lid. If a heavy terrine is unavailable, use a loaf pan wrapped with several layers of foil and bake in a water bath.

2. In a large mixing bowl thoroughly combine all ingredients except bay leaf and mix well. Turn into prepared pan, place bay leaf on top, and cover.

3. Bake for 1½ hours. Remove bay leaf. To serve, unmould the cooled pâté on a serving platter and completely cover the top of the pâté with coarsely ground black pepper for a bit of drama. This pâté tastes best aged for 2 to 3 days.

SEAFOOD SAUSAGE

Makes two 10-inch × 4-inch (25-cm × 10-cm) rolls

A delicately rich purée of scallops, studded with shrimp, crab and lobster and baked in puff pastry.

For sausage:

2 cups	milk	500 mL
4	egg yolks	4
3	eggs	3
1 cup	flour	250 mL
1 lb	white fish fillets (such as haddock or monkfish) cut into 1-inch (2.5-cm) pieces	450 g
2 cups	scallops, cut into 1-inch (2.5-cm) pieces (about 1 lb/450 g)	500 mL
½ lb	butter, cubed 1 inch (2.5 cm)	225 g
2 tsp	salt	10 mL
½ tsp	cayenne	2 mL
1 tsp	pepper	5 mL
1	egg white	1
1 cup	shelled raw shrimp, cut in 1-inch (2.5-cm) pieces	250 mL
1 cup	cooked crab meat	250 mL
1 cup	cooked lobster meat, cut in 1-inch (2.5-cm) pieces	250 mL

For pastry:

1 lb	puff pastry	450 g
1	egg, lightly beaten	1

1. In a small saucepan warm milk over medium heat. Do not boil. Set aside.

2. In a medium-sized saucepan beat the 4 egg yolks until light and creamy. Add 2 whole eggs and beat until incorporated. Beat in flour and slowly add the milk, whisking in over low heat. Cook, beating constantly, until very thick and no raw flour taste remains. Cool thoroughly.

3. In a food processor fitted with a steel blade combine ½ of the white fish and ½ cup of the scallops. Grind until fine. Add half of the butter. Process until incorporated. Add half the egg yolk-flour mixture, processing until well mixed. Transfer to a mixing bowl, and repeat with remaining fish, butter, egg yolk-flour mixture and another ½ cup of the scallops. Stir in salt, cayenne and pepper. Beat in 1 whole egg, then 1 egg white. Stir in shrimp, crab, lobster and remaining scallops.

4. Shape into two rolls, approximately 10 inches × 4 inches (25 cm × 10 cm). Wrap tightly in plastic wrap, then in foil or waxed paper, keeping rolls as round as possible. Put into freezer for 30 to 45 minutes, just long enough for rolls to become firm.

5. Preheat oven to 400°F (200°C).

6. Roll out puff pastry into two squares 12 inches × 12 inches (30 cm × 30 cm), about ⅛ inch (3 mm) thick.

7. Place one roll in the middle of each pastry rectangle. Wet edges of pastry with water. Pull sides of pastry up over roll and crimp closed. Wet crimped edge, folding and pressing again to ensure a complete seal. Place sausages, seam side down, on baking sheet. Decorate with pastry cut-outs and make 2 or 3 slits in pastry. Brush with lightly beaten egg and bake for 30 to 45 minutes, until pastry is brown and puffed. Serve warm with beurre blanc sauce, or at room temperature with a light hollandaise sauce.

BEURRE BLANC SAUCE

¼ cup	white wine	60 mL
¼ cup	white wine tarragon vinegar	60 mL
¼ cup	chopped shallots	60 mL
4 oz	butter, cubed ½ inch (1.25 cm)	110 g

1. In a medium-sized saucepan combine white wine, vinegar and chopped shallots over medium-high heat. Reduce volume to 2 Tbsp (30 mL). Let cool to lukewarm.

2. Over low heat gradually beat in butter. Sauce should be creamy and must be kept over warm water until served.

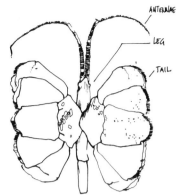

ANTENNAE
LEG
TAIL

A spectacular vermillion butterfly can be made from the shells of cooked lobster. Two lobster tails are wired together with a leg and two antennae pushed into the top of the leg shell.

ASPIC OF CHICKEN AND PIMENTO

Yields one 4-inch × 8-inch (10-cm × 20-cm) loaf

Each shimmering slice reveals layers of chicken, pimento and chicken livers. Garnish with leaves of radicchio or bibb lettuce and serve as a very special first course.

¾ lb	chicken livers, trimmed	340 g
2 Tbsp	dry sherry	30 mL
4	whole chicken breasts (about 4 lb/1.8 kg)	4
4 to 5 cups	strong chicken broth	1 to 1.25 L
2 Tbsp	butter	30 mL
to taste	salt and pepper	to taste
1 cup	diced ham ¼-inch (6-mm) cubes	250 mL
1 cup	diced pimento, ¼-inch (6-mm) cubes	250 mL
¼ cup	chopped fresh parsley	60 mL
3 Tbsp	gelatin	45 mL
4 Tbsp	water	60 mL
¼ tsp	ground dried rosemary	1 mL
1 tsp	salt	5 mL

1. In a small bowl marinate chicken livers in sherry for one hour, refrigerated.

2. Preheat oven to 400°F (200°C).

TO PREPARE A CLEAR ASPIC

1 Tbsp/15 mL gelatin
4 Tbsp/60 mL cold water
1 cup/250 mL hot water or clear chicken stock

1. In a small saucepan sprinkle gelatin over cold water and allow to soften. When gelatin has absorbed all the water, melt over low heat and add water or stock. Refrigerate and allow to partially set just until the consistency of egg whites.

3. Cut chicken breasts in half and place in a single layer, skin side up, in a large roasting pan. Add 1 cup (250 mL) chicken broth and cover tightly with foil. Poach in oven for 20 to 30 minutes. Remove from oven and cool completely in broth. Reserve broth. Remove chicken from bones and cut into ½-inch (1.25-cm) dice. Set aside.

4. Drain chicken livers. In a frying pan melt butter over medium-high heat. Add chicken livers and sauté until just cooked but still pink in the middle, about 4 minutes. Season with a little salt and pepper. Cool and cut into quarters.

5. In a small mixing bowl combine diced chicken, ham, pimento and parsley. Mix well and set aside.

6. In a small saucepan sprinkle gelatin over water and allow to soften. When gelatin has absorbed water, melt gently over low heat. Do not allow to boil.

7. Add chicken stock to reserved cooking liquid to make 3 cups (750 mL). Pour into a medium-sized mixing bowl and add melted gelatin, rosemary and salt. Mix well.

8. Lightly oil a 4-inch × 8-inch (10-cm × 20-cm) loaf pan. Place half of the chicken mixture into the pan. Pour in enough broth-gelatin mixture to cover. Press down with a spoon. Place chicken livers on top and cover with remaining chicken mixture. Press down lightly and pour in more broth-gelatin mixture to cover. Chill overnight, then unmould onto a large platter. If necessary, lower the pan, almost to the top, into a basin of hot water for a few seconds. Loaf will then slip out easily. Slice to serve.

9. If loaf is to be presented unsliced, as part of a buffet, you may wish to decorate the top. This decoration is placed in the bottom of the loaf pan before the layers of chicken and livers are added so that when the loaf is unmoulded onto the platter, the decoration will be on the top.

10. Prepare a clear aspic or clarified chicken-broth aspic and pour a ¼-inch (6-mm) layer into the bottom of the loaf pan. Then place thin vegetable cut-outs and sprigs of dill, parsley or chives in the aspic. Chill for ½ hour to firm, then add the chicken and liver mixtures as above.

pour in a layer of aspic.

allow to set.

Dip vegetable cut-outs in liquid aspic and position on gelled layer.

GALANTINE OF CHICKEN, PHILIPPINE STYLE

*Yields one pâté approximately 4 inches × 3 inches ×
8 inches (10 cm × 7 × 20 cm)*

*Exotically seasoned purée of chicken is wrapped in its own skin, then roasted to
golden brown succulence. Served hot, it is a flavourful entrée; cold, an elegant
first course.*

1	**4-lb (2-kg) chicken**	1
4	**Chinese sausages**	4
2 lb	**lean ground pork**	1 kg
4	**eggs**	4
1 cup	**finely chopped onions**	250 mL
½ cup	**coarsely chopped olives stuffed with pimento**	125 mL
4 cloves	**garlic, crushed**	4 cloves
1 cup	**sweet mixed relish**	250 mL
½ tsp	**pepper**	2 mL
2 tsp	**salt**	10 mL
1 Tbsp	**Worcestershire sauce**	15 mL
1 Tbsp	**soy sauce**	15 mL
2 Tbsp	**oyster sauce (optional)**	30 mL

oyster sauce

**Oyster sauce and Chinese
sausages can be pur-
chased in a store specializing in Oriental foods.**

1. Prepare the chicken. With a sharp knife remove tip and first
joint of wings. Remove the tail. Starting from the tail end and working towards the neck, separate the skin from the meat with a sharp
paring or boning knife and carefully pull away the skin. Do not
tear or cut the skin as it will be the casing for the meat. The skin
should come away easily and all in one piece. The only areas of
difficulty may be the legs and wings. The skin can be pulled gently
off the legs, inside out, just like a pair of socks. You may need to
use the knife at the end of the drumstick where the skin may still
be attached to the bone. When you reach the wings, the skin can
be removed in the same manner as the legs. Stitch neck end
closed and, if necessary, pull in the skin of the wings and legs so it
falls inside the skin of the body.

2. Preheat oven to 400°F (200°C).

3. Scrape meat off bones and cut into cubes. In a food processor fitted with a steel blade process the meat until finely ground.
Place in a large mixing bowl. Process the Chinese sausages until
finely chopped and add to chicken. Add ground pork, eggs,
chopped onions, chopped olives, crushed garlic, relish, pepper,
salt, Worcestershire sauce, soy sauce and oyster sauce. Mix together. Test flavour by frying a small amount of the mixture,
cooling, then tasting. Adjust seasonings if necessary.

4. Stuff chicken skin with mixture. Stitch the end closed. Pat
into a neat oblong shape and wrap with a double layer of foil.
Place on baking sheet and bake for 1¼ hours. Preheat broiler.
Open foil and brown the top of the galantine for 1 or 2 minutes.
Allow to cool for at least 5 minutes before slicing, to allow the
juices to set. May be served hot or cold.

GALANTINE OF CAPON STUFFED WITH VEAL AND PISTACHIOS

*Yields one pâté approximately 5 inches × 4 inches × 10 inches
(12 cm × 10 cm × 25 cm)*

Hot or at room temperature, this is a beautifully colourful and delicious first course. Serve slices with Cumberland sauce or any tart fruity relish.

For filling:

1 lb	ground veal	450 g
1	whole chicken breast, boned, skinned and cubed 2 to 3 inches (5 to 8 cm)	1
3	eggs	3
½ cup	softened butter	125 mL
¼ tsp	ground dried rosemary	1 mL
1 tsp	salt	5 mL
½ tsp	pepper	2 mL
3 cloves	garlic, peeled	3 cloves
1 Tbsp	grated lemon rind	15 mL
1 cup	shelled pistachio nuts	250 mL
1 cup	diced carrots	250 mL

For roll:

1	3- to 4-lb (1.5- to 1.75-kg) capon	1
2 Tbsp	softened butter	30 mL
¾ tsp	salt	3 mL
½ tsp	pepper	2 mL
1	10-oz (284-g) bag spinach, well-washed, trimmed, blanched, and well-drained	1

For seasoning:

¼ tsp	ground dried rosemary	1 mL
¼ tsp	salt	1 mL
⅛ tsp	pepper	0.5 mL
½ tsp	grated lemon rind	2 mL
2 tsp	softened butter	10 mL

1. Split capon along spine

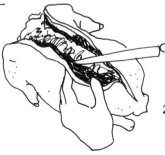

2. Keeping knife close to bone, use small cuts to free meat from bone.

1. Preheat oven to 450°F (230°C).

2. To prepare filling, combine ground veal, chicken breast, eggs, butter, rosemary, salt, pepper, garlic cloves and lemon rind in a food processor fitted with a steel blade. Process into a smooth paste. Remove to a medium-sized mixing bowl and stir in pistachios and diced carrots.

3. To prepare roll, split the back of the capon along the spine with a sharp cleaver. Remove the wing tip and first joint of the wings. With a sharp boning knife, bone the capon taking care, especially at the breastbone, not to pierce the skin. Keep the capon in one piece.

4. Place boned capon, skin side down, on a flat surface and flatten with a mallet or the side of a cleaver to distribute the meat somewhat evenly. Spread softened butter over the meat and sprinkle with salt and pepper. Cover the meat with an even layer of spinach. Spread the filling over the spinach and roll up into a log shape, about 15 inches (38 cm) long and 8 inches (20 cm) in diameter. Tuck in the skin at the ends to enclose the stuffing and, using a large sewing needle and heavy thread, stitch roll closed. Tie gently at regular intervals to hold the shape.

5. Season the roll by rubbing the outside with rosemary, salt, pepper and lemon rind. Dot with butter. Place in a roasting pan and bake for 1 hour. Remove from oven and allow to cool for at least ½ hour before slicing. May be served warm, at room temperature or cold.

3. At wing and thigh, cut through joints, freeing main bone structure.

4. Bone thighs and wings pulling meat inside-out so thighs and wings fall inside

5. Spread spinach and filling on capon.

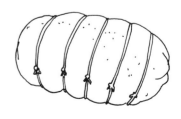

6. Roll up.

MUSHROOM PÂTÉ

Yields one pâté 8½ inches × 4½ inches × 2½ inches
(21 cm × 11 cm × 7 cm)

Mushrooms, wonderful mushrooms. Here's a pâté that celebrates their woodsy flavour laced with the smoothness of heavy cream. The mock puff pastry is made with butter and sour cream, so it won't get soggy from the filling.

For pâté:

¾ cup	regular oatmeal	175 mL
¾ cup	whipping cream	175 mL
3	eggs	3
3 Tbsp	butter	45 mL
3	shallots, finely chopped *or* 1 small onion, finely chopped	3
2 ribs	celery, finely chopped	2 ribs
1 lb	mushrooms, finely chopped and squeezed dry	450 g
½ cup	chopped fresh parsley	125 mL
⅛ tsp	ground dried rosemary	0.5 mL
pinch	ground dried basil	pinch
pinch	rubbed dried oregano	pinch
to taste	salt and pepper	to taste

For pastry:

½ cup	cold butter	125 mL
1 cup	flour	250 mL
¼ cup	sour cream	60 mL
1	egg, lightly beaten	1

1. Line an 8½-inch × 4½-inch (22-cm × 11-cm) loaf pan with parchment. Leave enough parchment on the sides to fold over the top and completely enclose the pâté.

2. In a large mixing bowl combine the oatmeal, cream and eggs. Allow the oatmeal to absorb the liquid for at least 30 minutes.

3. Preheat oven to 375°F (190°C).

4. In a small frying pan melt butter over medium heat. Add shallots or onion and sauté until translucent but not browned. Cool and add to oatmeal mixture. Mix in celery, mushrooms, parsley, rosemary, basil, oregano, salt and pepper. Turn mixture into prepared loaf pan. Fold over parchment to cover mixture. Seal pan with foil. Bake for 1½ hours. Remove from oven and immediately take foil off pan. Cool completely. Prepare pastry while pâté is cooling.

5. In a mixing bowl cut the butter into the flour with a pastry cutter until texture resembles coarse meal or process in food processor with several on/off pulses. Add sour cream and toss together lightly to combine. Turn out pastry onto a board dusted with flour and knead briefly until pastry holds together. It will be quite soft. Wrap and chill for at least ½ hour.

6. Preheat oven to 400°F (200°C). Line a baking sheet with parchment.

7. To assemble, roll out dough to a thickness of ⅛ inch (3 mm) in a rectangle large enough to completely wrap pâté. Place cooled pâté, smooth side down, on the rolled pastry and bring sides up and around to enclose pâté. Seal well with egg wash. Place on baking sheet, seam side down. Make two or three slits in the top to allow steam to escape. Decorate top with pastry cut-outs and brush top and sides with egg wash. Bake for 20 to 30 minutes, or until pastry is a golden brown.

VEGETABLE PÂTÉ

Yields one large pâté

This tri-coloured pâté, a favourite at the Cupboard, is a wonderfully light alternative to liver or meat terrines. Fresh and colourful, it's a real plus to any cook's repertoire.

1½	medium-sized cauliflowers, cut into florets	1½
1	small cooked potato, mashed	1
2 bunches	broccoli, cut into florets	2 bunches
1	10-oz (284-g) bag spinach, well washed and trimmed	1
4 Tbsp	butter	60 mL
2	leeks, well washed and sliced 1 inch (2.5 cm)	2
1	large zucchini, sliced 1 inch (2.5 cm)	1
2 bunches	carrots, peeled and sliced 1 inch (2.5 cm)	2 bunches
9	eggs	9
½ cup	whipping cream	125 mL
2 cups	fresh breadcrumbs	500 mL
2 tsp	mild curry powder	10 mL
2 tsp	salt	10 mL
¾ tsp	pepper	3 mL
⅛ tsp	rubbed dried oregano	0.5 mL
¼ tsp	dried mixed Italian herbs	1 mL
1½ tsp	dried tarragon	7 mL
3 Tbsp	tomato paste	45 mL
3 Tbsp	chopped fresh dill weed *or* 1 Tbsp (15 mL) dried dill weed	45 mL
4 Tbsp	butter, melted	60 mL

1. Preheat oven to 375°F (190°C). Line a 5-inch × 5-inch × 14-inch (12-cm × 12-cm × 36-cm) loaf pan with a sheet of parchment large enough to come up the sides of the pan and fold over the top to completely enclose the pâté.

2. In a large pot of boiling water blanch cauliflower florets for 3 to 4 minutes, or until tender. Drain well and chop finely in a food processor fitted with a steel blade. Place in cheesecloth and squeeze out excess moisture. Put into medium-sized mixing bowl. Mix in mashed potato. Set aside.

BAKING IN A WATER BATH

By baking the pâté in a water bath (bain-marie), you ensure even cooking. Place the pan of pâté in a larger pan and pour hot water between the sides, filling the larger pan almost to the top.

If you do not have a 14-inch (36-cm) loaf pan, use two small loaf pans, but the layers will not be as deep.

3. Blanch broccoli florets, drain, finely chop in a processor and squeeze dry. Put into a second medium-sized mixing bowl. Blanch spinach, drain, chop in a processor and squeeze dry. Add to broccoli. Set aside.

4. Melt 2 Tbsp (30 mL) of butter in a frying pan over medium heat. Add leeks and zucchini and sauté until tender. Chop finely in a food processor and add to broccoli mixture.

5. In food processor finely chop carrots. Melt 2 Tbsp (30 mL) of butter in frying pan, add carrots and sauté until tender. Place in a third mixing bowl.

6. In a fourth mixing bowl beat together the eggs and whipping cream. Add the breadcrumbs and soak until moisture is absorbed. Place a third of this mixture into each of the bowls of vegetables.

7. To the cauliflower mixture add curry powder, ¾ tsp (3 mL) salt, and ¼ tsp (1 mL) pepper. Stir to mix well.

8. To the broccoli mixture add oregano, Italian herbs, tarragon, ¾ tsp (3 mL) salt, and ¼ tsp (1 mL) pepper. Mix well.

9. To the carrots add the tomato paste, dill weed, ½ tsp (2 mL) salt and ¼ tsp (1 mL) pepper. Mix well.

10. Press the broccoli mixture evenly into the bottom of the lined pan. Press the carrot mixture on top of the broccoli in an even layer. Top with a layer of cauliflower mixture and smooth the surface. Pour the melted butter over the top and lift the parchment over the sides to cover the top. Cover all with a double layer of foil to keep in the steam as much as possible and place in a water bath. Bake for 2 hours. Cool, remove parchment and invert onto serving platter or serve sliced to reveal the colourful layers.

SALADS

TORTELLINI SALAD WITH FRESH TOMATO

Yields 8 to 12 servings

This salad is a "best-seller" at the Cupboard. It's perfect on a hot summer's day: tomatoes are at their sun-ripened best, and with the easy preparation you won't overheat the kitchen.

CHOOSING TOMATOES

Select tomatoes that are bright red, firm and yielding to the touch but not spongy. Tomatoes with dark blemishes or yellow spots and tomatoes that have split are not as good. In the summer, domestic tomatoes are at their true vine-ripened best. They burst with sun-touched flavour and even smell faintly sweet.

In winter, when most tomatoes, even those classified as vine-ripened, are picked ripe but slightly green, the best flavoured tomatoes bear labels from Israel or Hawaii. Those of you who have taken the time in summer to can or freeze some of the local harvest will be able to avoid the relatively high cost of these imports. Canned Italian plum tomatoes are another winter alternative and give excellent flavour to soups, stews and sauces.

2 lb	fresh meat or cheese tortellini	900 g
¾ cup	olive oil	175 mL
2 tsp	crushed garlic	10 mL
2¼ cups	diced tomatoes, ½-inch (1.25-cm) cubes (about 2½ lb/1 kg)	550 mL
½ cup	chopped fresh flat-leaf parsley or fresh basil or fresh coriander	125 mL
3 Tbsp	chopped fresh dill weed	45 mL
3 Tbsp	chopped Spanish onion	45 mL
4 tsp	salt	20 mL
1½ tsp	pepper	7 mL

1. In a large pot of salted boiling water cook tortellini over medium-high heat until tender. Drain and immerse in cold water. When fully cooled, drain tortellini and set aside in a large mixing bowl.

2. In a small frying pan combine olive oil and garlic and cook over medium-low heat until garlic has softened but not browned, about 2 to 3 minutes. Set aside to cool.

3. In a food processor fitted with a steel blade purée 1½ cups (375 mL) of tomatoes. Add to tortellini with remaining diced tomatoes. Add cooled garlic oil and all remaining ingredients. Toss to mix well. Serve cool or at room temperature.

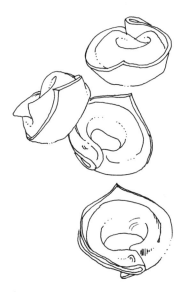

SEAFOOD PASTA SALAD

Yields 15 to 20 servings

Mussels, shrimp, crab and scallops are seasoned separately to bring out the individual flavours, then tossed with pasta and a confetti of vegetables.

For seafood:

1 lb	shrimp, cooked and shelled	450 g
2 Tbsp	olive oil	30 mL
4 tsp	lemon juice	20 mL
1 Tbsp	chopped fresh basil or dill weed or green onions	15 mL
3 lb	mussels	1.5 kg
1 to 1½ cups	white wine	250 to 375 mL
½ lb	fresh scallops	225 g
⅔ to 1 cup	lime juice or lemon juice	150 to 250 mL
1 lb	crab meat	450 g

For pasta and vegetables:

18 oz	penne or other fancy-shaped pasta	500 g
1 Tbsp	olive oil	15 mL
3 to 4 Tbsp	chopped fresh basil or coriander	45 to 60 mL
1	red bell pepper, cut in strips 2 inch × ⅛ inch (5 cm × 3 mm)	1
¾ cup	thinly diagonally sliced celery	175 mL
2½ cups	diced tomatoes	625 mL
1½ tsp	salt	7 mL
1 tsp	white pepper	5 mL
1 tsp	finely chopped hot pepper (optional)	5 mL

1. In a mixing bowl combine shrimp, olive oil, lemon juice and chopped basil. Toss to mix well and marinate in the refrigerator for at least 1 hour.

2. Scrub mussels well and remove beards. In a pot with a lid add wine to a depth of 1 inch (2.5 cm) and bring to boil over high heat. Add mussels, cover and steam until shells open, about 2 to 3 minutes. Remove from heat and, when cooled, remove from shells. Set aside.

3. Cut scallops in half if larger than bite size. Place in small bowl and add enough lime juice to cover. Marinate for at least 1 hour.

4. If using frozen crab meat, thaw, then drain. Set aside.

5. To prepare pasta bring a large pot of salted water to a boil. Cook pasta over medium-high heat until *al dente*. Drain and toss with 1 Tbsp (15 mL) olive oil in a large mixing bowl. Add basil, red pepper, celery, tomatoes, salt, pepper and hot pepper if desired. Toss together.

6. Add all seafood and marinades to pasta mixture and toss to mix well. Before serving, refrigerate for 1 hour to let flavours blend.

MARINATED VEGETABLE SALAD

Yields *approximately* 20 *servings*

A bright bouquet of vegetables in a very light marinade. Use any seasonal vegetable, whole or in big chunks, for a colourful mix.

For marinade:

½ cup	white wine vinegar	125 mL
¾ cup	olive oil	175 mL
2 Tbsp	brown sugar	30 mL
¾ tsp	dried mixed Italian herbs	3 mL
½ tsp	dried dill weed *or* 2 Tbsp (30 mL) fresh dill weed	2 mL
½ tsp	dried oregano *or* 2 Tbsp (30 mL) fresh oregano	2 mL
1 tsp	salt	5 mL
¼ tsp	pepper	1 mL

For vegetable mixture:

1 cup	green beans, ends removed	250 mL
1 cup	yellow wax beans, ends removed	250 mL
2 cups	broccoli florets, 2 inches (5 cm)	500 mL
3 cups	diagonally sliced parsnips, ¼-inch (6-mm) slices	750 mL
3 cups	diagonally sliced carrots, ¼-inch (6-mm) slices	750 mL
4 cups	cauliflower florets, 1½ inches (4 cm)	1 L
2 cups	Brussels sprouts, cleaned and trimmed	500 mL
2 cups	sliced zucchini, ¼-inch (6-mm) slices	500 mL
½ cup	sliced red bell pepper, long strips ¼ inch (6 mm) wide	125 mL
½ cup	sliced green bell pepper, long strips ¼ inch (6 mm) wide	125 mL
1 cup	snow peas, stems and strings removed	250 mL
1 cup	cherry tomatoes, stems removed	250 mL

1. To prepare marinade, combine white wine vinegar, olive oil, brown sugar, mixed Italian herbs, dill weed, oregano, salt and pepper in a small mixing bowl. Stir to dissolve brown sugar. Set aside. This marinade can be made ahead of time to allow the flavour of the herbs to infuse.

2. To prepare the vegetable mixture, bring to a boil a large pot of water over high heat. Blanch green and yellow beans, broccoli florets, parsnips, carrots and cauliflower in the boiling water for 2 minutes. Remove and run under cold water to stop the cooking and retain the bright colours. Place in very large mixing bowl or foil roasting pan. Blanch the Brussels sprouts for 3 to 4 minutes, until slightly cooked but still crunchy. Drain and run under cold

FLAVOURED VINEGARS

You may already use herb-scented vinegars, but have you tried spiced vinegar? To make your own, select a good wine vinegar and add a combination of whole spices. Cinnamon sticks with orange peel add warmth to a red wine vinegar. Chili peppers will make a white wine vinegar jump with flavour. Heat the vinegar with the spices and flavourings in a glass or enamelled saucepan, until just warm. Remove from heat and let the mixture infuse for about 30 minutes. If you prefer a stronger flavour, add more spices and flavourings and heat again.

water. Add to other blanched vegetables. Add raw zucchini, red and green bell peppers, snow peas and cherry tomatoes.

3. Pour marinade over the vegetable mixture and toss to mix well. Let stand for at least 30 minutes, stirring occasionally, before serving.

ORIENTAL VEGETABLE SALAD

Yields 8 to 12 servings

Crunchy, colourful vegetables are splashed with a light dressing. Terrific with barbecued steak.

1	**20-oz (567-g) can water chestnuts, drained and sliced into 4 rounds**	1
5 cups	**broccoli florets, blanched**	1.25 L
4 cups	**snow peas, tips and strings removed (about ¾ lb/330 g)**	1 L
2 cups	**sliced red bell pepper, ¼-inch (6-mm) strips**	500 mL
1½ lb	**asparagus, trimmed and cut diagonally into 2-inch (5-cm) lengths**	675 g
For dressing:		
½ cup	**rice vinegar**	125 mL
4 Tbsp	**sesame oil**	60 mL
4 Tbsp	**brown sugar**	60 mL
¾ tsp	**salt**	3 mL
¼ tsp	**pepper**	1 mL

1. In a large mixing bowl combine all the vegetables.

2. In a small mixing bowl combine all ingredients for dressing and mix well. Pour over vegetables, toss well and serve.

Water chestnuts are available fresh or canned. Light, sweet flavour and very crispy. Their crispy texture remains, even after cooking. If fresh are available, peel the brown, mud-covered skin before using. The work is a little messy, but the sweet, fresh flavour is worth it.

PASTA PRIMAVERA SALAD WITH LEMON

Yields 12 to 20 servings

Paper-thin slices of lemon add a surprising taste and texture to this pasta salad. A combination of different shapes—fusilli, bow tie, shells, penne, ruote—makes the munching fun.

LEMON-WISE

Pick lemons that have thin skins, indicated by a finely textured surface and a bit of suppleness when rolled in the hand. Lemons that are heavy for their size will be more juicy. And those that are slightly green will have more tartness.

2 lb	pasta of various shapes	900 mL
¾ cup	olive oil	175 mL
½ cup	lemon juice	125 mL
2 Tbsp	salt	30 mL
1 tsp	pepper	5 mL
2	lemons	2
3 cups	thinly shredded carrots	750 mL
3 cups	snow peas, julienned	750 mL
3 cups	thinly diagonally sliced celery or asparagus	750 mL
1½ cups	thinly sliced green onions	375 mL
garnish	chopped fresh herbs	garnish

1. Cook each type of pasta separately in salted boiling water until *al dente*; different shapes require different cooking times. Drain and run under cold water to cool. Drain well, then combine in a large mixing bowl. Add olive oil and toss well. Add lemon juice, salt and pepper, and toss again.

2. Cut lemons in half lengthwise, then cut into paper-thin slices. Add to pasta mixture. Add carrots, snow peas, celery or asparagus and green onions. Toss well and let stand at least 1 hour to allow flavours to blend. Transfer to serving dish and sprinkle with chopped herbs. If fresh herbs are unavailable, use chopped green onions.

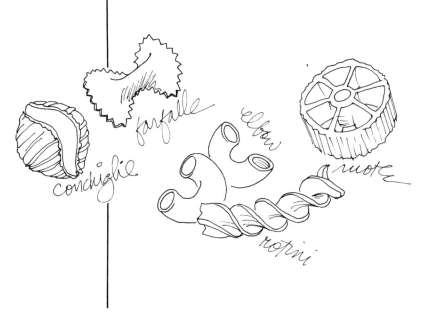

conchiglie   *farfalle*   *elbow*   *ruote*   *rotini*

SALAD ROLLS

Yields 8 large rolls

A fun way to eat a salad and a refreshingly delightful snack to be eaten in hand. A paper-thin rice wrapper encloses Chinese rice noodles, shredded chicken, bean sprouts, carrots and peanuts in a spicy sweet sauce, topped by a jaunty green-onion feather.

For sauce:

½ cup	rice vinegar	125 mL
1 Tbsp	brown sugar	15 mL
1 Tbsp	peanut butter	15 mL
1 Tbsp	soy sauce	15 mL
2 Tbsp	spicy soy sauce	30 mL
2 Tbsp	hoisin sauce	30 mL
¼ tsp	finely minced garlic	1 mL
1 tsp	grated fresh ginger	5 mL

For rolls:

5½ oz	rice noodles	150 g
16 rounds	Indonesian rice-paper wrappers	16 rounds
8	large leaves of lettuce, leaf or romaine	8
1 lb	chicken breast, poached, boned and julienned	450 g
1⅓ cup	bean sprouts	325 mL
2	small carrots, julienned	2
4 Tbsp	chopped peanuts	60 mL
8	green onions, trimmed	8

1. In a mixing bowl combine all the ingredients for the sauce and mix well. Set aside.

2. In a pot of boiling water cook rice noodles for 2 to 3 minutes and drain. Immerse in cold water, drain and place in a mixing bowl. Add ⅓ of the sauce and toss well. Set aside.

3. In a large bowl of warm water soak 2 rounds of rice wrapper for 1 to 2 minutes, or until softened. Remove and place one on top of the other on working surface. (As you are filling the wrappers, soak another 2 wrappers for the next roll.) Fold the top edge of the wrappers down about 1 inch (2.5 cm). Place a lettuce leaf on one end with the top ruffle extending over the folded edge of the wrapper. Put 1 green onion on top of the lettuce so it extends above the lettuce. Place ⅛ of the noodles, chicken, carrots and peanuts on top. Tuck lettuce edges around the noodles to enclose. Roll the wrapper across the filling, fold the bottom up, and continue rolling across until completely wrapped. Repeat with remaining ingredients. Serve with the rest of the sauce.

TO MAKE ROLLS:

Fold top down.

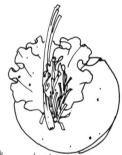

Place lettuce, green onion and filling on wrapper

Roll up.

INDONESIAN RICE PAPER

Thin, circular wrappers made from rice flour. Available in several sizes, most common size 8-inch (20-cm) diameter. Sold dried, must be soaked for 1 or 2 minutes to soften before use.

BRUNCH/LUNCH

CHICKEN HOBO PIES

Yields 4 individual pies

In our fanciful version of chicken pot pie the tasty filling is wrapped in phyllo pastry and tied like a hobo's knapsack.

5 Tbsp	butter	75 mL
10	large mushrooms, cleaned and halved	10
¼ cup	flour	60 mL
1 cup	milk	250 mL
½ cup	whipping cream	125 mL
½ tsp	ground or freshly grated nutmeg	2 mL
1 tsp	grated lemon rind	5 mL
to taste	salt and pepper	to taste
2	whole chicken breasts, slightly undercooked, boned, skinned and cubed 1 inch (2.5 cm)	2
2	carrots, cooked and sliced ½ inch (1.25 cm)	2
2	parsnips, cooked and sliced ½ inch (1.25 mm)	2
1	sweet potato, cooked, peeled and cubed ¾ inch (2 cm)	1
16 sheets	phyllo pastry	16 sheets
1 cup	melted butter	250 mL
4	9-inch (23-cm) lengths butcher's string	4

1. Preheat oven to 400°F (200°C). Line a cookie sheet with parchment.

2. In a small frying pan melt 1 Tbsp (15 mL) butter over medium-high heat. Add mushrooms and sauté for 1 or 2 minutes, just until juices are released. Set aside.

3. In a large frying pan melt 4 Tbsp (60 mL) butter. Add flour and brown slightly, stirring constantly. Slowly add milk and cream, whisking constantly. Bring to boil and season with nutmeg, lemon rind, salt and pepper. Fold in chicken, mushrooms and vegetables. Adjust seasoning if necessary. Cool.

4. Cut phyllo sheets into squares approximately 14 inches × 14 inches (36 cm × 36 cm). Work quickly to prevent sheets from drying out. Cover phyllo with a slightly damp tea towel. Remove 3 sheets and brush liberally with melted butter and place them squarely on top of each other. Set aside.

5. Brush another sheet of phyllo with melted butter. Place a quarter of the filling in the middle and fold up like an envelope to enclose the filling in a packet about 4 inches × 4 inches (10 cm × 10 cm). Place this packet in the middle of the three buttered sheets and draw up the sides and corners of the sheets, enclosing the chicken packet like a hobo's knapsack. Tie with butcher's string. Repeat with remaining phyllo and chicken, making four knapsacks. Place on baking sheet and bake for 20 to 30 minutes, or until golden brown.

POACHING CHICKEN

We have a special way of poaching chicken that retains all the flavour of the meat. First, cut the chicken into pieces appropriate to the recipe. Leave in the bones to add their considerable flavour. Place chicken, skin side up, in a single layer in a clean roasting pan. Add 3 or 4 cups of strong chicken stock to a level ½ inch (1.25 cm) deep in the pan. Do not cover chicken with liquid. Cover roasting pan with tightly fitting lid or double layer of foil. Place in an oven preheated to 375°F (190°C). Allow chicken to poach for 20 to 30 minutes, or just until done. Meat should be slightly pink.

For a simpler presentation, make four individual packets by rolling the filling in buttered phyllo, using the same folding technique as with egg rolls.

CHICKEN-APPLE PIE

Yields one 10-inch (25-cm) pie

A hint of maple syrup and the subtle sweetness of autumn apples sharpened with a generous addition of mustard add a special flavour to this chicken pie. The rich crust is freckled with Cheddar cheese.

For Cheddar cheese pastry:

2 cups	flour	500 mL
½ tsp	salt	2 mL
⅔ cup	cold butter, cubed 1 inch (2.5 cm)	150 mL
½ cup	grated Cheddar cheese	125 mL
4 to 6 Tbsp	cold water	60 to 90 mL

For filling:

1	4-lb (1.8-kg) chicken	1
¼ cup	flour	60 mL
2	medium-sized onions, sliced	2
2 Tbsp	olive oil	30 mL
2 Tbsp	butter	30 mL
4 Tbsp	dry mustard	60 mL
¼ cup	cider vinegar	60 mL
¾ cup	white wine	175 mL
2 Tbsp	brown sugar	30 mL
2 cloves	garlic, finely minced	2 cloves
to taste	salt and pepper	to taste
1 Tbsp	Honeycup or Russian-style mustard	15 mL
3	cooking apples	3
3 Tbsp	butter	50 mL
¼ cup	maple syrup	60 mL

1. Prepare Cheddar cheese pastry. In a food processor fitted with a steel blade, or in a mixing bowl, with a pastry cutter, cut together the flour, salt, butter and cheese until mixture resembles coarse meal.

2. Add water and mix just until dough holds together.

3. Remove from bowl and knead gently three or four times. Refrigerate while filling is prepared.

4. To make filling, cut chicken into frying pieces and dredge in flour.

5. In a large frying pan that has a lid sauté the sliced onions in the oil and butter. Add chicken pieces and brown.

6. While chicken is browning, mix together the dry mustard, vinegar, wine, sugar and garlic. Pour over the chicken and reduce heat. Cover and simmer for approximately 15 minutes, turning chicken often. The meat should be undercooked and slightly pink. Add salt and pepper. Adjust seasoning, adding more sugar or vinegar if necessary.

7. Cool chicken completely in sauce. When cool, take meat off bones and cut into cubes about 1¼ inches (3 cm).

8. Skim any excess oil off sauce and add Honeycup mustard. Put chicken back into sauce.

9. Preheat oven to 375°F (190°C).

10. Pare apples and cut into cubes about 1¼ inches (3 cm). Sauté in butter in a well-seasoned or non-stick frying pan for about 1 minute. Add the maple syrup and boil down over high heat for about 3 or 4 minutes, until apples are nicely glazed but still firm. Add to chicken.

11. Turn chicken-apple mixture into a deep 10-inch (25-cm) pie pan or casserole.

12. On a lightly floured board, roll out dough into a 14-inch (36-cm) circle. Cut steam vents in the middle and place over chicken-apple mixture. Crimp a decorative edge around the pie and bake for 30 to 45 minutes.

FOUR-BEAN BAKE

Yields 8 to 12 servings

This recipe is for my vegetarian friends. It's a wonderful blend of beans tenderly cooked together in a slow oven. Serve with buttered brown bread or mixed-grain soda bread.

1 cup	black-eyed beans	250 mL
1 cup	pinto beans	250 mL
1 cup	Romana or Lima beans	250 mL
1 cup	kidney beans	250 mL
4 cups	chopped Spanish onions	1 L
6 Tbsp	dry mustard	90 mL
1 Tbsp	salt	15 mL
1 cup	cider vinegar	250 mL
½ cup	butter	125 mL
3 cups	tomatoes cut into chunks	750 mL
¾ cup	dark molasses	175 mL
1 tsp	ground cinnamon	5 mL

1. In separate containers cover each type of bean with about 3 cups of water. Allow to soak overnight. Drain and put into separate saucepans. Cover with water and cook over medium heat until almost tender, about 1 to 2 hours. Add more water as necessary. Drain.

2. Preheat oven to 400°F (200°C).

3. In a Dutch oven combine beans and remaining ingredients. Stir well. Cover and bake for 15 minutes. Stir well again and reduce heat to 250°F (120°C). Bake, stirring occasionally, for about 3 hours, or until beans are really soft. Remove and serve hot.

Any combination of beans will work. Try mixing and matching.

A GREY CUP AFTERNOON

Grey Cup Day, television and old chums make for a comfortable afternoon. And baked beans served with soda bread seem just right. Marinated Vegetable Salad and Apple-Orange Coffee Cake round out the menu. For hors d'oeuvres? Potato chips and dip, of course.

BARRY'S TORTA RUSTICA

Yields 10 to 12 servings

Herb-scented layers of eggplant, ham, mushrooms, cheese and tomatoes form colourful layers in this intriguing Italian pie.

EGGPLANTS AND SALT

Before cooking, sprinkle eggplant slices with salt and allow to "sweat" for 20 minutes. Then pat dry and cook as desired. The salt draws out the slightly acrid juices of the eggplant. Salted, sweated eggplant will soak up less oil in cooking. Chinese eggplants do not have to be salted.

For dough:

2 pkg	active dry yeast	2 pkg
4 tsp	sugar	20 mL
1 cup	warm water	250 mL
2 tsp	salt	10 mL
½ cup	melted unsalted butter	125 mL
3 to 3½ cups	flour	750 to 875 mL
1 Tbsp	vegetable oil	15 mL

For filling:

1	medium-sized eggplant	1
1 Tbsp	salt	15 mL
⅓ cup	flour	75 mL
3 Tbsp	unsalted butter	45 mL
1 lb	mushrooms, cleaned and thinly sliced	450 g
½ cup	olive oil	125 mL
1 lb	thinly sliced cooked ham	450 g
4 Tbsp	dried mixed Italian herbs	60 mL
1 lb	thinly sliced firm white cheese (Jarlsberg, Gruyère, or Mozzarella)	450 g
2 or 3	firm tomatoes, thinly sliced	2 or 3

For glaze:

1	egg, lightly beaten	1

1. To make dough, in a large mixing bowl stir yeast, sugar and water together and allow yeast to dissolve and bubble up, about 5 minutes. Mix in salt and butter. Add about 1½ cups (375 mL) flour and beat until smooth. Add more flour to make a firm but moist dough. Turn out onto floured board and knead 3 to 4 minutes until dough is smooth, elastic and not sticky. Lightly oil a medium-sized bowl, add dough and turn over so top is oiled. Cover with a clean towel and allow to rise in a warm place for 2 hours.

2. To make filling, cut eggplant in ¼-inch (6-mm) slices. Sprinkle slices with salt and place in a large colander to drain for 15 minutes. Pat slices dry and dredge with flour.

3. In a large frying pan melt butter over medium-high heat. Add mushrooms and sauté just until mushrooms begin to release their juices. Remove and set aside. Heat oil in frying pan over medium heat. Add as many eggplant slices as can be accommodated in a single layer and fry until almost cooked and lightly browned. Remove and set aside. Repeat until all eggplant slices have been fried.

4. Punch down dough and roll out on a lightly floured surface into a circle about 15 to 20 inches (38 to 50 cm) in diameter. Line an 8- to 10-inch (20- to 25-cm) pie or springform pan with the dough, draping the excess over the sides. Arrange half the ham slices on the bottom and sprinkle with about 1 tsp (5 mL) herbs. Cover with a layer of half the cheese slices and a sprinkling of herbs, then a layer of half the tomatoes and a sprinkling of herbs, a layer of half the eggplant and more herbs, and a layer of all the mushrooms and a sprinkling of herbs. Form layers of the remaining ingredients in reverse order. Pull dough over the filling to form top crust. Brush with egg.

5. Preheat oven to 375°F (190°C). Allow torta to rest for 15 to 20 minutes before baking, then bake for 50 minutes, or until lightly browned. Serve at room temperature.

Line the dish with rolled-out dough

Layer in the filling

Bring up dough to cover the top

DEEP VEGETABLE QUICHE

Yields one 9-inch × 12-inch (23-cm × 30-cm) pie

The tasty whole-wheat crust can be made up in minutes, and the colourful filling is simply layered in, smothered in cream and eggs, then baked into a hearty egg pie.

For crust:

1½ cups	whole-wheat flour	375 mL
3 Tbsp	wheat germ or bran	50 mL
¾ cup	butter, melted	175 mL

For filling:

1	10-oz (284-g) bag spinach, well washed and trimmed	1
¼ cup	olive oil for sautéing	60 mL
1	medium-sized leek, well washed and chopped	1
2	small zucchini, sliced ¼ inch (6 mm)	2
2 cups	thickly sliced mushrooms	500 mL
2 cups	grated white cheese, such as Jarlsberg or Mozzarella (about ½ lb/225 g)	500 mL
2 cups	grated Cheddar cheese (about ½ lb/225 g)	500 mL
1½ cups	dry cottage cheese	375 mL
6	eggs	6
2 cups	whipping cream	500 mL
2 Tbsp	flour	30 mL
1 Tbsp	ground or freshly grated nutmeg	15 mL
1 Tbsp	dried tarragon, crushed	15 mL
1 tsp	dried fines herbes	5 mL
1 Tbsp	Dinah's Chive Salad Mix *or* dried chives	15 mL
½ tsp	salt	2 mL

1. Preheat oven to 400°F (200°C).

2. To make crust, combine whole-wheat flour and wheat germ in a small mixing bowl. Add melted butter and mix well.

3. Press into bottom and two thirds of the way up the sides of a 9-inch × 12-inch (23-cm × 30-cm) pan. Bake for fifteen minutes. Remove from oven and cool. Spread ½ of the white cheese, Cheddar cheese and cottage cheese on the bottom of the crust.

4. Lower oven temperature to 375°F (190°C).

5. Blanch the spinach briefly in boiling water. Drain well. Place in cheesecloth and squeeze dry. Spread a layer of spinach over the cheese.

6. In a frying pan heat 1 Tbsp (15 mL) of the olive oil over medium heat. Add leeks and sauté 2 to 3 minutes, or until soft. Spread evenly over spinach.

7. Sauté zucchini with 1 T (15 mL) of the olive oil for 2 minutes. Spread evenly over leeks.

SEAFOOD PIE

Use the Deep Vegetable Quiche recipe, but instead of white, Cheddar and cottage cheeses, substitute 1 lb (450 g) chèvre cheese. Instead of the vegetables, substitute: 1½ lb (675 g) shrimp, shelled, cleaned and cut into ½-inch (1.25-cm) pieces; 1 lb (450 g) scallops, cut into ½-inch (1.25-cm) pieces; and 1½ lb (675 g) crab meat, thawed and squeezed dry if using frozen. Substitute the herbs and spices with 1 Tbsp (15 mL) chopped fresh dill weed, 1 Tbsp (15 mL) dried tarragon, 1 tsp (5 mL) fines herbes and a pinch of nutmeg.

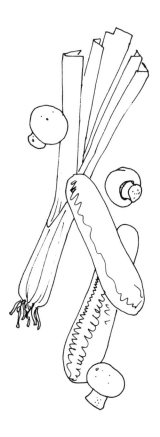

8. Sauté mushrooms in remaining olive oil just until juices run. Spread evenly over zucchini. Sprinkle the remainder of the white cheese, Cheddar cheese and cottage cheese on top.

9. In a medium-sized mixing bowl combine eggs, cream, flour, nutmeg, tarragon, fines herbes, Chive Salad Mix and salt. Beat lightly until blended. Pour over cheese.

10. Bake 50 to 60 minutes, or until a knife inserted into the centre comes out clean.

DINAH'S CHIVE SALAD MIX

A *blend based on chives, paprika and garlic.*

FINES HERBES

A *mixture of herbs, usually chervil, sage, rosemary and thyme.*

PASTA AND SCALLOPS IN BLACK BEAN SAUCE

Yields 4 to 6 servings

A pungent hint of black bean is a wonderful counterpoint to the natural sweetness of fresh scallops. Strips of snow peas, red peppers and green onions add their colourful zip.

½ lb	spaghettini or linguini	225 g
3 Tbsp	dried fermented black beans	45 mL
2 cloves	garlic	2 cloves
2 Tbsp	rice vinegar	30 mL
½ tsp	chopped fresh ginger	2 mL
2 Tbsp	soy sauce	30 mL
2 Tbsp	demerara sugar	30 mL
1 tsp	corn starch	5 mL
1 cup	water	250 mL
2 Tbsp	peanut oil	30 mL
½ lb	snow peas, julienned	225 g
½	red bell pepper, julienned	½
4	large green onions, julienned	4
1 lb	fresh whole bay scallops *or* fresh sea scallops, halved	450 g
to taste	soy sauce, salt and pepper	to taste

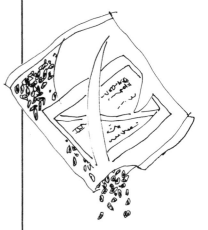

1. Into a large pot of rapidly boiling salted water gradually add spaghettini. Boil over high heat until *al dente*. Drain in colander. Keep warm.

2. In a food processor fitted with a steel blade combine black beans, garlic cloves, rice vinegar, ginger and soy sauce. Process until finely chopped. Add demerara sugar, corn starch and water and process until corn starch is fully incorporated.

3. In a large frying pan heat peanut oil over high heat until very hot. Add snow peas, red pepper and green onions. Stir fry for 1 to 2 minutes. Remove to a mixing bowl. Pour black-bean mixture into pan and bring to boil, stirring constantly until mixture thickens. Add scallops and cook for 1 minute. Return snow-pea mixture to the frying pan and stir to mix. Season to taste with soy sauce, salt and pepper. Serve immediately over cooked spaghettini.

CHINESE BLACK BEANS

Black Beans are dried, fermented soy beans used in Chinese cooking. Just a spoonful of these wrinkled little black dots will give a richly pungent flavour to vegetables, meat or fish. Sold in small plastic bags in stores specializing in Chinese foods, they should be transferred to a tightly lidded container and stored in a cool dark place, once the package is opened (if only to protect you from their strong odour).

TAMALE PIE

Yields 8 servings

The sunny flavours of corn, tomatoes and chili smothered in melted cheese. Serve with a salad for a light, nutritious, vegetarian meal or as a hearty accompaniment to spicy entrées like chunky chili and chicken mole.

1 cup	cornmeal	250 mL
3 cups	water	750 mL
7 Tbsp	chili powder	105 mL
to taste	salt	to taste
½ cup	oil	125 mL
1	large onion, diced	1
6 cloves	garlic, crushed	6 cloves
2	green onions, chopped	2
2 cups	broccoli florets, 1 inch (2.5 cm) (about ½ large head)	500 mL
2 cups	sliced zucchini, ½-inch (1.25-cm) slices (about 2 small)	500 mL
2 cups	sliced mushrooms, ¼-inch (6-mm) slices (about ½ lb/225 g)	500 mL
2 cups	diced tomatoes, 1-inch (2.5-cm) cubes (about 2 medium-sized)	500 mL
1	12-oz (341-mL) can niblet-style corn, drained *or* 1½ cups (375 mL) fresh corn cut off cob	1
1	19-oz (540-mL) can kidney beans, drained	1
½ cup	chopped fresh parsley	125 mL
¼ cup	chopped fresh dill weed *or* 4 tsp (20 mL) dried dill weed	60 mL
2 tsp	salt	10 mL
4 cups	grated Cheddar cheese (about 1 lb/450 g)	1 L
4	eggs, lightly beaten	4
2 cups	grated Mozzarella cheese (about ½ lb/225 g)	500 mL

1. Preheat oven to 375°F (190°C). Lightly grease a 9-inch × 12-inch (23-cm × 30-cm) rectangular casserole dish.

2. In a large saucepan combine cornmeal, water, 1 Tbsp (15 mL) chili powder and salt. Cook over medium-high heat until water is fully absorbed into cornmeal. Mixture will be very thick. Transfer to a large mixing bowl and cool slightly.

3. Heat oil in large frying pan over high heat. Sauté onions, garlic, green onions, broccoli, zucchini and mushrooms until cooked but still crunchy. Add tomatoes, corn, kidney beans, parsley, dill weed, remaining chili powder and salt. Stir to combine and remove from heat.

4. Combine ⅓ of vegetable mixture with the cooked cornmeal, Cheddar cheese and eggs.

5. Turn the remaining vegetable mixture into the prepared casserole dish, top with the cornmeal mixture and bake for 1 hour.

Two great accompaniments to this pie are guacamole and sour cream.

For a zippier version, add ½ to 1 cup (125 to 250 mL) chopped jalapeño peppers.

Tie a couple of bright bandanas around the baking dish for a colourful touch.

6. Top with the Mozzarella cheese 5 minutes before the end of cooking time.

POTATO MELTS

Yields 12 *servings*

Pan-browned potatoes smothered with a rainbow of chunky mixed vegetables and blanketed with lots of melted Cheddar.

3½ lb	potatoes, scrubbed	1.6 kg
2 cups	cauliflower florets	500 mL
3	parsnips, peeled and diagonally sliced ¼ inch (6 mm)	3
1½ cups	sliced carrots, ¼-inch (6-mm) slices	375 mL
2 cups	broccoli florets	500 mL
1 cup	cut green beans, each bean trimmed and cut in half	250 mL
6 Tbsp	butter	90 mL
4 Tbsp	olive oil	60 mL
½ cup	sliced onions	125 mL
1 cup	diagonally cut asparagus, each spear cut into 3	250 mL
2	zucchini, sliced ¼ inch (6 mm)	2
1 cup	snow peas, tips and strings removed	250 mL
1	red pepper, cut into ¼-inch (6-mm) strips	1
4 Tbsp	oyster sauce (optional)	60 mL
½ tsp	finely minced garlic	2 mL
1 tsp	pepper	5 mL
2 to 3 tsp	seasoned salt	10 to 15 mL
1½ lb	raw milk Cheddar or Mozzarella cheese, grated	675 g

One of the reasons why European cheeses taste so good is because they are made from raw or unpasteurized milk. Our health regulations do not permit this, with a few rare exceptions. Happily for Cheddar fans, naturally aged raw milk Cheddar is one. Its full, complex flavour is far superior to artificially aged Cheddars made from pasteurized milk.

Two other cheeses to try with Potato Melts: Appenzeller and Bagnes, so popular for raclette that it is often called Raclette cheese.

1. In a large saucepan cover potatoes with water and boil over medium-high heat until potatoes are cooked but still slightly crisp. Drain and cool. Cut cooled potatoes into 1-inch (2.5-cm) cubes. Set aside.

2. Bring a large saucepan of water to boil. Blanch cauliflower for 2 minutes. Remove cauliflower with a strainer and immediately plunge into cold water. Drain and set aside. Repeat with parsnips, carrots, broccoli and green beans, blanching each separately.

3. In a large frying pan heat 2 Tbsp (30 mL) butter and 2 Tbsp (30 mL) oil over medium-high heat. Add half the potatoes and sauté until browned, about 10 minutes. Sprinkle with half the seasoned salt and toss together. Remove from pan and set aside. Repeat with remaining potatoes.

4. Preheat oven to 375°F (190°C).

5. Add remaining butter and oil to frying pan and heat. Add

onions and sauté until transparent, about 5 minutes. Add the blanched vegetables and sauté for another 2 to 3 minutes. Add asparagus, zucchini, snow peas and red pepper and sauté an additional 2 to 3 minutes. Season with oyster sauce, garlic and pepper and toss together. (If you prefer not to use oyster sauce, season to taste with salt or soy sauce or lemon juice.) Remove from heat and keep warm.

6. In large gratin dish, paella pan or casserole dish spread fried potatoes evenly over the bottom. Add vegetables. Top with grated cheese and bake for 15 minutes, or until cheese has melted.

BAKED BRIE

Yields 30 to 40 servings

Why is this a most-requested recipe? Is it the heady flavour of wine pastry and French Brie melting into sugared nuts? Or is it the sensational look of luscious fresh strawberries piled around a huge pastry-wrapped wheel of Brie? Serve this baked Brie for brunch or as a dessert and decide for yourself.

1 recipe	wine pastry	1 recipe
1 whole	Brie, chilled and not too ripe about 13 inches/33 cm in diameter)	1 whole
1½ cups	brown sugar	375 mL
3 cups	walnut halves, toasted	750 mL
2 cups	pine nuts, toasted	500 mL
3 cups	sliced almonds, toasted	750 mL
1	egg, lightly beaten	1

1. Preheat oven to 475°F (240°C). Line a baking sheet with parchment. Baking sheet must be at least 15 inches (38 cm) in width.

2. On a lightly floured surface roll out a little less than half of the wine pastry into a circle about 15 inches (38 cm) in diameter, or about 2 inches (5 cm) larger than the wheel of Brie. Slide onto baking sheet. Place Brie in the centre, sprinkle with brown sugar, and cover with walnuts, pine nuts and almonds. Brush edge of pastry with egg wash.

3. Roll out remaining pastry. Cut into a circle about 18 inches (46 cm) in diameter. Gently lift onto Brie, covering completely. Press around edge to seal completely. Crimp all around, creating a large fluted edge about 1 inch (2.5 cm) high. Cut several slits in top of pastry to allow steam to escape. Decorate the top with cut-outs made from pastry scraps. Brush with egg wash. Fold foil to form a strip 1½ inches by 45 inches (4 cm by 115 cm) and encircle the fluted edge of the pastry tightly to hold fluting in place. The Brie may be prepared to this stage and kept in the refrigerator until baking time.

4. Bake 25 to 30 minutes, removing the foil after the first 15 minutes, until pastry has browned. Do not bake too long, or Brie

BEST BRIE

To choose a perfectly ripe Brie, look for one that is plump and softly springy to the touch. Avoid a Brie that has an ammonia smell (overripe), or is shrunken (old) or firm (not ripe). The white rind should look softly fuzzy, not dried or withered.

When choosing a cut Brie, look at the cut side. If it does not bulge, or has a white line of dense cheese through the middle, it is not ripe. If it smells of ammonia and is runny, it is overripe. The perfect Brie bulges generously at the cut and only threatens to run out.

will become runny and start bubbling out of the pastry. Let Brie stand for at least 1 hour before serving. In very hot weather, let stand for 2 hours. If it is served too soon, the cheese will be too runny. It should be slightly set but still lukewarm. Transfer carefully to large serving tray or basket and surround with fresh strawberries, grapes, blueberries or other seasonal fruit. In winter when fresh fruit is scarce, add dried figs, dates and apricots.

WINE PASTRY

½ lb	cold butter, cubed 1 inch (2.5 cm)	225 g
3½ cups	flour	875 mL
½ tsp	salt	2 mL
1	egg	1
6 Tbsp	white wine	100 mL
2 Tbsp	lemon juice	30 mL
4 Tbsp	vegetable oil	60 mL
½ rind	grated lemon rind	2 mL

1. In a food processor fitted with a steel blade combine butter, flour and salt. Process for 1 or 2 minutes with on/off pulses, or until texture resembles oatmeal. Transfer to a large mixing bowl and make a depression in the middle of the mixture, forming a well. Set aside.

2. In a small mixing bowl beat together the remaining ingredients and pour into well in butter-flour mixture. Mix lightly until dough holds together. Form into a ball, wrap with plastic wrap and refrigerate at least 20 minutes.

Cut pastry scraps into leaves and small circles to create this decoration for the top of the Brie.

COMPOSED VEGETABLE PLATTER

Yields 4 servings

An oversized plate is the canvas on which each artistic arrangement of vegetables is composed. A beautiful and bountiful meal that just happens to be very low in calories.

If you are preparing this platter ahead of time, lightly brush the blanched vegetables with oil to prevent them from drying out and to keep them looking fresh.

10	baby potatoes	10
6	small beets	6
20	snow peas or sugar peas	20
20	baby carrots *or* carrots cut into 20 lozenges ¾ inch × 2 inches (2 cm × 5 cm)	20
3	parsnips	3
8	Brussels sprouts	8
1 cup	broccoli florets	250 mL
1 cup	cauliflower florets	250 mL
12	asparagus stalks, trimmed	12
4	Chinese long beans	4
2	small zucchini	2
1 bunch	Chinese chives	1 bunch
1 cup	fresh peas	1 cup
2	small cucumbers	2
4	purple bell peppers	4
1	red bell pepper	1
1	yellow bell pepper	1
⅓ cup	olive oil	75 mL
2 Tbsp	caviar	30 mL
2 Tbsp	sour cream	30 mL
½ cup	alfalfa sprouts	125 mL
8	shiitake mushrooms	8
8	cherry tomatoes	8

1. Steam or boil potatoes and beets separately for 20 minutes or just until fork tender. Remove potatoes and put into a large bowl of cold water. Remove beets and put into a small bowl of cold water.

2. Bring a large pot of water to boil over high heat. Add snow peas and blanch for 15 seconds, or just until they turn bright green. Remove and put into cold water with potatoes. Keep pot of water boiling.

3. Peel and trim carrots into uniform shapes. Cut parsnips into sticks ¼ inch × ¼ inch × 3 inches (6 mm × 6 mm × 8 cm). Add carrots and parsnips to boiling water and blanch for 4 to 5 minutes, or just until cooked but still crisp. Remove and put into cold water with potatoes. Change water or add ice if water has become warm. Trim Brussels sprouts and cut an X through the stem end. Add to boiling water along with broccoli florets, cauliflower florets, asparagus and long beans. Blanch for 2 to 3 minutes or just until

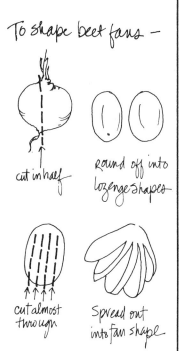

To shape beet fans —

cut in half

round off into lozenge shapes

cut almost through

Spread out into fan shape

broccoli turns bright green. Remove and add to potatoes in bowl of cold water.

4. Cut zucchini in half lengthwise, scoop out to form boats and blanch for 1 or 2 minutes, or just until tender. Remove and add to potatoes in cold water. Blanch chives for 15 seconds or just until limp. Remove and set aside. Blanch peas for 1 or 2 minutes, or until they turn bright green, then drain and run under cold water. Drain all vegetables and brush lightly with olive oil, keeping beets and peas separate from the rest of the vegetables.

5. Cut cucumber in half, trim and scoop out seeds, as illustrated, to make a basket. Fill each with 5 baby carrots and set aside. Cut off and discard the top 1 inch (2.5 cm) of each purple bell pepper. Remove seeds. Arrange florets of broccoli and cauliflower in each purple bell pepper and set aside. Fill each zucchini boat with peas and set aside. Cut each beet in half, trim into uniformly shaped lozenges and make several slices from tip end to within ⅛ inch (3 mm) of the stem end. Spread out into fan shape and set aside. Using a sharp cookie or aspic cutter cut heart shapes out of red and yellow bell peppers. Set aside. Cut each baby potato in half and top with a little caviar and sour cream. Set aside.

6. For each serving, arrange on plates as illustrated. Serve each plate with an assortment of dips presented in hollowed artichokes or artichoke bottoms.

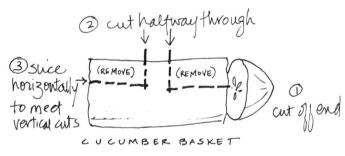

CUCUMBER BASKET

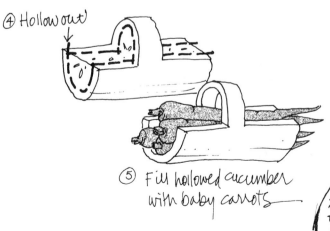

ARTICHOKES FILLED WITH DIP

Select two or three small unblemished artichokes per person. Hollow out each artichoke by cutting off and discarding the upper ⅓ and the stem. With a small knife dig out the centre leaves, then scrape out the bristly choke with a spoon. Trim away all but the bottom three or four rows of leaves. Rub well with lemon juice to prevent discolouration. Fill with dip and arrange on a small plate to serve with vegetable platter.

Serve with a choice of dips — hollandaise, green mayonnaise and herbed yoghurt.

GREEN MAYONNAISE
Yields 4 servings

½ cup/125 mL sour cream

½ cup/125 mL mayonnaise

1½ cups/375 mL thinly sliced cucumber

4½ tsp/22 mL chopped fresh dill weed

¼ tsp/1 mL salt
dash of white pepper

1. Combine all ingredients in a small mixing bowl and stir well to blend.

Fresh or frozen berries can be used in these pancakes. If using frozen, do not thaw, or their juice will discolour the pancakes.

BLUEBERRY YOGHURT PANCAKES

Yields about 2 dozen 4-inch (10-cm) pancakes

The sweet aroma of pancakes browning in the pan, images of stacks of pancakes filled with blueberries, drizzled with butter and blueberry sauce. Who needs an alarm clock when breakfast beckons thus?

5	eggs, separated	5
5 Tbsp	brown sugar	75 mL
1 cup	yoghurt	250 mL
1 cup	milk	250 mL
½ cup	cornstarch	125 mL
¼ cup	baking powder	60 mL
1 cup	flour	250 mL
½ tsp	salt	2 mL
2 cups	blueberries	500 mL
2 to	butter	30 to
4 Tbsp		60 mL

1. In a medium-sized mixing bowl beat egg yolks and sugar together. Beat in yoghurt and milk.

2. Sift together dry ingredients and stir into batter.

3. In a medium-sized mixing bowl beat egg whites to soft peaks. Fold egg whites and blueberries into batter.

4. Heat a large frying pan over medium-high heat. Brush very lightly with butter. Pour a ¼-cup (60-mL) measure of batter into the pan and cook until bubbles appear on the surface and the edges begin to look glossy. Flip over with metal spatula and cook the other side until browned, about 30 seconds. Butter the pan for each pancake. Serve with blueberry sauce.

BLUEBERRY SAUCE

¼ cup	frozen orange juice concentrate	60 mL
4 cups	fresh or frozen blueberries	1 L
½ cup	sugar*	125 mL

1. In a large saucepan combine the orange juice concentrate, blueberries and sugar over medium-low heat. Simmer until sugar has dissolved, about 5 minutes. Serve warm.

*If using frozen blueberries, sugar may have to be adjusted according to sweetness.

MAIN COURSES

LAMB SATAY ROAST

Yields 4 to 6 servings

Lamb is marinated in Indonesian peanut sauce for two days to give it tenderness and flavour. Then it's grilled to perfection on the barbecue.

2½ lb	leg of lamb	1.5 kg
For marinade:		
1	4-oz (125-g) bar unsweetened coconut cream	1
2 Tbsp	water	30 mL
6 Tbsp	natural peanut butter	90 mL
2 Tbsp	soy sauce	30 mL
2 Tbsp	spicy soy sauce	30 mL
3 Tbsp	bottled satay sauce	45 mL
1 Tbsp	brandy	15 mL
2 cloves	garlic, crushed	2 cloves

1. Trim off fat from lamb and remove bone, keeping meat in one piece. Cut into 3 or 4 large pieces about 4 inches × 4 inches × 2 inches (10 cm × 10 cm × 5 cm).

2. To make marinade, melt coconut cream with water in a small saucepan over medium heat. Pour into large mixing bowl and cool. Add the remaining ingredients and mix well. Remove a quarter of the mixture and reserve. Add lamb and spoon marinade over lamb to coat well. Marinate, refrigerated, for 2 days.

3. Light barbecue or preheat broiler.

4. Barbecue 15 to 20 minutes until medium rare, or broil 8 to 10 minutes per side. Brush with reserved marinade. Let sit for 10 to 15 minutes, then slice thinly and serve.

MENU

Stir-Fried Vermicelli Salad

Lamb Satay Roast
Green Mango Salad

Fresh Fruit served with Vanilla Cream

SPECIALTY SAUCES

If spicy soy sauce is unavailable, substitute with a mixture of 2 Tbsp (30 mL) regular soy sauce and ¼ tsp (1 mL) Chinese five-spice.

If satay sauce is unavailable, substitute with a mixture of 3 Tbsp (45 mL) soy sauce, 2 Tbsp (30 mL) peanut butter, a dash of sesame seed oil and a dash of hot pepper sauce.

PERSIAN LAMB

Yields 8 servings

*In this exotic tasting dish, slow-cooked onions melt into lamb scented with carda-
mom and saffron. Serve with rice garnished with toasted almonds or pine nuts.*

1 cup	butter	250 mL
18 cups	thinly sliced Spanish onions	4.5 L
4 Tbsp	red wine	60 mL
5 lb	leg or stewing lamb, cubed 1 inch (2.5 cm)	2.25 kg
½ tsp	ground coriander	2 mL
⅓ tsp	ground white cardamom	1.5 mL
1 tsp	grated fresh ginger	5 mL
5 tsp	ground cumin	20 mL
3 cloves	garlic, crushed	3 cloves
7½ tsp	ground cinnamon	37 mL
pinch	ground saffron	pinch
½ cup	ground almonds	125 mL
1 Tbsp	balsamic vinegar	15 mL
1½ tsp	salt	7 mL
4 Tbsp	raisins	60 mL

1. In a large frying pan melt butter over medium-high heat. Add onions and sauté until lightly browned. Transfer to a heavy sauce-pan with a lid and cook over very low heat for 4 to 5 hours, until the onions are caramelly brown and sweet and reduced to 2 to 3 cups (500 to 750 mL). Stir occasionally to prevent sticking or burning. Add red wine and set aside.

2. In a large heavy pot stir lamb over medium heat. Add corian-der, cardamom, ginger, cumin, garlic, cinnamon and saffron. Con-tinue stirring as lamb sautés in its own fat. Cook until juices are released from meat. Let meat stew in own juices for about 10 minutes. Increase heat to high and boil for 5 minutes. Lower heat and simmer, uncovered, for 1 hour. When meat is tender, add almonds, vinegar, salt and raisins. Serve with cooked onions spooned on top or stirred into lamb.

Serve Persian Lamb with with sautéd snow peas or sugar peas and steamed rice tossed with butter and cinnamon.

SUGAR PEAS

A sure sign of spring! These sweet plump pea-pods full of tiny peas are best just blanched for a few minutes, buttered and savoured au naturel. Add a bit of chopped fresh mint if you wish.

FRENCH BISTRO BEEF TENDERLOIN

Yields 4 *servings*

Straight from that little bistro in Paris—a silvery packet is delivered to the table and opened with a flourish, releasing a great puff of herb-scented steam and revealing a perfectly cooked roast. The presentation of this dish is so dramatic and the flavour so wondrously rich, it's hard to believe that the preparation is very simple.

5 lb	4-inch (10-cm) long marrow bones	2.25 kg
1 Tbsp	oil	15 mL
2 lb	piece of beef tenderloin	900 g
to taste	salt and pepper	to taste
1 tsp	Herbes de Provence	5 mL

1. Preheat oven to 500°F (260°C), or as high as possible.

2. Bring a large pot of water to a boil. Place the marrow bones in the pot, over medium heat, for 2 to 3 minutes, just long enough to loosen the marrow. Remove and push marrow out of bones, keeping pieces as large as possible. Discard bones and set marrow aside.

3. Heat a large heavy frying pan over high heat until very hot. Add oil. Just as oil begins to smoke, add tenderloin and turn to brown on all sides, approximately 5 minutes. Place tenderloin in the centre of a double piece of heavy aluminum foil about 17 inches × 24 inches (43 cm × 61 cm). Sprinkle liberally with salt and pepper and Herbes de Provence. Place marrow on top. Bring up sides of foil loosely around tenderloin and crimp the top and sides closed to form a tent, leaving a space of at least 2 inches (5 cm) over and around the meat. Roast 15 minutes for very rare, or 20 minutes for medium rare. Open the tent of foil at the table, slide tenderloin onto serving platter and slice. Serve immediately with juices and marrow. Thinly cut French fries are the perfect accompaniment.

PARSNIPS

This much-maligned but marvellous root is one of our favourite vegetables. The secret is not to over-cook as overcooking tends to make them mushy and unpleasant. Here are a few ideas for serving parsnips:

Glazed — Pare and slice diagonally, then steam or boil until tender. In a frying pan melt butter over medium-high heat. Add drained parsnips, a couple of spoons of brown sugar and a sprinkling of dry mustard. Toss in the pan until sugar melts and coats the parsnip slices. Salt to taste.

Bundled — Cut parsnips and carrots into strips about the size of French-fried potatoes. Steam or boil just until fork tender, about 8 minutes. Remove and, using blanched chives, green onions or leeks as ribbon, tie into bundles with 4 or 5 carrot strips and 4 or 5 parsnip strips in each bundle. Sprinkle with melted butter, salt and freshly ground pepper.

Puréed — Steam parsnips until fork tender and pu-rée with apples poached in cider. Add nutmeg, but-ter and salt to taste. Thin purée with a few spoons of whipping cream.

TERISUKI BEEF

Yields 8 servings

We've borrowed from two popular Japanese dishes — teriyaki and sukiyaki — to create this colourful dish.

3 Tbsp	butter	45 mL
1	small onion, sliced	1
1 cup	sliced mushrooms	250 mL
1	red bell pepper, sliced into long ¼-inch (6-mm) strips	1
1 cup	snow peas, tips and strings removed	250 mL
1 cup	sliced canned water chestnuts	250 mL
1 cup	sliced canned bamboo shoots	250 mL
2 cups	sliced deep-fried tofu cakes, ½-inch (1.25-cm) slices	500 mL
4 cups	bean sprouts	1 L
½ cup	Japanese soy sauce	125 mL
1 Tbsp	sherry	15 mL
4 Tbsp	brown sugar	60 mL
½ tsp	crushed garlic	2 mL
1 Tbsp	grated fresh ginger	15 mL
1¼ cups	beef stock	300 mL
2½ lb	sirloin tip or rib-eye beef, sliced very thinly ⅛ inch (3 mm)	1.15 kg
2 oz	cellophane vermicelli noodles soaked in water for 5 minutes, then drained	50 g

1. In a very large frying pan melt butter over high heat. Add onions and sauté for 2 minutes. Add mushrooms, red pepper and snow peas and sauté for another 2 minutes. Add water chestnuts, bamboo shoots, deep-fried tofu and bean sprouts and sauté again for 2 minutes. Remove to a large mixing bowl and set aside.

2. In the same pan combine soy sauce, sherry, brown sugar, garlic, ginger and beef stock. Bring to a boil over high heat. Drop in 4 to 6 pieces of beef, cook for 1 minute and add to vegetable mixture. Repeat until all beef slices have been cooked and added to vegetable mixture. Add well-drained vermicelli to pan and boil for 1 minute, just to heat through. Return vegetable-beef mixture to pan and toss to heat through. Remove to serving platter and serve immediately.

FOR THINLY SLICED BEEF

Ask your butcher to freeze and thinly slice (⅛ inch or 6 cm) a sirloin tip or rib-eye of beef for you. You can buy it already sliced from a store that specializes in Japanese food. Ask for sukiyaki beef.

Japanese soy sauce is a little milder than Chinese soy sauce and lighter in colour.

Bamboo Shoots

PEARL'S CURRIED GOAT

Yields 6 to 8 servings

The warm West Indies gave us Pearl. And Pearl gave us her wonderful curried goat, made in the traditional unhurried way of the Islands. Lamb or beef can be substituted for goat.

5 lb	goat meat, cubed 1 inch (2.5 cm)	2.25 kg
1	large onion, chopped	1
8 Tbsp	medium curry powder	120 mL
2 Tbsp	pepper	30 mL
1 Tbsp	ground dried thyme	15 mL
1 Tbsp	salt	15 mL
½ cup	butter	125 mL
1½ cups	water	375 mL
2	medium-sized potatoes, chopped	2

1. Put goat meat into a large mixing bowl and add chopped onions. Set aside.

2. Blend together curry powder, pepper, thyme and salt. Sprinkle over goat meat and onions. Toss to combine well. Refrigerate for at least 2 hours, or overnight.

3. In a large heavy pot that has a lid melt butter over medium-high heat until bubbling. Add goat mixture and stir well to coat all pieces with butter. Continue cooking, uncovered, for about 10 minutes, stirring frequently. Do not allow onions to brown.

4. Add 1 cup of water and lower heat to medium. Cover and cook for about 20 minutes, stirring occasionally.

5. Add chopped potatoes, turn heat to low, cover and simmer until tender, about 1 hour. Stir occasionally and add more water if necessary. The potatoes will break down and thicken the sauce as they cook. Serve with Rice and Peas or Fried Bakes.

FRIED BAKES

Yields 6 pieces

Our dear friends Dee and Grecia put together this recipe for Fried Bakes. The buttery flat bread is Caribbean in origin and, like Indian chapati, is ideal for wrapping, scooping, and sopping up curries and stews.

3 cups	flour	750 mL
2 tsp	baking powder	10 mL
1 tsp	salt	5 mL
1¼ cups	water	300 mL
2 Tbsp	cooking oil	30 mL
1 Tbsp	melted butter	15 ml

1. Combine flour, baking powder and salt in a medium-sized mixing bowl.

2. Add water, all at once, to dry ingredients. Stir together until incorporated. Remove from bowl and knead until smooth. Form into six 2-inch (5-cm) balls. Let rest 15 mintues.

3. In a small bowl combine oil and butter.

4. Roll out each ball on a well-floured board, as thin as possible (about the thickness of a penny). Spread with butter mixture.

5. Make a slash from the centre to the outer edge of one circle. Form the circle into a cone shape by wrapping it around your hand. Collapse the cone into a flat round by pushing the pointed end into the centre. The shape will resemble an unfilled Danish pastry. Repeat with each circle of dough. Cover and set aside for 20 to 25 minutes.

6. Roll each round to ⅛-inch (3-mm) thickness.

7. Heat heavy frying pan on medium-low setting. Grease lightly and fry each round 2 to 3 minutes on each side.

8. As each round is cooked, toss it lightly into the air, clapping it between your hand several times. This will separate the layers in the bread.

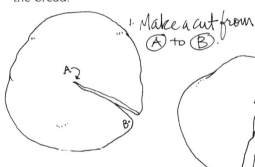

1. Make a cut from Ⓐ to Ⓑ.

2. Pick up dough holding along cut with Ⓐ at fingertips.

3. Wrap into cone-shape around hand with Ⓐ as the tip of the cone

4. Push tip Ⓐ into centre, collapsing cone into a thick, flat round.

RICE AND PEAS

Yields 6 to 8 servings

½ cup	kidney beans or pigeon peas	125 mL
3 cups	cold water	750 mL
1	fresh coconut, shelled and grated	1
3 cups	warm water	750 mL
1	green onion, chopped	1
1	small onion, chopped	1
4 Tbsp	butter	60 mL
½ tsp	ground dried thyme	2 mL
¼ tsp	salt	1 mL
2 cups	long-grain rice	500 mL

1. Wash kidney beans and put in saucepan with 3 cups water. Boil over medium heat for 30 minutes.

2. Place grated coconut in large mixing bowl and pour in half of the warm water. Knead, squeeze out and reserve the liquid: this is the coconut milk. Repeat with remaining warm water. Add coconut milk to beans and cook for an additional 30 minutes. Add green onion, onion, butter, thyme and salt. Stir well and cook for another 30 minutes, stirring occasionally. Add rice, reduce heat and simmer, covered, for 30 minutes or until rice is tender. Serve with curry.

If you have had a long day and don't feel like cracking coconuts, use this shortcut for making coconut milk: Melt a 7-oz/ 198-g bar of coconut cream in a saucepan over medium heat. Remove from heat and, beating constantly, slowly add 2½ cups/625 mL water in a steady stream. This liquid can be substituted for the coconut milk described in step 2.

FRUITED CURRY OF CHICKEN AND SHRIMP

Yields 8 servings

Coconut cream, apples and raisins add their subtle sweetness to a velvety curry of shrimp and chicken.

CURRY ACCOMPANIMENTS

- Toasted coconut
- Toasted almonds
- Sliced bananas
- Kumquats

COCONUT CREAM

Coconut oil sold in solid block form.

2 cups	white wine	500 mL
2 cups	whipping cream	500 mL
1 cup	strong chicken stock	250 mL
4 oz	unsweetened coconut cream	110 g
6 Tbsp	butter	90 mL
1 cup	chopped onions	250 mL
2 Tbsp	flour	30 mL
2 tsp	medium-hot curry	10 mL
1 tsp	ground cinnamon	5 mL
½ tsp	ground cardamom	2 mL
1 tsp	ground cumin	5 mL
½ tsp	ground or freshly grated nutmeg	2 mL
1 Tbsp	grated fresh ginger	15 mL
2 lb	shrimp, shelled (about 50)	1 kg
2	apples, cored and chopped	2
¼ cup	raisins	60 mL
4	whole chicken breasts, cooked, boned, skinned and cubed 1 inch (2.5 cm)	4

1. In a saucepan boil white wine over high heat to reduce volume by one half. Set aside.

2. In a heavy saucepan gently simmer whipping ..eam over medium-low heat until volume is reduced by half. Combine with reduced white wine and set aside. This mixture may be prepared ahead of time and stored in the refrigerator.

3. In a medium-sized saucepan combine reduced wine-cream mixture, chicken stock and coconut cream. Stir over medium-high heat until coconut cream has melted. Remove from heat and set aside.

4. In a Dutch oven or heavy casserole melt 4 Tbsp (60 mL) butter over medium-high heat. Add onions and sauté until translucent, about 5 minutes. Add flour and stir to brown lightly, about 2 minutes. Add curry powder, cinnamon, cardamom, cumin, nutmeg and ginger. Stir over medium heat for 2 minutes. Add coconut-cream mixture and simmer for 20 minutes.

5. In a large frying pan melt remaining 2 Tbsp (30 mL) butter over high heat. Add shrimp and sauté for 2 to 3 minutes, just until they begin to cook. Set aside.

6. Add chopped apples and raisins to simmering curry mixture. Turn up heat to high and bring to a light boil. Add sautéed shrimp and cubed chicken. Reduce heat to medium-low and simmer until shrimp and chicken are warmed through, about 5 minutes. Remove to platter and serve hot with rice and chutney.

LEMON FRIED CHICKEN

Yields 4 to 5 servings

In our tangy version of old-fashioned picnic chicken, matzo meal makes the coating extra crispy.

1	4- to 6-lb (1.75- to 2.75-kg) frying chicken	1
For marinade:		
2	lemons, unpeeled, cut into 1-inch (2.5-cm) pieces	2
1½ tsp	ground dried rosemary	7 mL
6 cloves	garlic, crushed	6 cloves
For coating:		
1 cup	flour	250 mL
1 Tbsp	salt	15 mL
1 Tbsp	pepper	15 mL
3	eggs, beaten	3
2 cups	matzo meal or cracker meal	500 mL
For frying:		
1 cup	olive oil	250 mL

1. Cut up the chicken into serving pieces.

2. In a food processor fitted with a steel blade coarsely chop lemons. Put into a large mixing bowl and add ground rosemary and crushed garlic. Add chicken pieces, combine well and marinate overnight in refrigerator.

3. In large bowl combine flour, salt and pepper. Remove chicken from marinade and shake off excess liquid. Bits of lemon will cling to the chicken. Dredge the pieces in the flour mixture.

4. Dip coated chicken pieces in beaten eggs and roll in matzo meal. Let stand 1 hour, refrigerated.

5. Heat olive oil in a large frying pan. Fry chicken pieces over medium-high heat until golden brown, about 10 to 15 minutes. Remove and drain on rack over paper towels. If pieces are large and not cooked through, finish cooking in a 400°F (200°C) oven for 10 to 15 minutes. Serve either warm or cold.

The key to successful deep frying is correct oil temperature. Hot oil will quickly crisp the outside, creating a wall that keeps the juice and flavour in and the oil out. Oil that is not hot enough will soak into the food before the wall has been formed. The ideal temperature varies according to the type of food being cooked, but 375°F (190°C) is a good rule of thumb. It is important to try to maintain this temperature while cooking.

A few hints:
Fry only a few pieces at a time because the addition of the food lowers the temperature of the oil.
Don't fry food straight from the refrigerator. Room temperature food will affect the oil's temperature less.
When removing the cooked food, use a utensil that will not draw off too much heat. Wooden tongs are a better choice than a large metal slotted ladle. Allow the oil to return to cooking temperature before adding another batch.

LEMON CHICKEN STUFFED WITH SPINACH

Yields 8 to 12 servings

Lemon-scented chicken breasts are plumped with a stuffing of mushrooms and spinach, then roasted to tender perfection.

8	whole chicken breasts	8
For marinade:		
5 cloves	garlic, crushed	5 cloves
1 Tbsp	grated lemon rind (about 2 lemons)	15 mL
½ cup	freshly squeezed lemon juice	125 mL
2 Tbsp	light soy sauce	30 mL
½ tsp	pepper	2 mL
For stuffing:		
3	10-oz (284-g) bags spinach, well washed and trimmed	3
½ cup	butter	125 mL
3 lb	mushrooms, cleaned and sliced	1.4 kg
12 cloves	garlic, crushed	12 cloves
2½ tsp	salt	12 mL
1½ tsp	pepper	7 mL
1½ cups	dry breadcrumbs	375 mL
16	lemon slices	16

1. Cut breasts in half along the breastbone and remove bone but leave skin attached to meat. In each piece cut pocket for stuffing by making a slit from the top as large as possible without piercing the sides, as diagrammed. Set aside.

2. Make marinade by combining crushed garlic, lemon rind, lemon juice, soy sauce and pepper in a large mixing bowl. Mix together and add chicken. Marinate overnight in refrigerator.

3. In a pot of boiling water blanch spinach for 10 seconds, drain and squeeze very dry in a piece of cheesecloth. Set aside.

4. In a large frying pan melt butter over high heat. Add mushrooms and sauté, stirring constantly until all juices have evaporated, about 5 to 8 minutes. (Do not use a non-stick pan because the coating will prevent juices from evaporating.) Add garlic, salt and pepper. Sauté for one minute. Remove to cool.

5. In a food processor fitted with steel blade process half the spinach by pulsing on/off a few times. Add half the cooled mushroom mixture and pulse on/off a few times. Add half of the breadcrumbs and pulse on/off a few times. Remove mixture from workbowl and repeat with remaining half of spinach, mushrooms, and breadcrumbs. Mixture should be finely chopped but not puréed.

6. Preheat oven to 450°F (230°C).

7. Remove chicken from marinade and discard marinade. Divide the stuffing into sixteen portions and spoon one portion into

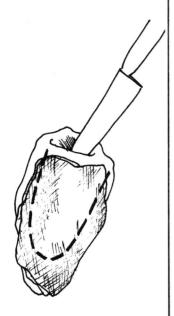

FIDDLEHEADS

We remember spring so-journs down country roads to search out the first shoots of woodland ferns — called fiddleheads because the tightly curled baby fronds resemble the head of a fiddle. The morning of gathering would yield a precious basketful and we would travel back to the city anticipating the evening meal.

Now, fiddleheads are available fresh at the market during their short season, and frozen — retaining a respectable degree of flavour and texture — throughout the year. And even though they are more easily available now, we still treasure every bite when buttered, steamed fiddleheads come to our table.

the pocket of each piece of chicken. Tuck ends into pocket to keep stuffing in, as diagrammed. Sprinkle with salt and pepper. Place on roasting pan. Top each piece with a slice of lemon and roast for 12 to 15 minutes.

CHICKEN-ARTICHOKE CASSEROLE

Yields 8 to 10 servings

A splash of lemon awakens the gentle flavours of chicken and artichoke — a glorious combination.

12 lb	chicken breasts	5.5 kg
4 to 5 cups	strong chicken stock	1 to 1.25 L
⅓ cup	butter	75 mL
½ cup	flour	125 mL
½ cup	white wine	125 mL
¼ to ⅓ cup	lemon juice	60 to 75 mL
1 tsp	grated lemon rind	5 mL
to taste	salt and pepper	to taste
2 Tbsp	whipping cream	30 mL
1	14-oz (398-mL) can artichoke hearts, drained and quartered	1
For topping:		
½ cup	melted butter	125 mL
2 cups	dry breadcrumbs	500 mL
8 cloves	garlic, finely minced	8 cloves
to taste	salt	to taste

PARMESAN PLUS

Optional for cheese lovers: Add ¼ cup (60 mL) freshly grated Parmesan cheese to topping ingredients.

1. Preheat oven to 400°F (200°C).

2. Cut whole chicken breasts in half and place in a single layer, skin side up, in two roasting pans. Add 1 cup chicken broth to each pan and cover tightly with foil. Poach in oven for 20 to 25 minutes, or until just slightly undercooked. Cool chicken completely, remove from bones, and cut into 1-inch (2.5-cm) cubes. Strain cooking stock into large measuring cup and add chicken stock to make 3 cups (750 mL). Reserve.

3. In a large frying pan melt butter. Add flour and stir over medium heat for 2 to 3 minutes, or until straw-coloured. Add reserved stock, white wine, lemon juice (amount required depends on sourness of the lemons) and grated lemon rind. Add salt and pepper to taste. Whisk over medium heat until thickened. Stir in whipping cream. Add artichoke hearts and cubed chicken. Pour into 9-inch × 12-inch (23-cm × 30-cm) shallow casserole.

4. To prepare topping, combine melted butter, breadcrumbs and garlic in a small mixing bowl. Mix thoroughly. Sprinkle over chicken mixture. Bake 20 minutes, just until bubbly and chicken has warmed through.

ORIENTAL FRIED CHICKEN

Yields 4 servings

Crispy chicken scented with Oriental flavours of sesame, ginger and garlic.

1	3- to 4-lb (1.5- to 1.75-kg) chicken	1
For marinade:		
1½ tsp	grated fresh ginger	7 mL
8 cloves	garlic, crushed	8 cloves
1 Tbsp	sesame oil	15 mL
1 tsp	white vinegar	5 mL
2½ Tbsp	soy sauce	37 mL
For frying:		
2	egg whites	2
4 Tbsp	cornstarch	60 mL
1½ cups	oil for deep frying	375 mL

1. Cut chicken into serving pieces and set aside.

2. In a large mixing bowl combine all ingredients for marinade. Add chicken pieces and toss well to coat. Marinate, refrigerated, for at least 2 hours. Turn occasionally for even marination.

3. In a small mixing bowl lightly beat egg whites until frothy. Pour over chicken and marinade, mixing well to coat each piece. Sprinkle on cornstarch and rub into all pieces to coat well with the paste that forms.

4. In a large heavy frying pan heat oil for deep frying to 375°F (190°C) over medium-high heat. Lower a few pieces of chicken, skin side down, into the oil. Fry for 5 to 7 minutes then turn over and fry other side for 5 to 7 minutes, or until golden brown. Remove to drain on rack over paper towels. Repeat until all chicken is cooked. Delicious served hot or at room temperature.

WALNUT CHICKEN

Yields 6 to 8 servings

Spiced walnuts tossed with peas and peppers are served over sautéd chicken.

7 lb	chicken breasts	3 kg
3 Tbsp	sherry	45 mL
1 Tbsp	soy sauce	15 mL
2 cups	walnut halves	500 mL
¾ cup	sugar	175 mL
½ tsp	Chinese five-spice	2 mL
3 to 4 cups	oil for deep frying	0.75 to 1 L
For sautéing:		
7 Tbsp	corn starch	105 mL
1½ tsp	salt	7 mL

In the summer, the store is busy with orders for picnics. Little romantic grapevine baskets for two. Great oversized hampers brimming with food for eight. It's a wonderful time of year when everyone delights in a picnic, whether in the countryside, at the beach, or in the back of a limousine.

A FAMILY OUTING

Pâté Maison

A Cheese Assortment

Crackers or Baguettes

Primavera Pasta with Lemons

Fried Chicken

Butter Tarts

Chocolate Cake

½ tsp	pepper	2 mL
4 Tbsp	vegetable oil	60 mL
½ cup	butter	125 mL
3 cups	strong chicken stock	750 mL
3 Tbsp	grated fresh ginger	45 mL
2 cloves	garlic, crushed	2 cloves
⅓ cup	sherry	75 mL
1 Tbsp	soy sauce	15 mL
3 Tbsp	spicy soy sauce	45 mL
2 Tbsp	rice vinegar	30 mL
to taste	salt and pepper	to taste
½ lb	snow peas, tips and strings removed (about 2 cups/500 mL)	230 g
2 cups	sliced red bell peppers	500 mL

1. Skin and bone chickens. Cut meat into strips about ½ inch × ½ inch × 3 inches (1.25 cm × 1.25 cm × 8 cm). In a large mixing bowl mix together sherry and soy sauce and add chicken pieces. Toss to coat well and marinate at least 1 hour.

2. In a pot of boiling water blanch walnut halves for 2 to 3 minutes. Drain and set aside in mixing bowl. In a small bowl combine sugar and Chinese five-spice, then add to hot walnuts. Toss to coat well.

3. Heat oil for deep frying to 375°F (190°C) in a heavy sauce-pan over medium-high heat, or in deep fryer. Line a baking sheet with a brown bag. (Nuts will stick to paper towels.) Deep fry a quarter of the nuts at a time, until golden brown. Set aside to drain on prepared baking sheet.

4. In a small bowl mix together 5 Tbsp (75 mL) of the corn starch, 1½ tsp (7 mL) salt and ½ tsp (2 mL) pepper. Sprinkle over chicken, mixing well to coat each piece with the paste that forms.

5. In a heavy frying pan melt together about 1 Tbsp (15 mL) each of oil and butter. Over high heat sauté a quarter of the chicken until just undercooked, about 2 to 3 minutes. Toss constantly to brown all sides. Remove to foil roasting pan or large Dutch oven and keep warm in oven. Repeat with remaining chicken.

6. In a medium-sized saucepan combine chicken stock, ginger, garlic, sherry, soy sauce, spicy soy sauce, vinegar and remaining corn starch. Stir well to blend corn starch completely into the liquid. Bring to boil over high heat, then continue cooking for 2 to 3 minutes until mixture has thickened. Season to taste with salt and pepper. Reduce heat and keep just warm.

7. In a frying pan melt 2 Tbsp (30 mL) butter over medium-high heat. Add snow peas and sauté for 2 to 3 minutes. Season to taste with salt and pepper. Texture should still be crispy. Remove from pan and set aside. Melt remaining butter in frying pan. Add red peppers and sauté for 2 to 3 minutes. Season to taste with salt and pepper.

8. Combine chicken, snow peas and red peppers. Place on serving platter and pour sauce over all. Top with walnuts. Serve hot.

SPICY SOY SAUCE

If you can't get spicy soy sauce, use ordinary soy sauce and add a pinch of Chinese five-spice.

STRONG CHICKEN STOCK

Yields 7 cups (1.75 L)

Many of our recipes call for strong chicken stock. It gives an extra boost of flavour to many dishes.

7 lb/3 kg
  chicken bones
7 quarts/7 L
  cold water

1. **Put chicken bones into a large pot and cover with water. Bring to boil over high heat, then immediately lower heat and simmer for 4 to 6 hours. Remove from heat and strain out bones. Strain stock again through cheese-cloth. Return to pot and simmer over low heat until stock is reduced to one-quarter of the original volume.**

ROAST PARTRIDGE WITH RED CABBAGE

Yields 6 servings

These little game birds are filled with a stuffing of wild rice, pine nuts and chanterelles and served in ``nests`` of brandied red cabbage and apples.

For port sauce:

1 cup	red currant jelly	250 mL
½ cup	orange juice	125 mL
½ cup	raisins	125 mL
4 Tbsp	lemon juice	60 mL
4 Tbsp	port	60 mL
2 Tbsp	grated orange rind	30 mL
1 Tbsp	grated lemon rind	15 mL
1 tsp	dry mustard	5 mL
pinch	ground ginger	pinch

For stuffing:

1 cup	wild rice	250 mL
1 ½ cups	water	375 mL
1 Tbsp	butter	15 mL
½ lb	chanterelles or other mushrooms, cleaned and diced ½ inch (1.25 cm)	227 g
to taste	salt and pepper	to taste
⅓ cup	roasted pine nuts	75 mL

For nests:

3 Tbsp	olive oil	45 mL
1	medium-sized red cabbage, shredded	1
½	medium-sized onion, sliced	½
3	unpeeled apples, julienned	3
to taste	salt and pepper	to taste
2 Tbsp	Calvados or brandy	30 mL

To assemble:

6	partridges	6
to taste	salt and pepper	to taste
1 ¼ lb	pork fat, cut into thin slices	560 g
to dust	flour	to dust

1. Make port sauce the day before or at least 6 hours ahead. In a medium-sized saucepan combine jelly, orange juice, raisins, lemon juice, port, orange rind, lemon rind, mustard and ginger. Simmer for 3 minutes. Remove from heat and set aside.

2. For stuffing, wash wild rice in several changes of cold water to remove any foreign particles. Drain well and add to a medium-sized saucepan with a lid. Add water and bring to boil. Cover, reduce heat to low and simmer for 35 minutes, or until rice is tender.

3. In a frying pan melt butter over medium-high heat and sauté mushrooms 2 to 3 minutes.

CHANTERELLES

Bright golden yellow in colour with funnel-shaped caps. Has a wonderfully warm, fruity flavour when fresh. The flavour of freeze-dried chanterelles is almost better than fresh, but the texture is a bit spongy.

4. Add mushrooms to rice. Season to taste with salt and pepper. Cool. Add pine nuts.

5. For "nests," heat olive oil in a large frying pan over medium heat. Add cabbage, onions and apples and sauté 20 minutes, or until softened. Remove from heat. Season with salt and pepper and stir in Calvados and port sauce. Place in roasting pan large enough to hold partridges. Set aside.

6. Wipe partridges dry with paper towels. Season cavities with salt and pepper. Between skin and breast meat of each bird insert a small piece of pork fat (or 2 pieces, one on each side of breast bone).

7. Divide stuffing into 6 equal portions and stuff the partridges. Close cavity by sewing with heavy thread or skewering with a toothpick.

8. Preheat broiler.

9. Dust partridges lightly with flour and season with salt and pepper. Broil 5 minutes per side, or until browned. Remove from oven.

10. Preheat oven to 375°F (190°C).

11. Place half of the remaining slices of pork fat on top of cabbage mixture in roasting pan. Place partridges on cabbage, breast side down. Place remaining slices of pork fat on birds. Roast for 15 minutes, then turn over and cook an additional 10 to 15 minutes.

12. To serve, place partridges on a "nest" of cabbage.

FRENCH BEANS

Blanch for 2 or 3 minutes in boiling water and enjoy with a light vinaigrette or with a drizzle of lemon juice, melted butter and chopped fresh herbs. Long and thin, these wonderful beans are an elegant alternative to green beans and wax beans.

ZUCCHINI

Tasty and versatile, zucchini can be steamed, stir fried, breaded and deep fried, stewed with tomatoes, chopped and added to potato pancake batter, grated into zucchini bread, or eaten raw with dip, just to name a few ways.

Zucchini blossoms are absolutely delightful deep fried in a light batter.

FRUIT-STUFFED TURKEY MILLEFEUILLE

Yields 20 servings

A harvest of fruits and nuts are spiked and spiced, then rolled into whole, boned turkey. A golden wrap of puff pastry completes the tender package.

1 lb	dried apricots, diced	450 g
1 lb	dried dates, diced	450 g
1 lb	dried prunes, diced	450 g
2 cups	brandy	500 mL
1½ cups	Triple Sec	375 mL
½ lb	candied ginger, diced	225 g
4	cooking apples, pared, cored and chopped	4
1 cup	walnut pieces, lightly toasted	250 mL
2	10-lb (4.5-kg) turkeys	2
6 Tbsp	butter, softened	90 mL
2 tsp	salt	10 mL
1 tsp	pepper	5 mL
4 lb	puff pastry	1.8 kg
1	egg, lightly beaten	1

1. For stuffing, combine dried apricots, dates, prunes, brandy and Triple Sec in a large mixing bowl. Allow to soak for 24 hours. Mix in ginger, apples and walnuts.

2. To bone turkeys, cut off wings at joint and slit the skin along the back bone. With a boning knife or small paring knife, carefully scrape meat away from bones. For more detailed boning instructions, see page 76.

3. Preheat oven to 425°F (220°C).

4. Spread out each boned turkey, skin side down, and rub with butter. Sprinkle with salt and pepper. Spread half of the stuffing on each turkey. Roll up each one, starting from the tail end and rolling towards the neck end. When completely rolled, tie securely with butcher's string. Place on roasting pan, leaving adequate space between rolls for circulation of heat. Roast for 1 hour and 15 minutes. Let cool completely. If you wish, turkeys can be prepared to this stage the day before serving and kept in the refrigerator.

5. Preheat oven to 400°F (200°C).

6. For each rolled turkey, roll out 2 lb (900 g) of pastry to a thickness of ¼ inch (6 mm) and large enough to wrap turkey. Cover from the top and tuck ends underneath, sealing with beaten egg. With leftover pastry, cut out appliqués to decorate the rolls. Place on baking sheet. Prick all over with fork.

7. Brush entire roll with beaten egg. Bake for 30 minutes, or until golden brown. May be served hot or cold with Red Currant Sauce.

RED CURRANT SAUCE

2 cups/500 mL
  red currant jelly
¾ cup/175 mL
  frozen orange juice concentrate, undiluted
¾ cup/175 mL
  brandy
¾ cup/175 mL
  balsamic vinegar
  or ½ cup (125 mL)
  red wine vinegar

1. Melt all ingredients together in a small saucepan over medium-high heat. Serve warm.

CHRISTMAS DINNER

Shrimp Rolls
Raw Oysters on Half Shells

Fruit-Stuffed Turkey Millefeuille
Fan Potatoes
Oriental Vegetable Salad

Eggnog Applemince Pie

RAGOUT OF DUCK

Yields 10 to 12 servings

Beautifully glazed slices of boneless duck garnished with poached pear make a perfect dish for a buffet.

3	ducks	3
9 Tbsp	brown sugar	135 mL
⅝ tsp	ground cinnamon	3 mL
10 Tbsp	white wine vinegar	150 mL
3	Bosc or other cooking pears	3
1 tsp	lemon juice or vinegar	5 mL

1. Cut up each duck into pieces — breasts, thighs and legs. Set aside. Cut up remaining bones and put into stock pot. Cover with water and bring to boil over high heat. Lower heat and simmer for 1½ to 2 hours. Strain, remove fat and return stock to medium-high heat. Reduce until stock is quite concentrated, to about 1 to 2 cups (250 to 500 mL). Measure out ¾ cup (175 mL) for use in glaze and poaching liquid. The balance can be frozen for use at another time.

2. With a fork prick skin of meat all over. In a frying pan fry 2 or 3 pieces of duck over high heat until golden brown on one side, about 5 to 6 minutes. Turn and fry other side for 5 minutes, pricking skin again to release as much fat as possible. Drain off fat as necessary. Remove duck and repeat with remaining pieces. Meat should be medium rare. Drain off fat.

3. To make glaze, reduce heat to medium-high and add 8 Tbsp (120 mL) sugar to frying pan. Cook until melted, stirring and watching carefully, as sugar burns easily. Add 8 Tbsp (120 mL) wine vinegar and bring to boil. Sprinkle in ½ tsp (2 mL) cinnamon and stir out any lumps. Add fried duck, a few pieces at a time, and turn over once or twice to coat well with glaze. Remove and repeat with remaining duck. If glaze becomes too thick, add a little duck stock as required. When all the pieces of duck have been glazed, remove pan from heat and set aside.

4. Allow duck to cool completely, then remove bones. Slice meat about ¼ inch (6 mm) thick, cutting diagonally across the grain. Discard bits of excess fat and skin. Arrange slices, skin side up, in a large attractive baking dish, alternating rows of breast meat with rows of leg and thigh meat. Set aside.

5. Preheat oven to 350°F (180°C).

6. Peel pears and cut into quarters, removing cores. Brush with lemon juice to keep from discolouring.

7. Reheat frying pan containing glaze over medium-high heat. Add remaining duck stock, wine vinegar, brown sugar and cinnamon. Bring to boil. Add pear quarters and poach about 5 minutes, until cooked but still crisp. Remove and cool just enough to handle. Starting at the bottom of the pear, make 3 or 4 cuts towards the stem end but stop about ¼ inch (6 mm) from the top. Spread out the slices to resemble a fan. Arrange pear fans on sliced duck and pour remaining glaze over top. Bake for 20 to 30 minutes, just to heat through. Do not overcook or meat will become tough. Serve immediately.

Serve Ragout of Duck with Wild Rice with Pine Nuts and steamed asparagus spears or assorted baby vegetables.

BABY VEGETABLES

There are few things more disarming and precious than babies: baby girls, baby birds, puppies ... and, yes, even baby vegetables. We see them popping out on the vegetable stands in springtime, and we are charmed by them. Tiny carrots, little golden beets, baby sugar peas, new potatoes, French beans. Like other babies, they are sweet, tender and fleeting. They soon grow up to be big and demanding, so enjoy them when you can — just barely cooked and very lightly seasoned.

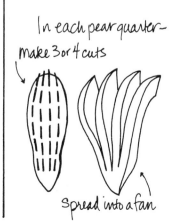

In each pear quarter—
make 3 or 4 cuts

Spread into a fan

ARTICHOKES

Globe artichokes are terrific to serve when you are entertaining as they can be served at room temperature. Trim and steam them ahead of time and make the accompanying vinaigrette dip well in advance. Be sure to trim off the tops of the outer leaves, which are tipped with sharp thorns.

Baby artichokes are available in spring and fall and can be fried and eaten whole because the leaves are very tender. Or poach them whole, just until tender, in a mixture of white wine, olive oil and rosemary. Delicious!

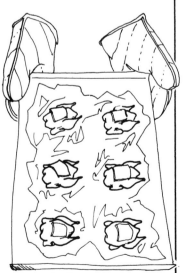

crumple the foil around the birds to keep them upright

QUAILS STUFFED WITH SWEETBREADS

Yields 6 first-course or 3 main-course servings

These tiny, succulent birds are roasted to perfection with a savoury stuffing of herbed sweetbreads and mushrooms.

1 lb	veal sweetbreads	450 g
4 Tbsp	butter	60 mL
1 cup	diced onions	250 mL
1 cup	diced celery	250 mL
4 oz	mushrooms, diced	110 g
1 tsp	fresh thyme *or* ¼ tsp (1 mL) dried thyme	5 mL
1 tsp	chopped green onions	5 mL
1 Tbsp	dry red wine	15 mL
1 Tbsp	demi-glace (page 27)	15 mL
pinch	ground or freshly grated nutmeg	pinch
to taste	salt and pepper	to taste
6	quails	6
10 oz	pork fat, thinly sliced into pieces 1 inch × 2 inches (2.5 cm × 5 cm)	280 g
6	6-inch (15-cm) lengths of butcher's string	6

1. Soak sweetbreads overnight in water. Drain and rinse under cold water until water runs clear. In a medium-sized saucepan cover sweetbreads with cold water. Bring to boil over high heat, reduce heat and simmer for 15 minutes. Drain and rinse in cold water to stop the cooking. Wrap sweetbreads in several layers of paper towels and place between two plates. Put a weight (such as a brick or a few heavy cans) on top to press out excess moisture, and let sit for at least 1 hour or as long as overnight. Peel away membrane and connective tissue. Chop coarsely and set aside.

2. Preheat oven to 450°F (230°C). On a baking sheet crumple a large sheet of aluminum foil to form 6 evenly spaced shallow "nests" on which to place each stuffed quail. This will keep the birds upright during roasting and ensure even browning.

3. In a large frying pan melt butter over medium-high heat. Add onions and sauté for 2 minutes. Add celery and sauté for an additional 2 minutes. Add mushrooms and sauté, stirring constantly until juices have evaporated and mixture is fairly dry. Add chopped sweetbreads, thyme, green onions, red wine, demi-glace, nutmeg, salt and pepper. Stir together and remove from heat. Cool mixture before stuffing the birds.

4. Pat quails dry, inside and out, with paper towels. Sprinkle salt and pepper inside and out. Divide stuffing into 6 equal portions and stuff one portion into the cavity of each bird. Thread a toothpick through cavity opening to hold stuffing in place. Tie the legs of each bird together with a length of butcher's string. Place stuffed quails on prepared baking sheet. Top each breast with a slice of pork fat. Bake for 15 to 20 minutes, or until browned. Before serving, remove toothpicks, string and pork fat.

PORK CHOPS WITH CLAMS

Yields 4 servings

A hearty dish, Portuguese in spirit, that combines pork and shellfish in a most inspired way. Terrific teamed with fried potatoes and watercress.

4	1-inch (2.5-cm) thick pork chops or pork steaks	4
1 Tbsp	flour	15 mL
1 Tbsp	olive oil	15 mL
1 cup	sliced onions	250 mL
pinch	salt	pinch
½ tsp	pepper	2 mL
8 cloves	garlic, crushed	8 cloves
½ cup	white wine	125 mL
2 lb	clams, well cleaned	900 g
4 Tbsp	chopped fresh parsley or green onions	60 mL

1. Dredge pork chops with flour and set aside.

2. In a large frying pan with a lid, heat oil over high heat. Add pork chops and brown on both sides. Add onions and fry for 2 minutes. Add salt, pepper, garlic and wine. Take care not to add too much salt; clams have a natural saltiness. Reduce heat to low, cover and simmer until tender, about 45 minutes. In the last 10 to 15 minutes of cooking, add the clams, cover and cook until clams open. Remove to serving dish and sprinkle liberally with chopped parsley or chopped green onions.

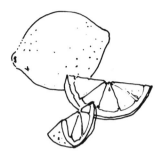

LEMON FRIED POTATOES

Yields 4 servings

1½ lb/675 g
    new potatoes

3 Tbsp/45 mL
    butter

2 Tbsp/30 mL
    olive oil

3 Tbsp/45 mL
    lemon juice

to taste
    salt and pepper

1. Wash potatoes and slice into ¼-inch (6-mm) thick rounds.

2. In a large frying pan melt butter with olive oil over medium-high heat. Add potatoes and fry, turning frequently, for about 15 minutes, or until all slices are tender and have browned. Sprinkle with lemon juice, salt and pepper and shake pan to distribute seasonings. Serve immediately.

KINGFISH WITH PICKLED ONIONS

Yields 6 to 8 servings

Thick-cut steaks of fish smothered in glazed onions make a great summer or picnic dish. Kingfish has a wonderfully meaty texture, but any firm fish can be prepared in this style.

Thick-cut steaks of halibut can be prepared in this style. Or lotte, also known as monkfish, whose flavour and texture are often compared to lobster.

4 lb	kingfish, cut into 1-inch (2.5-cm) steaks	1.8 kg
1½ tsp	salt	7 mL
1 Tbsp	pepper	15 mL
2 to 3 cups	vegetable oil (or enough for 1-inch/2.5-cm depth in frying pan)	500 to 750 mL
8 cups	sliced Spanish onions	2 L
1⅓ cups	white vinegar	325 mL
4 tsp	sugar	20 mL
1 tsp	salt	5 mL

1. Liberally sprinkle fish fillets with salt and pepper, adding more to taste, if desired. The fish should taste peppery.

2. Pour oil into large heavy frying pan to a depth of 1 inch (2.5 cm) and heat to 375°F (190°C). Gently lower fish steaks into oil, placing them in a single layer. Fry until crispy and browned on the outside, about 10 minutes. Only fry as many at a time as frying pan will accommodate without crowding. Allow oil to return to 375°F (190°C) between fryings. Remove fish to serving platter and arrange in a single layer.

3. Remove all but 4 Tbsp (60 mL) of oil from frying pan. Add onions to pan and sauté over high heat for 5 minutes. Add vinegar, sugar and salt and bring to boil. Lower heat to medium and cook until onions are translucent but still crisp, about 5 to 10 minutes. Adjust seasonings, if necessary, by adding more vinegar, sugar, salt or pepper. The taste should be slightly more sour than sweet, and not too overpowering. Remove from heat and pour over fish. This dish is equally good served warm, at room temperature, or snitched cold from the fridge as a midnight snack.

Fresh fish is firm and plump. The flesh springs back to the touch and the gills are tinged with bright red.
Sunken and cloudy eyes are a sign that the fish is not fresh.

SALMON EN CROÛTE

Yields 6 to 8 servings

Tender, herbed salmon beautifully wrapped in wine pastry. Follow the easy step-by-step directions for decorating the pastry and you'll have a show-stopping dish that looks as exceptional as it tastes.

2½ lb	**side of boneless salmon**	1.15 kg
2 Tbsp	**lemon juice**	30 mL
4 Tbsp	**olive oil**	60 mL
1 tsp	**salt**	4 mL
1	**10-oz (284-g) bag spinach, well washed and trimmed**	1
1 cup	**fresh parsley, washed and stems removed**	250 mL
1 cup	**fresh dill weed, washed and stems removed**	250 mL
1 recipe	**wine pastry (see page 133)**	1 recipe
1	**egg, lightly beaten**	1

1. Remove any bones from salmon. Place in a shallow dish and sprinkle with lemon juice, olive oil and ½ tsp (2 mL) salt. Allow to marinate, refrigerated, for 30 to 60 minutes.

2. Preheat oven to 425°F (220°C). Line a baking sheet with parchment.

3. In a large pot of boiling water blanch spinach for 10 seconds. Remove from water, drain and squeeze very dry in a piece of cheesecloth; there should be about 4 oz (110 g) after squeezing.

4. In a food processor fitted with a steel blade process parsley, dill, blanched spinach and ½ tsp (2 mL) salt until finely chopped. Remove to a piece of cheesecloth and squeeze out excess moisture. Set aside.

5. Roll out pastry and cut into shapes as diagrammed: (a) bottom body and tail, (b) top body and tail, (c) scales — about 3 to 4 dozen, (d) upper fin, (e) lower fin, (f) eye, (g) mouth, (h) gill cover.

6. Place (a) pastry for bottom body on prepared baking sheet. Sprinkle chopped spinach mixture on pastry to within 1 inch (2.5 cm) of edge, with none on the tail. Top with salmon, cutting or folding salmon to conform to the shape of the pastry. Brush edge of pastry with egg. Place the (b) top body piece over salmon and crimp edge to seal well. Cut a gill-shaped slit in the gill area of the body to allow steam to escape. Brush the pastry body with egg and apply the (d) upper fin, (e) lower fin, (f) eye, (g) mouth and (h) gill cover. Place the (c) scales, starting from the tail end, overlapping the rows, and ending at the gill. Brush scales with egg and bake for 20 to 22 minutes, taking care to not overbake. Let stand at least 10 minutes before serving. This dish is also very good served at room temperature. Serve with hollandaise or dill cucumber mayonnaise.

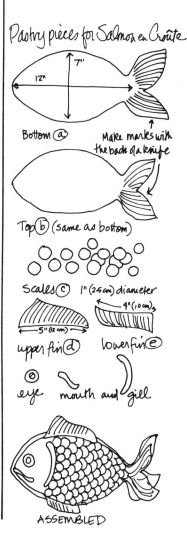

Pastry pieces for Salmon en Croûte

7"
12"
Bottom (a)
Make marks with the back of a knife

Top (b) (same as bottom)

Scales (c) 1" (2.5 cm) diameter
4" (10 cm)
5" (12 cm)
upper fin (d)   lower fin (e)

eye   mouth   and   gill

ASSEMBLED

COULIBIAC OF FRESH LOBSTER AND SALMON

Yields 15 servings

The plump brioche conceals layers of pink decadence . . . lobster cloaked in a cheesy wine sauce and salmon dressed with rice. An extravagant dish perfect for a gathering of very special friends.

For cheese sauce:

6 Tbsp	butter	90 mL
6 Tbsp	flour	90 mL
3 cups	table cream (18%)	750 mL
1 cup	grated Gruyère cheese (about ¼ lb/110 g)	250 mL
¾ cup	white wine	175 mL
1 tsp	ground or freshly grated nutmeg	5 mL
to taste	salt and pepper	to taste

For rice mixture:

¾ cup	parboiled rice cooked in 1 cup (250 mL) water	175 mL
3	eggs, hard-boiled and diced ¼ inch (6 mm)	3
⅓ cup	finely chopped green onions	75 mL

For filling:

9	1½-lb (675-g) lobsters, cooked, shelled and diced ½ inch (1.25 cm)	9
4 Tbsp	fresh tarragon *or* 1 Tbsp (15 mL) dried tarragon	60 mL
4 Tbsp	chopped fresh dill weed *or* 1 Tbsp (15 mL) dried dill	60 mL
4 Tbsp	chopped fresh parsley *or* 1 Tbsp (15 mL) dried parsley	60 mL
3 lb	salmon fillets, sliced diagonally, ⅛ inch (3 mm), as one would slice smoked salmon	1.4 kg
to taste	salt and pepper	to taste

For brioche:

1½ pkg	dry active yeast	1½ pkg
3 Tbsp	warm water	45 mL
3 Tbsp	sugar	45 mL
¾ tsp	salt	3 mL
3 Tbsp	butter, melted and cooled	45 mL
9 Tbsp	milk	140 mL
3	eggs, lightly beaten	3
2½ cups	flour	625 mL

Parboiled rice, such as Uncle Ben's Converted, is ideal for this dish. The grains stay perfectly shaped and separate and will absorb a lot of liquid without becoming mushy.

1. To make cheese sauce, melt butter in a small heavy saucepan over medium heat. Whisk in flour and brown lightly. Slowly add cream, whisking continuously. Still whisking, bring mixture to a light boil. It will be thick at this point. Turn off heat. Stir in cheese until melted. Add wine, nutmeg, salt and pepper. Whisk until smooth and well blended. Set aside.

2. In a mixing bowl combine cooked rice, diced eggs, green onions and ¾ cup (175 mL) of cheese sauce.

3. In another bowl mix diced lobster and herbs with remaining cheese sauce.

4. Lightly butter a 9-inch × 12-inch (23-cm × 30-cm) shallow baking dish. Spread the rice and egg mixture in an even layer on the bottom. Then, layer on half of the salmon slices and season with a little salt and pepper. On top of that, spread the lobster mixture. Finish with the remaining salmon slices, seasoned with a little salt and pepper. (The dish can be refrigerated at this point, to be finished as much as a day later. Remove from the refrigerator 2 hours before baking.)

5. Preheat oven to 400°F (200°C).

6. For brioche, dissolve yeast in warm water sprinkled with sugar. Mix in salt, butter, milk, eggs and 1½ cups of flour. Beat with electric beater on low speed to blend ingredients. Increase beater speed to medium and beat for 2 minutes. Add remaining flour. Beat until smooth and let rise in a warm place for ½ to 1 hour, or until doubled in bulk. Stir down with a spoon and pour over casserole, spreading gently to cover filling. Let stand, uncovered, for 10 minutes.

7. Bake for 30 to 45 minutes, or until top is golden brown and filling is heated through. After removing from the oven, brush the crust with melted butter, if you wish. The coulibiac is a great dish for a buffet, since it will retain its own heat for a long time, and is good at room temperature as well. Serve with Herb and Lemon Sauce.

HERB AND LEMON SAUCE

2 cups/500 mL
   whipping cream

4 Tbsp/60 mL
   butter

6 Tbsp/90 mL
   lemon juice

5 Tbsp/75 mL
   chopped mixed fresh herbs, such as tarragon, parsley, dill and chives, or 4 tsp (20 mL) dried herbs
to taste
   salt and cayenne

1. In a small heavy saucepan scald cream; do not let cream boil. Add remaining ingredients, then remove from heat.

A large scallop shell makes an unusual container for the lemon sauce. Put the shell on a small plate and place wads of wet paper towels around the base of the shell to hold it steady. Conceal the paper towels with a leafy ring of parsley. Rest small glass or silver ladle on the side.

Flowers cut from red and green peppers complement the rich colours of paella.

Or surround the pan with clusters of fresh-cut sunflowers, black-eyed susans and asters of golden hues.

Parboiled rice, such as Uncle Ben's Converted, is ideal for this dish. The grains stay perfectly shaped and separate and will absorb a lot of liquid without becoming mushy.

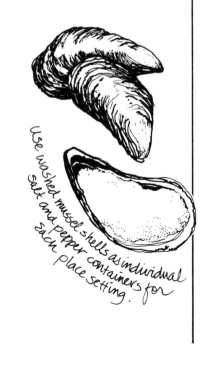

Use washed mussel shells as individual salt and pepper containers for each place setting.

DINAH'S PAELLA

Yields 6 to 8 servings

In our version of this Spanish favourite, the ingredients are seasoned and cooked separately to enhance the individual flavours.

For marinade:

4 Tbsp	olive oil	60 mL
2 Tbsp	lemon juice	30 mL
2 cloves	garlic, crushed	2 cloves
½ lb	shrimp, shelled and cleaned	225 g
½ lb	scallops	225 g
1 cup	parboiled rice	250 mL
1½ cups	extra-strong chicken stock	375 mL
2	large tomatoes, coarsely chopped	2
4	green onions, chopped	4
¼ tsp	crushed saffron	1 mL
2 cloves	garlic, crushed	2 cloves
2 tsp	ground cumin	10 mL
1 Tbsp	olive oil	15 mL
1 Tbsp	butter	15 mL
to taste	cayenne and salt	to taste
1 cup	white wine	250 mL
1 lb	mussels in the shell, scrubbed clean	450 g
1 lb	clams in the shell, scrubbed clean	450 g

For sautéing:

1 Tbsp	olive oil	15 mL
1 Tbsp	butter	15 mL
to taste	salt and pepper	to taste
½ cup	chopped fresh coriander	125 mL

1. Make marinade by combining olive oil, lemon juice and garlic. Divide equally into two bowls. Add shrimp to one bowl, scallops to the other. Marinate at least 1 hour, refrigerated.

2. Cook rice with chicken stock in a small covered saucepan. Stir in tomatoes, green onions, saffron, garlic, cumin, olive oil, butter, cayenne and salt. Transfer to a large paella or flan pan. Keep warm in oven.

Ten minutes before serving:

3. Bring wine to boil in a large covered frying pan. Add clams and mussels, replace lid and steam just until shells open.

4. Drain shrimp and scallops. Separately sauté over very high heat in butter and olive oil for 2 to 3 minutes, just until cooked. Sprinkle with salt and pepper. Add seafood and cooking juices to rice and toss.

5. Tuck the steamed mussels and clams (complete with shells) into the rice, spooning on some of their juices. Sprinkle liberally with chopped fresh coriander. Serve immediately in the paella or flan pan.

Variation: Add ½ cup (125 mL) finely diced cooked ham to rice just after cooking.

ACCOMPANIMENTS

ROAST POTATOES WITH GARLIC

Yields 8 servings

Dare to devour the whole roasted garlic cloves and you'll be surprised by their gentle flavour. Mild-mannered potatoes are a wonderful foil for garlic and the similarity of texture is intriguing.

These can also be roasted beside a rib of beef or a chicken.

8	large baking potatoes, washed and scrubbed	8
1 cup	olive oil	250 mL
30 to 40	separated garlic cloves, unpeeled	30 to 40
to taste	salt and pepper	to taste

1. Preheat oven to 400°F (200°C).

2. Cut each potato into three, or four if very large. Bring a large pot of water to a boil and blanch the potatoes for 5 to 7 minutes, until slightly softened. Drain and set aside.

3. Pour olive oil into a shallow roasting pan and heat over high heat for 5 minutes. Add hot potatoes and unpeeled garlic cloves and toss to coat with oil. Add salt and pepper to taste.

4. Place roasting pan in oven and roast for 1 hour, turning and basting potatoes every 10 minutes. Add more salt and pepper if desired. Serve several cloves of garlic with each portion of potatoes.

FRITTATA-STUFFED POTATOES

Yields 8 stuffed potatoes

We've taken our popular potato frittata and baked it in potato skins to make a gently flavoured accompaniment to savoury meats like spicy Italian sausage. To serve them on their own as a nourishing snack, add cubed ham, fried sausage slices or smoked salmon bits to the filling.

8	large baked potatoes	8
3 Tbsp	butter	45 mL
1	medium-sized onion, chopped	1
2	medium-sized tomatoes, seeded and cut into 1-inch (2.5-cm) chunks	2
5	eggs	5
⅓ cup	whipping cream	75 mL
1½ tsp	salt	7 mL
¼ tsp	pepper	1 mL
4 dashes	Tabasco sauce	4 dashes

1. Preheat oven to 375°F (190°C).

2. Cut off and discard the top ½ inch (1.25 cm) of each potato. Scoop out the pulp, leaving about ¼ inch (6 mm) of pulp attached to the skin. Place skins on a baking sheet and set aside.

GREEN POTATOES
You may notice a bit of green on a potato now and again. This is caused by exposure to light and indicates the presence of a toxic substance. Cut off any green parts before using.

3. Remove one quarter of the scooped-out potato pulp and discard or save for use at another time. In a frying pan over medium-high heat melt 2 Tbsp (30 mL) butter. Fry remaining pulp until lightly browned. Remove to bowl and set aside. In frying pan melt remaining butter over medium-high heat, add onions and fry 2 or 3 minutes, or until translucent. Add tomatoes and fry 1 minute, just to heat through. Remove and add to potatoes.

4. In a large mixing bowl beat together remaining ingredients. Add potato mixture and mix well. Spoon into potato skins, adding as much filling as each skin will hold. Bake for 30 to 35 minutes, or until edges have browned and an inserted knife comes out clean. Serve warm or at room temperature.

POTATO PANCAKES

Yields 1 dozen 4-inch (10-cm) pancakes

Crispy and golden on the outside, creamy and chewy on the inside, these potato pancakes are delicious with sour cream and chives. For a hearty breakfast, serve with a mixed grill of sausages, kidneys, mushrooms and lamb or pork chops.

4	**slices bacon, cut into ¼-inch (6-cm) pieces**	4
6	**medium-sized baking potatoes, peeled and quartered (about 2¼ lb/1 kg)**	6
2	**eggs, lightly beaten**	2
4 Tbsp	**chopped onions**	60 mL
½ cup	**flour**	125 mL
1 tsp	**baking powder**	5 mL
1 tsp	**salt**	5 mL
1 tsp	**pepper**	5 mL
2 to 4 Tbsp	**olive oil**	30 to 60 mL
2 to 4 Tbsp	**butter**	30 to 60 mL

1. In a frying pan briefly sauté diced bacon to remove some of the fat. Drain and set aside.

2. In a food processor fitted with a steel blade process potatoes with on/off pulses until chopped into small bits, but not puréed. Remove to medium-sized mixing bowl. Add fried bacon, eggs, chopped onions, flour, baking powder, salt and pepper. Beat lightly until well blended.

3. Heat olive oil to a depth of ⅛ inch (3 mm) in a frying pan over high heat. Add equal amount of butter and melt. Pour ¼ cup (60 mL) batter into pan to form a 4-inch (10-cm) pancake. Cover and cook for about 1 or 2 minutes. Turn over and cook, uncovered, for another 2 to 3 minutes. Repeat until all batter has been used, adding more olive oil and butter to the pan as required. High heat and a generous amount of oil and butter are necessary to give these pancakes their characteristic texture. The pancakes can be kept warm in the oven for a short time. Serve with sour cream.

TO BAKE POTATOES

For light, fluffy texture, choose starchy, mealy potatoes such as Russets and Idahos. To prepare potatoes for the oven, simply scrub clean and prick with a fork. Do not wrap in foil, as this creates steam. For crisp skin, bake bare; for soft skin, rub with butter or oil. Bake at 375°F (190°C) for about 1 hour, or until potato can be pierced through easily with a fork.

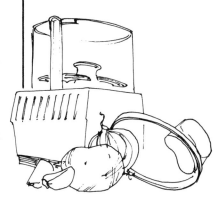

SPAGHETTI SQUASH WITH SPINACH SAUCE

Yields 4 *servings*

Some vegetables are just more fun than others; spaghetti squash is definitely one of them. As it cooks, it separates into long, spaghetti-like strands that can be buttered and served with sauce, just like pasta. Light and fresh in flavour, this dish can be served as a vegetable with a main course or on its own.

1	spaghetti squash	1
6 Tbsp	butter	90 mL
1	10-oz (284-g) bag spinach, well cleaned and trimmed	1
2 cloves	garlic, crushed	2 cloves
1 tsp	ground or freshly grated nutmeg	5 mL
to taste	salt	to taste
1	medium-sized onion, chopped	1
1 cup	sliced mushrooms	250 mL
2 Tbsp	sesame seeds, toasted	30 mL

1. Place whole squash into a large pot. Cover with water and bring to a boil. Let simmer for 1 to 1½ hours over medium-low heat, or until tender (when a fork will go in easily). Remove and cut in half across the width. Scoop out and discard the seeds. Gently scoop out the flesh, fluffing lightly to separate the strands.

2. To prepare the sauce, in a frying pan melt 4 Tbsp (60 mL) of the butter over medium-high heat. Add spinach and sauté with garlic, nutmeg and salt, just until spinach is wilted, about 5 minutes. Remove from frying pan to food processor fitted with steel blade. Purée and pour over squash.

3. Sauté onions in remaining butter until soft. Add mushrooms to the pan and sauté just until their juices begin to run. Spoon over the spinach.

4. Sprinkle sesame seeds on top and serve.

Here's a 15-minute method for cooking the squash, if you haven't time to boil it whole:
1. Cut squash across the width into 2-inch (5-cm) slices. (Don't cut the squash lengthwise or you will cut all the strands in half, as they grow laterally.) Scoop out seeds and discard.
2. Steam squash for 15 minutes, or until just tender.
3. Gently scrape cooked squash away from skin. Discard skin. Place squash on warmed platter, fluffing lightly to separate strands. Keep warm while preparing the sauce.

Try spaghetti squash a la panna. In a big frying pan heat together precooked, peeled squash and a little butter. Add some heavy cream and boil for a few minutes, just to reduce cream slightly. Add nutmeg and freshly grated Parmesan cheese. Season with salt and freshly ground pepper.

FRESH TOMATO SAUCE

An easy and elegant sauce for spaghetti squash or pasta. Try it in summer when field tomatoes are plentiful and taste their very best. Don't hesitate to chop into the pan whatever your garden offers: fresh basil, green bell peppers, zucchini . . .

1 Tbsp	olive oil	15 mL
2 or 3	tomatoes, peeled and diced	2 or 3
3 cloves	garlic, minced	3 cloves
1	green onion, chopped	1
to taste	salt and pepper	to taste

1. Heat oil in frying pan over high heat until very hot but not smoking. Add diced tomatoes and garlic and sauté just until heated, about 1 or 2 minutes. Stir in green onions and season with salt and pepper. Pour over cooked spaghetti squash and serve.

GARDEN STIR-FRY

Yields 20 servings

Bright, crispy vegetables are fried quickly over high heat to retain their texture and colour. With pre-blanching, the frying process is shortened and requires less oil than in a traditional stir-fry. Use any vegetables that are in season.

1 lb	parsnips, diagonally sliced ¼ inch (6 mm)	450 g
1 lb	green beans, cut 1½ inches (4 cm)	450 g
1 lb	yellow beans, cut 1½ inches (4 cm)	450 g
1	medium-sized cauliflower, cut into small florets	1
2 bunches	broccoli, cut into small florets	2 bunches
2 bunches	medium-sized carrots, diagonally sliced ¼ inch (6 mm)	2 bunches
½ to 1 cup	butter and olive oil for sautéing	125 to 250 mL
1	large red onion, cut into ¼-inch (6-mm) wedges	1
2	zucchini, sliced ¼ inch (6 mm)	2
⅓ cup	soy sauce	75 mL
to taste	salt and pepper	to taste
4 cloves	garlic, minced	4 cloves
2	red bell peppers, cut into ¼-inch (6-mm) strips	2
1	yellow bell pepper, cut into ¼-inch (6-mm) strips	
1 lb	snow peas or sugar peas, strings removed	450 g
4 Tbsp	lemon juice (optional)	60 mL

1. Bring a large pot of salted water to a boil. Blanch parsnips for several minutes, until slightly softened but still crispy. Drain and run under cold water to stop the cooking. Repeat process with beans, then cauliflower, then broccoli, then carrots. This can be done a few hours ahead of serving time.

2. Preheat oven to 300°F (150°C). Have ready a large casserole or foil roasting pan large enough to hold the vegetables. A half-hour before serving, heat enough olive oil over medium-high heat to coat the bottom of a large frying pan. Add a little butter. Sauté onions for a minute, add zucchini and stir for another minute, sprinkling on a little soy sauce, salt and pepper, and a little garlic. Transfer to large pan and keep hot in oven.

3. To the frying pan add more oil, butter, garlic and as much of the blanched vegetables as can be tossed and sautéed at one time. Sauté quickly for 2 to 3 minutes, sprinkling with a little soy sauce, salt and pepper. Transfer to large pan in oven. Repeat until all blanched vegetables have been sautéed. Peppers and snow peas should be cooked last; they require only 1 to 2 minutes. Combine everything in the large pan. Season to taste and sprinkle with lemon juice, if desired.

BROCCOLI

If your recipe calls only for florets of the broccoli, don't throw away the stems. Once peeled, they become very tender and can be sliced and added to a stir-fry or steamed until just tender (about 5 minutes), then cubed and tossed into a potato or vegetable salad.

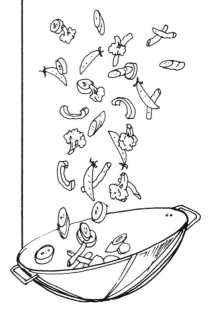

VEGETABLES IN PHYLLO

Yields 8 side servings

A colourful assortment of vegetables wrapped in crispy leaves of phyllo pastry and served with Creamy Tomato Sauce. These can be made a day in advance and baked just before serving.

CREAMY TOMATO SAUCE

2 tsp/10 mL
butter

1 Tbsp/15 mL
minced onion

1 medium-sized
tomato,
chopped finely

1 Tbsp/15 mL
white wine

pinch
sugar

to taste
salt and pepper

1 cup/250 mL
table cream

1. In a medium-sized saucepan melt butter over medium-high heat. Add onion and sauté until translucent, about 2 minutes. Add tomato and cook for another 4 to 6 minutes, or until very soft. Add wine, sugar, salt, pepper and cream and cook stirring constantly, for an additional 3 to 5 minutes, or until sauce has thickened a little. Remove from heat and strain sauce through a sieve. Serve immediately with baked Vegetables in Phyllo.

2 tsp	butter	10 mL
½	small onion, thinly sliced	½
½ cup	julienned snow peas	125 mL
½ cup	julienned asparagus	125 mL
½ cup	sliced mushrooms	125 mL
¼	green bell pepper, julienned	¼
¼	red bell pepper, julienned	¼
1	large carrot, julienned	1
1 rib	celery, julienned	1 rib
1	medium-sized tomato, diced	1
¼ tsp	dried mixed Italian herbs	1 mL
1 clove	garlic, crushed	1 clove
4 tsp	white wine	20 mL
1 cup	grated Swiss cheese (about 4 oz/110 g)	250 mL
16	sheets phyllo pastry	16
½ cup	melted butter	125 mL

1. Melt butter over medium-high heat in a large frying pan. Add onions and sauté until translucent, about 2 minutes. Add remaining vegetables and cook for an additional 3 to 5 minutes. Add herbs, garlic and wine and cook for another 2 minutes. Add grated cheese and stir until cheese melts. Tilt pan and pour off all liquid. Reserve this liquid for the Creamy Tomato Sauce. Set vegetable mixture aside to cool completely.

2. If baking immediately, preheat oven to 400°F (200°C).

3. Cut each sheet of phyllo pastry into 2 pieces: a square approximately 12 inches × 12 inches (30 cm × 30 cm) and a rectangle about 12 inches × 4 inches (30 cm × 10 cm). Cover phyllo with a slightly damp cloth to keep it from drying out, and work with just a few sheets of phyllo at a time. Brush 2 squares of phyllo with butter, coating well. Place one on top of the other. Butter one of the rectangles, fold in three to make a square about 4 inches × 4 inches (10 cm × 10 cm) and place in the centre of the buttered larger squares. Spoon one-eighth of the filling onto the middle of the pastry and draw up the sides, handkerchief-style. Gather at the top and tie with a length of butcher's string. Repeat with remaining phyllo and filling, making 8 pouches.

Pouches may be made ahead to this point. Brush well with butter, cover with plastic wrap and refrigerate. Remove from refrigerator about 15 minutes before baking.

Place on baking sheets and bake for 8 to 12 minutes, or until phyllo is golden brown. Serve with Creamy Tomato Sauce.

FOUR-GRAIN SODA BREAD

Yields two 6-inch (15-cm) round loaves

Steaming hot from the oven and slathered with butter, this freckled brown bread is the perfect accompaniment to a thick chili, homebaked beans or country stew.

2 cups	whole-wheat flour	500 mL
1 cup	rye flour	250 mL
1 cup	all-purpose flour	250 mL
1 cup	oatmeal	250 mL
1 tsp	baking soda	5 mL
1 Tbsp	baking powder	15 mL
4 Tbsp	vegetable oil	60 mL
2	eggs, lightly beaten	2
1½ cups	buttermilk	375 mL
1 Tbsp	molasses	15 mL

1. Preheat oven to 375°F (190°C). Grease a large baking sheet.

2. In a large mixing bowl blend together whole-wheat flour, rye flour, all-purpose flour, oatmeal, baking soda and baking powder.

3. In a small mixing bowl beat together vegetable oil, eggs, buttermilk and molasses. Pour all at once into the bowl of dry ingredients and mix until ingredients are well incorporated. Knead for 5 to 8 minutes until dough is smooth.

4. With lightly floured hands shape dough into two round loaves and place them well apart on the prepared baking sheet. Bake for about 25 to 30 minutes, or until loaves have browned and produce a hollow sound when tapped. Best eaten the same day, or toasted the next.

Add ½ cup (125 mL) grated Cheddar cheese and/or ½ cup (125 mL) of sautéed chopped onions to the dough for a distinctive flavour.

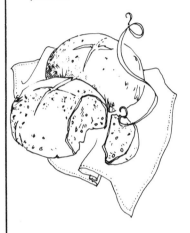

MOLASSES BRAN MUFFINS

Yields 12 large muffins

Dark, moist and full of rich molasses flavour.

2	eggs	2
1 cup	sour cream	250 mL
½ cup	molasses	125 mL
½ cup	honey	125 mL
¼ cup	butter, melted	50 mL
1 tsp	vanilla	5 mL
1 cup	whole-wheat flour	250 mL
¾ cup	bran	175 mL
½ tsp	salt	2 mL
¾ tsp	baking soda	3 mL
2 Tbsp	sugar	30 mL
1 tsp	ground cinnamon	5 mL
½ cup	raisins	125 mL

CHOLESTEROL CORNER

Balance the nutritious goodness of Molasses Bran Muffins with a sinful slathering of butter. How could it hurt?

Date Butter
Chop ¼ cup (50 mL) dates and purée with ¼ cup butter (50 mL) and a little orange zest.

Spiced Honey Butter
Cream together ¼ cup (50 mL) butter, ¼ cup (50 mL) honey, ½ tsp (2 mL) ground cinnamon and a pinch of cardamom.

1. Preheat oven to 425°F (220°C). Line a muffin tin with paper muffin cups.

2. In a large mixing bowl beat together eggs, sour cream, molasses, honey, butter and vanilla.

3. In a small bowl mix the flour, bran, salt, baking soda, sugar and cinnamon very well. Add all at once to the liquid mixture. Stir together, just until well blended. Do not overmix. Fold in raisins.

4. Fill muffin cups almost full. (This batter will not rise much.) Bake for 15 to 20 minutes, or until a toothpick inserted into the middle of a muffin comes out clean.

DATE-NUT-FIG LOAF

Yields one 8½-inch × 4½-inch (22-cm × 11-cm) loaf

The marvellous engaging flavours of fruit and nuts marry in this rich, dark loaf.

Create a little oasis of comfort in your hectic day. Brew up a pot of hot tea and make a little plate of tea sandwiches. Then put your feet up.

Tea Sandwiches: In food processor fitted with steel blade chop ⅓ cup (75 mL) pecans with 2 tsp (10 mL) brown sugar and 2 Tbsp (30 mL) butter. Spread between thin slices of Date-Nut-Fig Loaf.

1 cup	water	250 mL
1 tsp	baking soda	5 mL
1 cup	diced dates, ½-inch (1.25-cm) cubes	250 mL
1 cup	diced dried figs, ½-inch (1.25-cm) cubes	250 mL
½ cup	butter, softened	125 mL
1 cup	brown sugar	250 mL
1	egg, lightly beaten	1
1 tsp	vanilla extract	5 mL
1½ cups	flour	375 mL
½ cup	bran	125 mL
1 tsp	ground cinnamon	5 mL
1 cup	whole shelled nuts (use a variety, including hazelnuts, walnuts, almonds, Brazil nuts, pine nuts or sunflower seeds)	250 mL

1. Preheat oven to 350°F (180°C). Line a 8½-inch × 4½-inch (21-cm × 11-cm) loaf pan with parchment, or butter and dust with flour.

2. In a large saucepan bring water to a boil over high heat. Add soda, dates and figs. Turn off heat. Cover and let sit while rest of loaf is prepared.

3. In a medium-sized mixing bowl cream butter. Add sugar and egg and beat until light and fluffy. Beat in vanilla.

4. In a small bowl mix together flour, bran, cinnamon and nuts. Fold into butter mixture and add date and fig mixture, stirring just until batter is blended. Pour batter into prepared loaf pan. Bake for 1 hour, or until a toothpick inserted into the centre of the loaf comes out clean.

DESSERTS

CHOCOLATE RUFFLE CAKE

Yields one 10-inch (25-cm) double layer cake

Rich with chocolate and cream, and completely covered in large ruffles of dark chocolate, this cake is spectacularly decadent on the outside and angel light on the inside.

For cake:

12	eggs, separated	12
½ cup	sugar	125 mL
8 oz	semi-sweet chocolate, melted	230 g

For filling:

3 cups	whipping cream	750 mL
8 oz	semi-sweet chocolate, melted	230 g

For ruffles:

5 oz	semi-sweet chocolate, melted	150 g

1. Preheat oven to 350°F (180°C). Line the bottom of two 10-inch (25-cm) springform pans with parchment.

2. In a large mixing bowl beat the egg yolks and half of the sugar with an electric beater for about 15 minutes, or until the mixture is thick and very light in colour.

3. In another large bowl beat the egg whites until soft peaks form, gradually add the remaining sugar and continue beating until mixture holds a stiff peak.

4. Gently fold 8 oz (230 g) melted chocolate into the yolks, making sure chocolate has cooled first. Fold the chocolate mixture into the beaten egg whites. Pour half of the batter into each of the prepared pans. Bake for 30 minutes, or until a toothpick inserted into the middle of the cake comes out clean. Let cake cool in pans. They may fall slightly or have uneven surfaces. When cakes have cooled fully, remove them from the pans and peel off the parchment.

5. To make the filling, beat the whipping cream in a medium-sized bowl until stiff. Gradually fold in 8 oz (230 g) cooled, melted chocolate and set aside.

6. To make the ruffles, spread about half of the melted chocolate thinly on the back of a baking sheet. Refrigerate for about 10 minutes. Using a metal spatula or a clean paint scraper, scrape the chocolate off the baking sheet, pushing forward to form pleats or ruffles. If chocolate breaks off unevenly in small slivers, the chocolate is too cold. Let it stand at room temperature for a few minutes. If chocolate bunches up onto the scraper, it is too warm and must be returned to the refrigerator briefly. If you find ruffle-making all too daunting, spread and chill the chocolate in the same way but just scrape off the chocolate in thin, flat shards. These can be piled at different angles on the filling to form an attractive garnish.

7. To assemble the cake, use a serrated knife to split each cake in two to produce four layers. Place the first layer on the cake plate. Spread with filling and top with another layer of cake. Repeat with remaining layers, finishing with filling on top. Spread remaining filling around the sides. Cover cake generously with

---

Chocolate is for lovers

Phenylethylamine — that's a chemical produced in the body when people fall in love, giving the "high" that lovers find so propelling. It's also found in chocolate, long considered an aphrodisiac. Nutritionists say that the phenylethylamine in chocolate has no effect on the body. But lovers might disagree.

MELTING CHOCOLATE

• Chop chocolate into small pieces, place in the top of a double-boiler and heat gently over simmering water. Stir occasionally. Or melt in microwave oven by heating for 3 to 4 minutes on low setting, removing to stir every few minutes.

• Excessive heat or even a drop of water can cause melting chocolate to seize and harden irreversibly.

• The addition of vegetable oil will give your chocolate a shiny finish. For 1 lb (450 g) of chocolate add 2 tsp (10 mL) oil.

FOR RUFFLES —
Spread chocolate on marble slab or chilled cookie sheet.

chocolate ruffles, using the largest curls on the top. Refrigerate for at least two hours, or overnight.

Note: It is best not to double this recipe as quantities will be too large for standard-sized equipment.

MUM'S CHOCOLATE CAKE

Yields one triple-layer cake

Velvety mocha filling is sandwiched between triple layers of dark, moist, semi-sweet chocolate cake. Dramatically tall and iced in white, it'll draw lots of oohs and aahs.

For cake:

1¼ cups	butter, softened	300 mL
1½ cups	mayonnaise	375 mL
2⅔ cups	brown sugar	650 mL
1 Tbsp	vanilla	15 mL
6	eggs	6
3 cups	flour	750 mL
1 Tbsp	baking soda	15 mL
¾ tsp	salt	3 mL
1½ cups	cocoa	375 mL
2 cups	hot water	500 mL

For mocha filling:

1½ cups	sifted icing sugar	375 mL
4 Tbsp	butter, softened	60 mL
4 Tbsp	very strong cold coffee	60 mL
3 oz	unsweetened chocolate, melted	90 g
1 tsp	vanilla	5 mL
1	egg	1

For whipped butter icing:

1 cup	unsalted butter, softened	250 mL
1½ cups	sifted icing sugar	375 mL
½ cup	whipping cream	125 mL
½ cup	boiling water	125 mL

1. Preheat oven to 350°F (180°C). Line the bottoms of three 9-inch (23-cm) layer pans with parchment, or butter and dust with flour.

2. In a large mixing bowl cream together butter, mayonnaise, brown sugar and vanilla. Add eggs and beat until light and fluffy.

3. In a medium-sized mixing bowl sift together, 3 times, the flour, baking soda, salt and cocoa. Alternately add the dry ingredients and hot water to the mayonnaise mixture, starting and ending with ⅓ of the dry ingredients. After each addition beat only enough to blend ingredients thoroughly.

4. Pour into prepared pans and bake for 30 to 40 minutes, or until a toothpick inserted into the centre of a cake comes out almost clean. A few bits of cake should still cling to the toothpick

A CHILD'S BIRTHDAY

Our mothers used to bury a shiny new penny in our birthday cake as a prize for the lucky child who found it in his or her slice.

Things were simpler then. Now, when catering children's parties, we find ourselves surrounded by mimes, magicians, ponies, popcorn vendors and talking parrots. Cakes full of pennies might seem to pale in comparison.

But not so. Children still await the presentation of the birthday cake with the same undisguised eagerness that once filled our little hearts. And their incredulous eyes widen when a wonderfully tall cake, like this Chocolate Cake, is brought to the table for the ritual of candle and song.

for a truly moist cake. Cool in pans for 10 minutes, invert onto cooling racks, remove parchment and cool completely before icing.

5. To make mocha filling, blend icing sugar, butter, coffee, chocolate and vanilla in a small mixing bowl. Add egg and stir just until blended.

6. Fill a larger bowl with ice cubes and place small bowl containing filling on top of ice. Stir until mixture thickens to spreading consistency. If necessary, add a little icing sugar.

7. To make butter icing, cream together butter, icing sugar and whipping cream with an electric beater until well blended.

8. Add boiling water, 1 teaspoon (5 mL) at a time, beating constantly until all water is incorporated and icing is light and fluffy.

9. To assemble, place one layer of cake on cake plate. Spread with half of the mocha filling. Place second layer on top and spread with remaining mocha filling. Top with third layer. Spread whipped butter icing over top and sides, covering cake completely. This icing is very smooth and silky. Serve cake at room temperature. If cake is refrigerated, bring back to room temperature before serving or icing will be very hard.

CARROT-COCONUT CAKE

Yields one 2-layer 9-inch (23-cm) round cake

Blue jeans, tisanes and carrot cake — comforting reminders of the sixties. In this unusual version orange rind, browned butter and sesame seeds contribute their warm, nutty flavours, and coarsely chopped carrots add moistness.

1¼ cups	butter	300 mL
4 cups	very coarsely chopped carrots (about 5 large carrots), use steel blade in food processor	1 L
1 cup	honey	250 mL
2 tsp	vanilla	10 mL
4	eggs	4
½ tsp	ground or freshly grated nutmeg	2 mL
2 tsp	ground cinnamon	10 mL
2 cups	whole-wheat flour	500 mL
2 tsp	baking soda	10 mL
1¼ cups	demerara sugar	300 mL
½ tsp	grated orange rind	2 mL
1 cup	flaked or shredded coconut	250 mL
1 cup	sesame seeds	250 mL
1 cup	sunflower seeds	250 mL
¼ tsp	salt (optional)	1 mL

1. Preheat oven to 375°F (190°C). Prepare two 9-inch (23-cm) round cake pans by lining the bottom of each with a circle of parchment paper, or by buttering and dusting with flour.

All our recipes use all-purpose flour, unless otherwise specified.

All-purpose is a blend of hard and soft flours that is suitable for most cooking and baking.

Cake and pastry flour has a higher content of soft flour which has less gluten, therefore less elasticity, than hard flour, so is ideal for short, crisp preparations like cookies and flaky pastry.

Extra-fine cake flour has an even lower gluten content and will yield very tender cakes.

Bread flour is high in gluten and captures all the leavening for light, high loaves.

Different regions blend their flour in different proportions, so you may find that a recipe that works well in Paris doesn't yield the same results in Vancouver.

2. Melt butter in small frying pan and heat over medium-low heat until butter turns a delicate brown. Watch carefully because butter burns very quickly.

3. Combine browned butter, carrots, honey, vanilla and eggs in a mixing bowl.

4. In a second mixing bowl combine nutmeg, cinnamon, whole-wheat flour, baking soda, demerara sugar, orange rind, coconut, sesame seeds, sunflower seeds and salt. Toss to mix thoroughly.

5. Pour the carrot mixture into the dry ingredients and stir to blend completely.

6. Pour half the batter into each prepared pan. Bake for 35 to 45 minutes, or until a toothpick inserted into the middle of the cake comes out clean. Remove from oven and cool in pans for 10 minutes, then turn onto racks to cool completely before icing. Use the Classic Carrot-Cake Icing if you like a rich, not too sweet topping; or the Seven-Minute Citrus Icing if you prefer your topping light and fluffy.

CLASSIC CARROT-CAKE ICING

1 lb	cream cheese	450 g
½ cup	icing sugar	125 mL
1 tsp	vanilla	2 mL

1. Beat cream cheese until soft and fluffy. Beat in sugar and vanilla.

SEVEN-MINUTE CITRUS ICING

2	egg whites	2
⅓ cup	freshly squeezed orange juice	75 mL
⅛ tsp	grated orange rind	0.5 mL
1½ cups	demerara sugar	375 mL
3 tsp	corn syrup	15 mL

1. Place all ingredients in the top of a double boiler over simmering water. Beat with electric beater for about 7 minutes, or until very fluffy and stiff.

TISANES

Herbal teas will soothe and relax. They can also cure what ails you. Maté tea, full of caffeine, will give you an energy boost. If you have a cold, an infusion of ginger root and lemon grass with honey will make you feel better. A strong brew of camomile mixed with mint will soothe you to sleep.

PEACH MELBA CAKE

Yields one 10-inch (25-cm) cake

Lofty layers of puff pastry, buttery génoise, peaches and raspberries sprinkled with Kirsch are enveloped in a dreamy light cloud of rum butter cream.

For génoise layers:

6	eggs	6
1 cup	sugar	250 mL
½ tsp	vanilla	2 mL
1 tsp	almond extract	5 mL
1 cup	sifted cake flour	250 mL
½ cup	melted, cooled butter	125 mL
3 Tbsp	Kirsch	45 mL
1 Tbsp	water	15 mL

For pastry layers:

3 lb	puff pastry	1.5 kg

For whipped butter icing:

1½ lb	butter	675 g
4½ cups	icing sugar	1.125 L
1½ cups	whipping cream	375 mL
6 Tbsp	dark rum	90 mL
1½ cups	boiling water	375 mL

For filling:

2 cups	peach jam	500 mL
2 cups	sliced peaches, fresh or canned	500 mL
4 cups	raspberries, fresh or flash frozen	1 L
1 cup	sliced almonds, toasted	250 mL

1. For the génoise layers, preheat oven to 350°F (180°C). Line the bottoms of three 10-inch (25-cm) springform pans with parchment.

2. Combine eggs and sugar in a large mixing bowl placed over a pot of simmering water. With electric beater on medium speed, beat together until soft peaks form, about 7 to 10 minutes. Remove from heat, add vanilla and almond extract and beat until cool, about 3 minutes. Do not beat on high speed as this will create large air holes in cake. Sift one quarter of the flour over egg mixture. Fold in with 7 or 8 strokes, or just enough to incorporate most of the added flour. Repeat three times, using the remaining flour and folding with as few strokes as possible. Slowly drizzle butter over the batter and fold in, scraping the bottom of the bowl with each stroke because the butter tends to sink to the bottom. Use as few strokes as possible.

3. Pour a third of the batter into each prepared pan. Bake 20 to 25 minutes. Tops will not be dry and a small depression will remain when touched, but they do not require longer baking. Any longer than 25 minutes will make them dry. Cool in pans, then release from springform and remove parchment.

4. In a small bowl combine Kirsch and water. Sprinkle over génoise layers. Set aside. Cover with plastic wrap if not assembling immediately.

5. For pastry layers, preheat oven to 425°F (220°C). Roll out pastry to ⅛-inch (3-mm) thickness and 3 squares approximately 14 inches × 14 inches (36 cm × 36 cm). Place on baking sheets, prick entire surface with fork and bake for 15 minutes, or until golden brown. Halfway through the baking, check if pastry is rising unevenly or higher than ½ inch (1.25 cm). If pastry is rising too much or unevenly, place an empty baking sheet on top to act as a weight. When pastry has cooled completely, cut each square into a circle 9½ inches (24 cm) in diameter. Set aside.

6. For butter icing, in a medium-sized mixing bowl cream butter with electric beater on high speed. Add icing sugar and beat in. Add whipping cream and rum and beat in. Beating constantly on high speed, add a spoonful of boiling water. When water has been completely incorporated, about 15 seconds, add another spoonful of boiling water. Continue adding water until all has been incorporated and icing is white, light and very fluffy. If mixture curdles, just keep beating. Set aside.

7. To fill and assemble, place a paper doily on cake plate. Place four strips of waxed paper around edge to keep doily and plate clean while assembling and decorating cake. Place a circle of pastry on the plate. Spread with half the jam. Place génoise layer on top and spread with a ¼-inch (6-mm) layer of icing. Arrange half of the peach slices and a third of the raspberries on top. Sprinkle with half the toasted almonds. Roughly spread another layer of pastry with icing and place, icing side down, on top of fruit. Spread the rest of the jam on pastry. Repeat layering of génoise, icing, peaches, raspberries, almonds, icing and pastry. Spread a layer of icing on pastry and top with last layer of génoise. With a serrated knife trim the side of the cake so it is straight and even. Use remaining icing to cover the top and sides of cake completely. Decorate top with remaining raspberries. Slide out strips of waxed paper and serve.

Layering the cake

- puff pastry
almonds -
- peaches and raspberries
buttercream -
- génoise
- jam on puff pastry
almonds -
- peaches and raspberries
buttercream -
- génoise
- jam on puff pastry

COOKING WITH APPLES

It's important to choose the right apples for cooking. They should be slightly tart, full flavoured, firm and juicy but not watery. Romes are perfect for baking. Northern Spy are delicious. Cortland and Greening are also good. You can use McIntosh, if they are very firm, and Granny Smith. But Delicious apples will turn to flaccid mush and belie your efforts in the kitchen.

SOUR-CREAM APPLE PIE

Yields one deep 9-inch (23-cm) pie

This favourite has the creamy richness of cheesecake and the wholesome freshness of chunky apples — all in a homey graham wafer crust.

For crust:

1½ cups	graham wafer crumbs	375 mL
¼ cup	sugar	60 mL
½ cup	butter, melted	125 mL

For filling:

3 Tbsp	flour	45 mL
1 cup	sugar	250 mL
1 tsp	ground cinnamon	5 mL
2	eggs, lightly beaten	2
¾ tsp	vanilla	3 mL
1½ cups	sour cream	375 mL
6	medium-sized baking apples, peeled, cored and cut into 1-inch (2.5-cm) chunks	6

For topping:

⅓ cup	sugar	75 mL
⅓ cup	flour	75 mL
¾ tsp	ground cinnamon	3 mL
3 Tbsp	butter, cold	45 mL

1. To make the crust, combine graham wafer crumbs, ¼ cup (60 mL) sugar and melted butter in a medium-sized mixing bowl. Mix well and press into the sides and bottom of a deep 9-inch (23-cm) pie pan. Refrigerate while preparing the filling and topping.

2. Preheat oven to 400°F (200°C).

3. For the filling, combine 3 Tbsp (45 mL) flour, 1 cup (250 mL) sugar, 1 tsp (5 mL) cinnamon, eggs, vanilla and sour cream in a medium-sized bowl. Beat together. Stir in the apple chunks and pour mixture into the crust.

4. Bake for 15 minutes. Reduce heat to 350°F (180°C) and bake for an additional 30 minutes.

5. For the topping, combine the remaining sugar, flour and cinnamon in a small bowl. Cut the butter into the dry ingredients until crumbly.

6. Raise temperature to 400°F (200°C). Sprinkle topping over pie and bake for 12 to 15 minutes, or until crust is lightly browned.

MOCHA ALMOND FUDGE PIE

Yields one deep 9-inch (23-cm) pie

An absolute winner: a crunchy chocolate crust filled with rich ganache, fudgy and piled mile-high with mocha whipped cream. For the best flavour, use the finest quality chocolate — Belgian, French or German.

For crust:

1	7-oz (200-g) package chocolate wafers, finely crushed	1
¼ cup	brown sugar crystals, crushed*	60 mL
2 Tbsp	chocolate chips, crushed	30 mL
½ cup	chopped almonds, toasted	125 mL
½ cup	butter, melted	125 mL

For filling:

12 oz	semi-sweet chocolate	350 g
½ cup	unsalted butter	125 mL
½ cup	chopped almonds, toasted	125 mL
1 cup	whipping cream	250 mL

For topping:

1 tsp	gelatin	5 mL
4 tsp	cold water	20 mL
2 cups	whipping cream	500 mL
½ cup	icing sugar	125 mL
1 tsp	concentrated mocha flavouring	5 mL

COFFEE SUGAR CRYSTALS

Sparkling in the sugar bowl like rough cut jewels, coffee sugar crystals add an elegant touch to tea time. Or, as in our Mocha Almond Fudge Pie, an unusual crunch to a crumb crust. These dark brown rock sugar crystals are available in specialty coffee and tea stores.

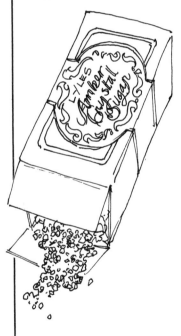

1. In a mixing bowl combine all ingredients for crust. Mix well. Reserve ½ cup (125 mL) of the mixture to dust the top of the finished pie. Press the remaining crumb mixture firmly into the bottom and sides of the deep 9-inch (23-cm) pie pan. Chill in refrigerator while preparing the filling and topping.

2. To make the filling, combine chocolate and butter in the top of a double boiler over hot water. Stir occasionally until completely melted. Add almonds and whipping cream and stir to blend completely. Remove from heat and allow to cool slightly, but not to thicken. Pour into crumb crust and place in the refrigerator until filling sets.

3. In a small saucepan sprinkle gelatin over cold water and allow to soften. Melt over low heat. Do not allow gelatin to boil. Cool to room temperature.

4. In a medium-sized mixing bowl combine whipping cream, icing sugar and mocha flavouring with the cooled gelatin. Beat with electric beater just until the mixture holds a firm peak. Mound on top of chocolate filling and sprinkle with reserved crumbs.

5. If you wish, garnish the pie further with chocolate curls or candy mocha beans. Served with espresso or continental coffee, this pie will be a sensation. Worth every sinful calorie.

*If unavailable, omit.

EGGNOG-APPLEMINCE PIE

Yields one deep 9-inch (23-cm) pie

We've combined traditional Christmas flavours in an untraditional way for a pie for all seasons.

For crust:		
2 cups	finely crushed gingersnap cookies (one 8-oz/225-g package)	500 mL
4 Tbsp	butter, melted	60 mL
For filling:		
2 Tbsp	butter	30 mL
2	medium-sized baking apples, minced, unpeeled	2
½ cup	mincemeat	125 mL
For topping:		
1½ tsp	gelatin	7 mL
2 Tbsp	cold water	30 mL
4 Tbsp	rum	60 mL
6	egg yolks	6
¾ cup	sugar	175 mL
to taste	ground or freshly grated nutmeg	to taste
2 cups	whipping cream	500 mL

Crush cookies in a food processor fitted with a steel blade, one third of a package at a time, or crush between sheets of waxed paper with a rolling pin.

1. Preheat oven to 350°F (180°C).

2. In a mixing bowl toss the gingersnap crumbs with the melted butter until well blended. Reserve ½ cup (125 mL) of the crumb mixture for dusting on top of the finished pie. Press the remaining crumbs firmly into the bottom and sides of a deep 9-inch (23-cm) pie pan. Bake 5 minutes. Remove and cool completely.

3. In a frying pan melt butter over medium-high heat. Add minced apple and sauté until cooked but still crispy, about 5 minutes. Stir in mincemeat and set aside.

4. In a small saucepan sprinkle gelatin over cold water and allow to soften. Stir over low heat just until gelatin melts. Do not allow gelatin to boil. Add rum and cool to room temperature.

5. In a mixing bowl beat egg yolks, sugar and nutmeg until soft peaks form, about 8 to 10 minutes. Set aside.

6. In a large mixing bowl combine gelatin mixture and whipping cream. Beat until firm peaks form. Gently fold in egg-yolk mixture.

7. To assemble pie, spoon cooled apple-mincemeat filling into crust. Mound topping over filling and sprinkle on reserved crumbs. Chill at least 1 hour to firm before serving.

CHRISTMAS PIE

For a festive touch, garnish this pie with an edible wreath: Colour marzipan with green food colouring. Roll out to a thickness of ⅛ inch (3 mm) and cut out holly-leaf shapes with a cookie cutter. Colour a small amount of marzipan with red food colouring and roll between your fingers to form little balls. Arrange the "leaves and berries" on top of the pie.

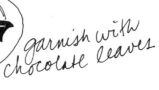

garnish with chocolate leaves

RASPBERRY CREAM SOUFFLÉ

Yields 12 to 20 servings

Luscious raspberries — whipped with heavy cream and fluffed into a heavenly cloud of egg whites. A light, refreshing dénouement to any meal.

3	19-oz (424-g) packages frozen sweetened raspberries	3
2 Tbsp	gelatin	30 mL
½ cup	cold water	125 mL
4	egg whites	4
½ cup	sugar	125 mL
4 cups	whipping cream	1 L

1. Thaw raspberries, purée in blender, and pass through a sieve to remove seeds.

2. Sprinkle gelatin over cold water in a small bowl. When water has been absorbed completely, melt gelatin over low heat. Do not allow to boil. Add melted gelatin to the puréed, sieved raspberries and stir to blend completely. Refrigerate until slightly set.

3. Beat egg whites with half of the sugar until soft peaks form. Do not overbeat.

4. Beat cream with remaining sugar until soft peaks form.

5. Fold beaten egg whites into slightly gelled raspberries, then fold in whipped cream.

6. Pour into a large decorative bowl and refrigerate until completely set and ready to serve.

Lemon ruffles, fresh garden mint leaves and fresh raspberries all make delightful garnishes for the top of this soufflé. In winter when these items may be scarce, generous dollops of winter-white whipped cream will be just as appealing — sprinkled perhaps with toasted almonds or chocolate curls.

For an added touch of sweetness, serve a strawberry-raspberry sauce with the soufflé. Add fresh sliced strawberries to a sweetened purée of raspberries or strawberries, flavoured with your favourite liqueur.

If raspberries are not flavourful enough, add raspberry syrup to taste.

CHOCOLATE-CHIP COOKIES

Yields about 2 dozen 4-inch (10-cm) cookies

Crispy on the outside and brownie-soft on the inside, these chewy nuggets are thick, rich and polka-dotted with lots and lots of chocolate chips.

CHOCOLATE-CHUNK COOKIES

For total indulgence, substitute chocolate chips with 12 oz (350 g) of fine quality semi-sweet chocolate roughly cut into ¹/₂- to 1-inch (1.25- to 2.5-cm) chunks.

1⅓ cups	butter, softened	325 mL
1½ cups	brown sugar, lightly packed	375 mL
4	egg yolks	4
1 tsp	vanilla	5 mL
½ tsp	salt	2 mL
3 cups	flour	750 mL
1 tsp	baking soda	5 mL
1 tsp	hot water	5 mL
2 cups	chocolate chips	500 mL

1. Preheat oven to 425°F (220°C). Lightly grease baking sheet.

2. In a medium-sized mixing bowl cream butter together with sugar until light and fluffy. Add egg yolks, vanilla and salt. Beat well. Stir in half the flour.

3. In a small dish dissolve baking soda in hot water and mix into dough. Stir in remaining flour. Knead in chocolate chips.

4. Press dough into a ¼-cup (50-mL) measuring cup and drop onto prepared baking sheet. Do not flatten out. Leave at least 2 inches (5 cm) between cookies and repeat until cookie sheet is full. Bake for 10 minutes. Do not overbake or cookies will be cakey instead of chewy.

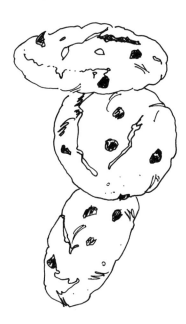

FOOD BY DESIGN

Looks too good to eat? Never! Food that looks good tastes better. A platter or table should always be visually inviting: the eye's promise to the palate that life just got a little better.

Like a bow on a present, a lovely garnish says "This is special." Meals presented attractively will be savoured and appreciated, so give your food the attention it deserves.

Within this chapter are some simple, easy methods for food presentation that will surely establish your reputation as a most creative cook — your signature with a flourish!

BORDERS AND BASES

The easiest way to pretty up a dish is to frame the food on the platter. Simply tuck sprigs of parsley, leaf lettuce, or slices of tomato, cucumber or lemon around the starring entrée.

Always remember to wash and dry garnishes thoroughly before placing them with the food. A tiny, curious caterpillar peeking out from unwashed endive can really ruin a meal. And just a few grains of sand left in the leeks will turn a delicious morsel into an unpleasant mouthful.

CURLY ENDIVE — The pale green curly tendrils offer an attractive alternative to the often overworked parsley. Its intriguingly bitter flavour may encourage diners to munch on it — something they often neglect to do with other garnishes. Other leafy alternatives to consider: radicchio, travise (a type of radicchio), kale.

RED CABBAGE — Shredded, it provides a dramatic backdrop of rich deep red, or, whole leaves can cup the food and fan around it to create a giant rose. The larger outer leaves, often discarded, are the prettiest.

FRESH HERBS—Garden-fresh thyme, parsley, mint, savory, to name a few, will add enchanting visual appeal and a subtle aroma that lingers throughout dinner. You don't need fistfuls, as some store-bought herbs can be expensive. A few well-placed sprigs tucked into a border of kale or leaf lettuce will give the desired effect.

VEGETABLES — You can save on table space and dishwashing by garnishing the main course with the vegetable course. Bright green peas, broccoli florets, julienned carrots, sliced zucchini, whatever your vegetable choice, can be piled in a generous border around a roast or row of chops in a charmingly informal presentation. Or they can be overlapped in orderly rows — such as fans of snow peas or rows of marinated cucumber slices.

RICE, PASTA OR SMALL POTATOES—These can be used with the same success as vegetables in the above method but may benefit from a light dusting of paprika, chopped parsley, grated cheese or nuts for colour.

SAUCES—Ladled carefully into a pool in the centre of the plate, a sauce or vegetable purée makes an elegant backdrop upon which to place a single tournedos or breast of chicken.

FLOWERS — Used discreetly, they can be delightful. Colour and size of blossoms should complement the food. Try to use edible flowers (squash blossoms, wild roses, nasturtiums) or flowers that have edible cousins (protea with artichokes, sweetpeas with snow peas) and beware of poisonous plants (poinsettia, oleander, etc.). Cloyingly scented flowers should also be avoided. Just a few select blossoms, nestled in parsley or curly endive, will enhance and never overpower. In the case of flowers with food, less is always more . . . except when the theme is tropical. Then, let your excesses run riot and create a floral jungle as extravagant as your budget allows.

SIMPLE GARNISHES

Here are a few little tricks that can be used to create pretty garnishes with a flick of the knife. Use them often. They take but a minute to make, yet add such a memorable touch.

LEMON RUFFLES

For each ruffle:

1. Cut lemon through width.

2. Make another cut ⅔ of the way through, about ⅛ inch (3 mm) away from first cut.

3. Make third cut completely through, ⅛ inch (3 mm) from second cut.

4. Cut through ruffle from the centre to bottom.

5. Twist "A" to the back and "B" to the front.

6. Several of these ruffles can be clustered together to form a border. A single ruffle can be used with a caper or bit of parsley in the centre to garnish a breast of chicken or slice of fish.

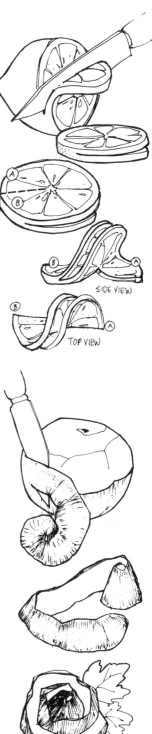

TOMATO ROSE

For one rose:

1. Starting at blossom end, pare a firm tomato in a continuous strip, about ¾ inch (2 cm) wide, spiralling around to the opposite end of the tomato. Pare rather roughly so strip is not overly thin, about ⅛ inch (3 mm) thick, and width is not too even, varying ½ to ¾ inch (1.25 to 2 cm). This creative abandon adds to the character of the finished rose.

2. With skin side out, wind the strip around and around in a spiral and a rose will form. The size of the rose will vary according to the size of the strip.

3. Use one as a single beauty, or make many of varying sizes to cluster with sprigs of parsley or leaves of fresh basil.

ARTICHOKE ROSE

1. Pry the leaves of the whole artichoke outward and press open from the centre to reveal the pale yellow-pink inner leaves that are close to the choke. It's a good idea to wear rubber gloves while doing this to avoid pricking your fingers on the thorny leaf tips. Artichokes that are a bit stale or have been left unrefrigerated for a day will open easier than really fresh ones.

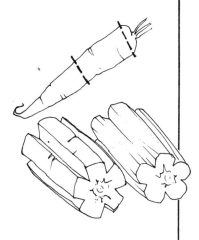

CARROT DAISY

1. Pare and trim carrot into 3- to 4-inch (8- to 10-cm) lengths.

2. Cut out five V-shaped grooves along length of carrot, spacing grooves evenly around the circumference. Use a small wood chisel with a V-tipped blade, if you have one.

3. Trim each groove to round off the petals.

4. Slice into individual flowers.

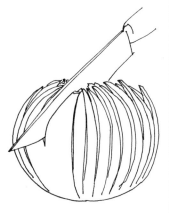

ONION CHRYSANTHEMUM

1. Peel onion and trim off tip and roots.

2. Slice straight down from tip to within ⅛ inch (3 mm) of root end.

3. Continue making radial slices from top to bottom, taking care not to slice all the way through the onion.

4. Soak slice onion in cold water for at least two hours and it will slowly open into a flower. Food colouring may be added to the water so the flower takes on colour while it is opening. Red onions can be used for their lovely natural colour.

LEEK CHRYSANTHEMUM

1. Trim roots and green top off leek.

2. Slice through leek from cut end to within ⅛ inch (3 mm) of root end. Continue making radial slices in this fashion until entire leek is cut.

3. Soak in cold water for at least three hours, or until leek has opened out completely into a beautiful spider mum.

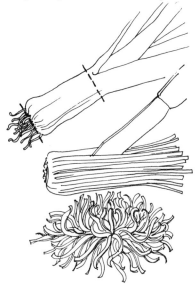

GREEN-ONION FLOWER

1. Trim roots and green top off green onion.

2. Starting ⅛ inch (3 mm) from root end, slice a V into the centre of the green onion.

3. Repeat around the green onion to form 4 or 5 petals.

4. Soak in cold water for at least an hour.

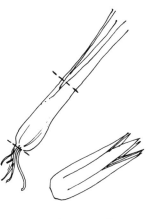

CARROT LILY

1. Make a four-sided point at the end of a carrot, just as if you were sharpening a pencil.

2. Holding knife parallel to first side, make a cut to within ⅛ inch (3 mm) of the very tip of the point.

3. Repeat cut on all other sides. Cuts will probably overlap, creating little pointed petals between the four larger petals.

4. Gently snap flower off the carrot end.

5. Immerse in cold water to keep flower fresh looking.

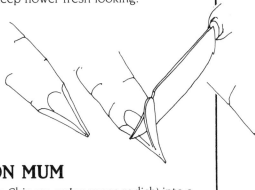

CARROT OR DAIKON MUM

1. Trim carrot or daikon (white Chinese or Japanese radish) into a straight-sided block as large as possible.

2. Slice very thinly lengthwise into rectangular pieces.

3. Soak pieces in salted water (1 part salt to 8 parts water) for about 30 minutes, or until they are very limp.

4. With each piece, fold in half lengthwise and slice from ⅛ inch (3 mm) of cut edge through folded edge. Continue slicing along the length of the folded piece.

5. Roll the length up snugly and secure with a piece of toothpick.

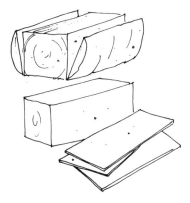

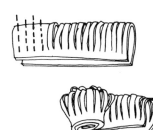

APPLE FEATHERS

1. Cut unpeeled apple into five or six wedges.

2. Cut each wedge into four V-shaped layers.

3. Extend layers of each wedge to form long "feather."

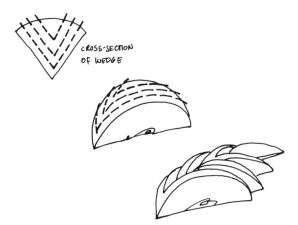

PEPPER LILIES

1. Select small chili peppers. It is best to wear rubber gloves while working with these peppers as their oils may burn your skin or eyes.

2. Make an incision close to the base of the pepper and cut up to the tip. Rotate pepper and make similar cut ¼ inch (6 mm) away from the first cut. Continue, making 5 or 6 cuts from base to tip around the pepper.

3. Immerse cut pepper in ice water and refrigerate for at least 2 hours or until pepper opens out into a flower.

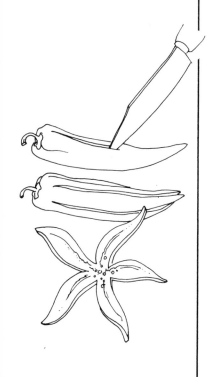

DESSERT GARNISHES

FROSTED ROSE AND MINT LEAVES

1. Select a rose or any other fresh-cut bloom.

2. Beat an egg white until frothy.

3. With a small paintbrush coat both sides of each petal of the flower thoroughly with the egg white.

4. Dust each side of each petal generously with granulated sugar. Shake off excess gently.

5. Allow sugared flower to dry completely on a cake rack.

6. For mint leaves, use the same method, but place leaves to dry on a convex surface, such as a rolling pin, so they retain their natural form.

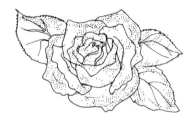

CHOCOLATE LEAVES

1. Select firm, non-toxic leaves, such as Benjamina or holly, and wipe clean.

2. Spray liberally with vegetable oil spray, or brush with oil.

3. Spread a thin layer, about 1/16 inch (2 mm) thick, of melted coating (or tempered) chocolate on the underside of each leaf.

4. Refrigerate for 20 minutes, or until chocolate has hardened completely.

5. Gently peel away leaf from hardened chocolate. Keep chocolate leaves in a cool, dry place.

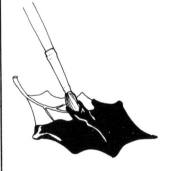

CHOCOLATE BUTTERFLIES

1. Place melted, cooled chocolate in piping bag fitted with a plain 1/8-inch (3-mm) decorating tube.

2. Draw butterfly outline on a double thickness of tinfoil. Make a crease in tinfoil down the centre of the body of the butterfly.

3. Pipe chocolate onto tinfoil following outline.

4. Angle sides up slightly along crease and refrigerate for about 20 minutes, or until chocolate has hardened. Gently peel away tinfoil. Keep in cool, dry place.

CANTALOUPE LEAVES

1. Cut melon in half and remove seeds. Pare away outer rind very thinly, leaving on as much green rind as possible.

2. Cut melon into leaf shapes.

3. Carve leaf markings out of green rind and notch leaf edges.

MELON FLOWERS

1. Cut a ½-inch (1.25-cm) slice off the bottom of melon to keep it from rolling around.

2. Pare away the outer rind, leaving some green.

3. With tip of paring knife, score petal outline about ½ inch (1.25 cm) deep. Continue around melon, making about 5 or 6 petals.

4. Pare away a ¼-inch (6-mm) thick layer of fruit above the cut lines.

5. Form outer layer of petals by carefully cutting out a thin wedge behind each petal.

6. Trim the fruit behind first row of petals into a smooth ball.

7. Score a second petal outline so that the petals are offset from the first layer. Cut into the fruit, following the outline, and remove the centre core. Scoop out seeds.

8. If the melon is very large, you can make three rows of petals.

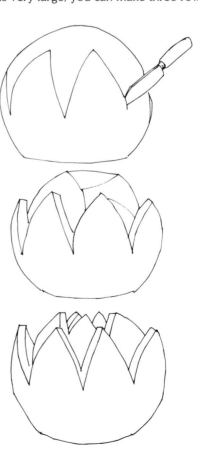

CONTAINERS AS GARNISHES

LEMON BASKET FOR SAUCE OR RELISH

1. Cut a ⅛-inch (3-mm) slice off one side of lemon. This flat base will keep the finished basket from rolling or tipping.

2. Cut away a wedge from the left and right sides of lemon, leaving a ¼-inch (6-mm) strip in the middle.

3. Scoop out pulp with a teaspoon, taking care not to tear the strip which will be the handle of the finished basket.

4. Cover finished basket in plastic wrap and store in refrigerator until ready to use.

WATERMELON BASKET

1. Use same method as for lemon basket, leaving a 2-inch (5-cm) strip as a handle. Work only on watermelon that has been left at room temperature overnight; a cold, swollen melon may split uncontrollably as you cut it. If you have a small ice-cream scoop, use it to remove the pulp. The giant melon balls will make an impressive fruit salad.

2. Wind lengths of ivy around handle and edge, securing with paperclips that have been broken into U-shaped halves. Tuck small flowers into ivy.

3. Fill with assorted fruit and/or scoops of ice-cream.

SMALL SQUASHES WITH LIDS

1. Cut the top quarter off the squash and reserve as a lid. Cut a thin slice off the bottom to keep it from tipping.

2. Scoop out seeds and some of the flesh of the squash to create a vessel for sauce or dip.

3. Fill and replace lid, slightly offset to reveal the sauce inside.

CRUDITÉ TABLESCAPE

Think of an abandoned garden growing in the woods: wild herbs and windflowers poking through clumps of overgrown cabbages, strawberry vines tumbling over swollen melons. This is the scene you set when you lay a crudité tablescape — a spectacular presentation that celebrates nature's bounty and your creativity. Fresh fruits, vegetables and dips, pâté, cheese and crackers are the food components. The rest is up to your imagination.

Savoy or ornamental cabbage arranged with flowers in a large basket.

Tuck small flowers and herbs between leaves

Small basket of shiny red apples

Cover the whole table with large cabbage leaves

Fresh herbs and kale tucked into corners

Fill the cabbage leaves with assorted raw vegetables that have been trimmed and cut into bite-size pieces.

Wheels of cheese on board

W e have varied this theme in many ways. For a Miami party, we added pink and green tulle, giant shells, palm leaves, orchids and plastic pink flamingos in the centre of the tablescape. For a summer party, we added a touch of whimsy by hanging dozens of strawberries on a large Benjamina tree and placing it in the centre of a round crudité table. We've found that regardless of the variation, a tablescape is a gorgeous way of presenting food for a cocktail party.

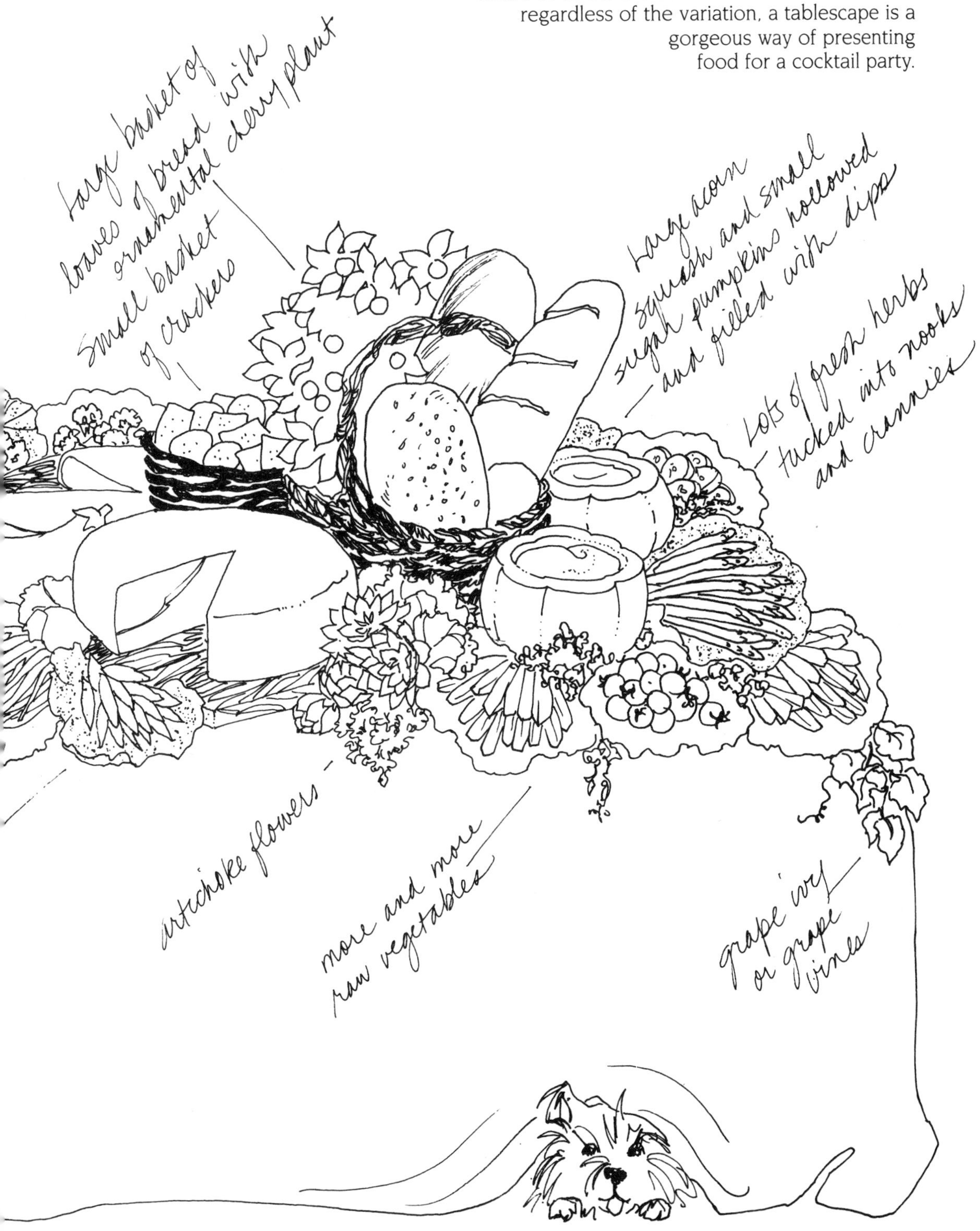

large basket of loaves of bread with ornamental cherry plant

small basket of crackers

Large acorn squash and small sugar pumpkins hollowed and filled with dips

Lots of fresh herbs tucked into nooks and crannies

artichoke flowers

more and more raw vegetables

grape ivy or grape vines

CREATING A CRUDITÉ TABLESCAPE

Here is a list of ingredients and materials, and directions for creating the tablescape on the previous page.

Order your cheeses and pâtés well in advance and get your greengrocer to help you select the varieties of fruits and vegetables best for the season. Make the dips a day in advance and prepare the vegetables the night before so you will only need two or three hours on the day of the party to arrange everything on the table.

Materials needed for tablescape for 75:

table, about 3 feet × 8 feet (90 cm × 240 cm)
assorted baskets
sheet of clear plastic cut to size of tabletop (optional)
tablecloth
pâté and cheese knives
assorted cut flowers, 2 or 3 dozen stems
2 pots of flowers or miniature fruit

Vegetables:

5	savoy cabbage, plus 3 or 4 dozen outer leaves, well washed (your greengrocer usually discards these leaves; ask him to keep them for you)
8 heads	kale, well washed
3 heads	curly endive, well washed
4 heads	leaf lettuce, well washed
3 bunches	assorted herbs (optional)
3	red cabbage, hollowed out for dip
3	large squash or sugar pumpkins, hollowed for dip
8	zucchini, cut into strips ¹/₂ inch × ¹/₂ inch × 4 inches (1.25 cm × 1.25 cm × 10 cm)
4 bunches	baby carrots, well washed, *or* 2 lb (1 kg) carrots cut into strips ¹/₂ inch × ¹/₂ inch × 4 inches (1.25 cm × 1.25 cm × 10 cm)
3 bunches	asparagus, trimmed
1 lb (450 g)	green beans, tips removed
1 lb (450 g)	wax beans, tips removed
2 heads	broccoli, cut into large florets
1 head	cauliflower, cut into large florets
1 lb (450 g)	snow peas or sugar peas, tips and strings removed
5	green bell peppers, cut into rings
5	red bell peppers, cut into rings
1 lb (450 g)	mushrooms, brushed clean

ARTICHOKE-SPINACH DIP

1 (14-oz/398-mL can
  artichoke hearts
1 (10-oz/284-g) bag
  spinach
3 cloves
  garlic, chopped
³/₄ cup/225 mL
  mayonnaise
2 Tbsp/30 mL
  lemon juice
¹/₂ tsp/2 mL
  Worcestershire
  sauce
¹/₂ tsp/2 mL
  grated lemon rind
to taste
  Tabasco sauce
  salt and pepper

1. Chop artichoke hearts in food processor fitted with steel blade. Set aside.

2. Wash spinach well. Blanch in boiling water, drain, squeeze dry and chop in food processor. Add chopped artichoke hearts and remaining ingredients, and process just until blended.

Fruit:

2 quarts (2 L) strawberries
2 dozen apples
6 bunches grapes

Cheese:

1 lb (450 g) Cheddar
1 lb (450 g) Brie
1 lb (450 g) Emmenthaler
½ lb (225 g) Gorgonzola
½ lb (225 g) Chèvre

Pâté:

2 Pâté Maison

Extras:

assorted loaves of bread
assorted crackers
2 cups Herbed Yoghurt Dip
2 cups Artichoke-Spinach Dip
2 cups Smoked Salmon Dip

1. Cover table with cloth and plastic sheet. Arrange baskets on table. Fill large baskets with loaves of bread and some of the cabbages, apples, cut and potted flowers. Put crackers in a few of the smaller baskets. Arrange remaining cabbages around the baskets. Place the hollowed red cabbages and hollowed squash around the table at regular intervals. Cover the surface of the table completely with large outer leaves of cabbage, leaf lettuce, kale and curly endive, fanning them around in an attractive pattern.

2. Arrange cheese and pâté close to baskets of bread and crackers and stick pâté knives into them. Cluster fruit around cheese. Pile prepared vegetables in groupings of contrasting colour around the table so that every inch of the table is covered. Fill hollowed cabbages and squash with dips.

HERBED YOGHURT DIP

2 cups/500 mL
natural yoghurt
½ cup/125 mL
chopped chives
2 cloves
garlic, chopped
¼ cup/60 mL
chopped fresh herbs (parsley, dill, rosemary or thyme)
to taste
salt and cayenne

1. **Blend all ingredients together.**

SMOKED SALMON DIP

½ cup/125 mL
smoked salmon bits
1 cup/250 mL
sour cream
½ cup/125 mL
cream cheese
¼ cup/60 mL
chopped Spanish onion
to taste
salt and pepper

1. **Combine all ingredients in food processor fitted with steel blade and process until blended.**

PEACOCK FRUIT TABLESCAPE

The traditional peacock platter is a celebrated Chinese appetizer plate in which assorted meats and vegetables are cut into tiny shapes and intricately overlapped to form a colourful peacock. We have taken this ancient concept and blown it up to big, breezy Canadian proportions. Made entirely from fruit, our peacock spreads his fabled tail across the whole table.

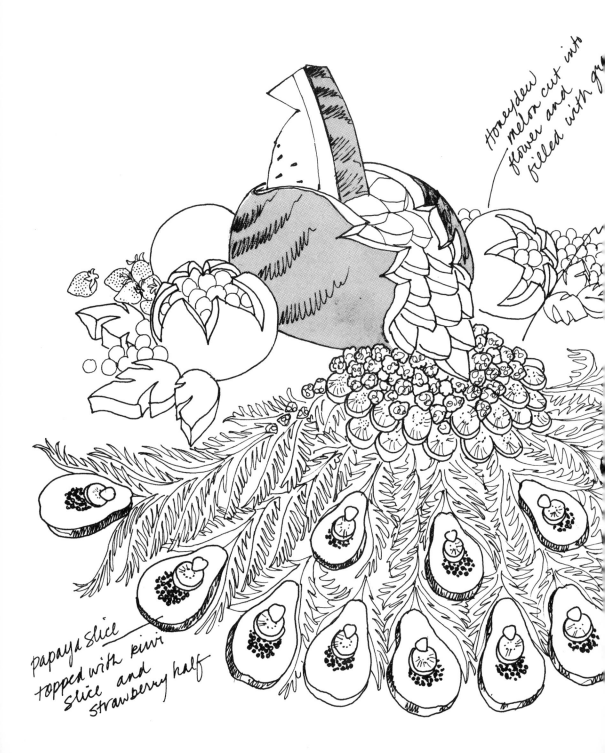

Honeydew cut into flower and filled with gr...

papaya slice topped with kiwi slice and strawberry half

This presentation is fabulous as a dessert table for a grand banquet, or as a sweet table at a large cocktail party. Last summer, we made a peacock table, poolside, for a client who had very special houseguests and wanted refreshing fruits available for them as they swam and sunbathed.

berries, kiwi
es and
sp berries

melon 'feathers'

leave seeds in
papaya slices

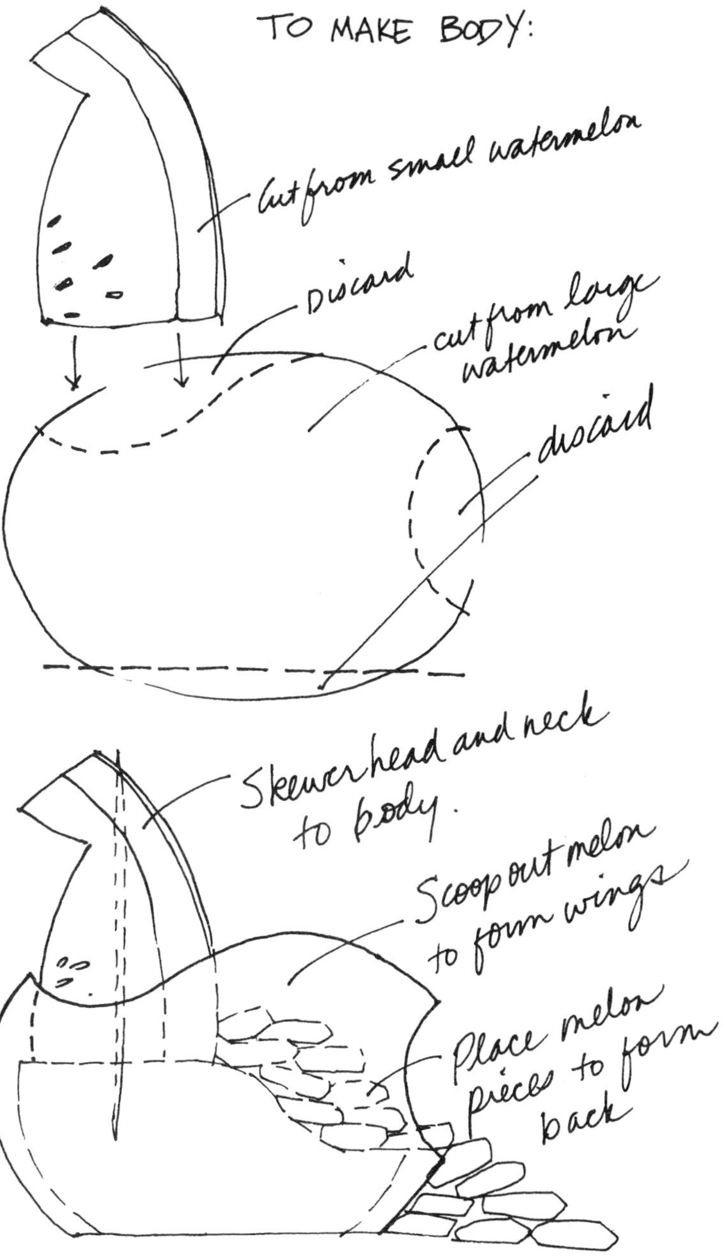

TO MAKE BODY:

Cut from small watermelon

Discard

cut from large
watermelon

discard

Skewer head and neck
to body.

Scoop out melon
to form wings

Place melon
pieces to form
back

To make feathers

melon

seeds
papaya slice
kiwi slice
strawberry half

FOR A PEACOCK TABLESCAPE

Fruit:

2	**watermelons**
3	**small cantaloupe melons, cut into flowers (page 188)**
3	**large cantaloupe melons, peeled and cut into ½-inch (1.25-cm) wedges**
2	**small honeydew melons, cut into leaves (page 188)**
5	**large honeydew melons, peeled and cut into ½-inch (1.25-cm) wedges**
1	**Santa Claus melon, peeled and cut into ½-inch (1.25-cm) wedges**
5	**papayas, sliced ½ inch (1.25 cm), seeds left in**
6	**kiwi, peeled and sliced ¼ inch (6 mm)**
3 pints (750 mL)	**strawberries, 6 berries sliced**
1 pint (250 mL)	**blueberries, blackberries or raspberries**
3	**red apples, cut into feathers (page 186), soaked in lemon juice**
5	**bunches green and purple grapes**

Materials:

3	**bunches Mexican palm leaves (from your florist)**

clear plastic sheet cut to the size of the tabletop

1. Cut 1 watermelon into body, as in diagram A. Carve remaining watermelon into head and neck, as in diagram B. Using a large skewer, secure head to body. Cut triangular slices out of watermelon cuttings for feathers. Pile feathers up behind neck and along back.

2. Make diagonal slashes in all melon wedges, as in diagram C.

3. To assemble: Cover table with cloth and clear plastic sheet. Cover the entire surface of the table with palm leaves. Place the body in the upper left quadrant of the table. Rearrange any feathers that have fallen out of place. Place 12 of the papaya slices, evenly spaced, in an arc as far out from the body as the size of the table allows. Place rows of honeydew wedges leading from each papaya slice forming feathers to the back of the body. Place 6 papaya slices two thirds of the way up the first feathers and place rows of cantaloupe and Santa Claus melons from these slices in the same manner as the first row of feathers. Place apple feathers along back where body meets tail. Place a row of blueberries along the "spine" of each feather. Place 1 kiwi slice on each papaya slice, slightly overlapping onto the seeds, and a slice of strawberry slightly overlapping on each kiwi slice. See diagram D for feather pattern. Arrange the large melon flowers around the bird with the honeydew leaves, grapes, and remaining strawberries.

TABLETOPS

Parties are a little like theatrical events. Just as a set design establishes the mood of a scene, table decoration plays an important role in defining the ambience, so let your creativity flow and be as imaginative as you dare with tablecoverings and centrepieces. Here are a few designs to inspire you to new dramatic heights.

ENGLISH COUNTRY GARDEN

Centrepiece: Fill a wicker basket full of assorted freshly cut flowers and fern fronds. The basket can be natural or painted in a pastel colour. If you wish, tuck a little moss around the base of the basket. For a touch of whimsy, form a little nest of straw and fill it with a few small brown eggs. Perch a little artificial bird nearby.

Tablecovering: Spatter a length of canvas with pastel-coloured latex paint. You don't have to be an artist to achieve a beautiful effect, just splash small brushfuls of paint randomly on the fabric and let the colours work for you.

BEACH BLANKET BINGO NIGHT

Centrepiece: Pour clean sand, available from aquarium stores, directly on the tablecovering in a large neat hill. Push several candles into the sand, making sure they will stand without tipping.

For a fun look, arrange assorted seashells, a pair of sunglasses and a bottle of suntan lotion in the sand. If you really want to cause a sensation, put a goldfish swimming in a small fishbowl at the top of each place-setting. But don't serve fish for dinner!

For an elegant look, paint a few dried tree branches black and stand them upright in the sand. Arrange seashells and large, interesting blossoms, such as orchids or rubrum lilies, on the sand. To keep the blossoms fresh, place them in floral picks, available from any florist.

Tablecovering: For a fun look, spread a large beach towel on the table and use napkins in different colours to match the beach towel.

For an elegant look, use shiny black or deep blue vinyl, available at large hardware stores or upholstery fabric shops.

CARING FOR CUT FLOWERS

As soon as you get home from the florist, cut the stems on an angle and put into water. If possible, hold the stems under water as you cut them to prevent air bubbles from being drawn up into the stems.

Packages of special nutrient for cut flowers are available from your florist and should be added to the water to prolong their life. Or, you can stir a few drops of bleach and a spoonful of sugar into the water. Add fresh water every day and remove any deteriorating greenery.

Droopy flowers can be revived, or reluctant buds can be opened, by putting them in a container of very hot water. The water level should be halfway up the stems.

FLORAL FOAM

Floral foam, such as Oasis, will make flower-arranging easy for you by anchoring stems exactly where you want them. It is a highly absorbent foam that comes in blocks. You simply cut off a piece to fit the size of your container and soak it in water. When it is completely saturated, place it in the container, securing with tape if necessary. The stems of greenery and flowers can then be stuck into the foam to form an arrangement. Fill the container with water to keep the foam saturated, and replenish the water when necessary.

CANDELIGHT AND ROSES

Centrepiece: Twine lengths of ivy around a large five-branch candelabra or a cluster of candlesticks. Secure the ivy in place with bows of satin ribbon. Just before your guests arrive, tuck small tea roses into the ivy and place a single rose on the napkin of each place-setting. Candelabras can be rented and roses and ivy can be ordered from your florist or begged from the garden of a green-thumbed friend.

Tablecovering: For elegance and formality, use a white floor-length damask linen tablecloth and white lace napkins. The tablecloth can be rented and the napkins can be made by cutting a length of dressmaking lace into large napkin-sized rectangles or by sewing lace trim onto large men's handkerchiefs.

For Proustian lushness, use a multi-coloured, cabbage-rose chintz cloth with matching napkins or a floor-length russet-coloured velvet cloth covered with a small square of old lace.

For Erté elan, use a floor-length white tablecloth covered with a small square of black velvet trimmed with ribbons and tassels in an art deco style. The tablecloth can be a new white bedsheet with the corners tucked under for a billowing look. And the velvet square can be made from fabric, ribbon and tassels purchased from a dressmaker's supply store. Don't like to sew? Hems can be ironed up and taped in place and ribbon can be attached with fabric glue or double-sided tape. Just a bit of stitching — you do have to bring out the needle and thread to attach a tassel to each corner.

A small pot of flowers dropped into a brightly coloured paper bag makes a pretty and inexpensive centrepiece. Stuff coloured tissue paper around the flowers to fill out the top of the bag.

MINIATURE GARDENS

Centrepiece: Sometimes the table is too small for a centrepiece. This is the time to make individual mini-arrangements of flowers to put at the top of each place-setting. Use little containers such as Chinese teacups, crystal liqueur glasses or tiny ceramic baskets. Place a water-saturated cube of floral foam (available from any florist) in each container and cover with a piece of sheet moss. Arrange several small flowers in each container. Tea roses, ixia, statice, heather and individual alstroemeria blossoms are ideal.

Tablecovering: Use a pastel-coloured tablecloth and cover it with a layer of nylon net, available at fabric stores. Using narrow satin ribbon, tie bows onto the nylon net, with a single blossom in each bow, if desired.

INDEX

sb indicates sidebar information

sb indicates sidebar information

sb indicates sidebar information

G-H-I-J

L

M

sb indicates sidebar information

N-O

P

sb indicates sidebar information

sb indicates sidebar information

sb indicates sidebar information

sb **indicates sidebar information**